PRAISE FOR *SLOW TRAINS TO ISTANBUL*

"*Tom Chesshyre is a kind of railway flâneur, drifting across Europe, taking trains as and when he pleases. It's a simple formula, but hugely enjoyable books are the result.*"

Andrew Martin, author of *Night Trains*

"*If you were ever in doubt over how wonderful Interrail is, just read* Slow Trains to Istanbul. *Wonderful prose that captures the rhythm of the trains as Tom Chesshyre navigates his way across Europe.*"

Nicky Gardner, *hidden europe*

"*Chesshyre's journey is an act of middle-aged rebellion, interrailing eastwards with no particular purpose other than to get to Istanbul. En route he rattles across the points of Europe, both literally and metaphorically. Combining a train geek's delight with a keen eye for history, and interacting with everyone he meets.*"

Andrew Eames, author of *The 8.55 to Baghdad*

"*Wry, funny and perceptive, very little escapes Tom Chesshyre's piercing eye on this entertaining odyssey on the rails across Europe. I loved this book.*"

Michael Williams, author of *On the Slow Train*

"*Tom Chesshyre is the consummate traveller, who makes you want to experience all his adventures and mishaps for yourself. Every encounter is turned into a story, giving insights into every place he visits. His journey becomes your journey. And as ever, he demonstrates that trains are the best form of travel.*"

Christian Wolmar, author of *British Rail: The Making and Breaking of Our Trains*

"*A love letter to the InterRail Pass and the endless possibilities and serendipities of train travel. This book will probably send you dashing to the nearest station, eager to set off on your own rail adventure.*"

Sarah Baxter, author of *A History of the World in 500 Railway Journeys*

"*An entertaining and eye-opening tale that transports you onto the rails for the most epic of European train adventures. Chesshyre's sharp wit, journalistic eye and knack for finding colourful characters make for cracking travel writing.*"

Ben Clatworthy, *The Times*

PRAISE FOR *TICKET TO RIDE*

"*This is an engaging, enjoyable and warm-hearted book that will appeal as much to general readers as to lovers of trains.*"

Simon Bradley, author of *The Railways: Nation, Network and People*

"*Like mini-odysseys, Chesshyre's railway journeys are by turns gentle and awesome, and full of surprises.*"

John Gimlette, author of *Elephant Complex: Travels in Sri Lanka*

PRAISE FOR *SLOW TRAINS AROUND SPAIN*

"*A lovely book.*"

Michael Portillo

"*Chesshyre takes us on a wondrously hypnotic meander across Spain… a highly relaxing and subtly addictive read.*"

Glen Mutel, *National Geographic Traveller*

"*I found myself quickly falling into step beside Tom Chesshyre, charmed by his amiable meanderings, pointed observations and meetings with strangers.*"

Fergus Collins, *BBC Countryfile Magazine*

"*Readers should perhaps prepare themselves for a whole new wave of Whither England? type books in the months and years ahead, and Chesshyre's is a not unwelcome early attempt to answer that seemingly urgent question.*"

Ian Sansom, *Times Literary Supplement*

PRAISE FOR *PARK LIFE*

"*A delightfully personable and impressively global gazetteer.*"

Travis Elborough, author of *A Walk in the Park*

"*This timely guide to urban escapes will not only add dozens more to your to-do list, but also help you appreciate your own local little wonder a little more, too.*"

Wanderlust magazine

PRAISE FOR *TO HULL AND BACK*

"*Tom Chesshyre celebrates the UK... discovering pleasure in the unregarded wonders of the 'unfashionable underbelly' of Britain. The moral, of course, is that heaven is where you find it.*"

Frank Barrett, *The Mail on Sunday*

"*You warm to Chesshyre, whose cultural references intelligently inform his postcards from locations less travelled.*"

Iain Finlayson, *The Times*

TOM CHESSHYRE

SLOW TRAINS TO ISTANBUL

...And Back: A 4,570-Mile Adventure on 55 Rides

summersdale

SLOW TRAINS TO ISTANBUL

An Hachette UK Company
www.hachette.co.uk

Summersdale Publishers
Part of Octopus Publishing Group Limited
Carmelite House
50 Victoria Embankment
LONDON
EC4Y 0DZ
UK

www.summersdale.com

Printed and bound by Clays Ltd, Suffolk, NR35 1ED

ISBN: 978-1-83799-273-7

This FSC® label means that materials used for the product have been responsibly sourced

MIX
Paper | Supporting responsible forestry
FSC
www.fsc.org
FSC® C104740

Substantial discounts on bulk quantities of Summersdale books are available to corporations, professional associations and other organizations. For details contact general enquiries: telephone: +44 (0) 1243 771107 or email: enquiries@summersdale.com.

For all train lovers

ALSO BY TOM CHESSHYRE

How Low Can You Go?
To Hull and Back
Tales from the Fast Trains
A Tourist in the Arab Spring
Gatecrashing Paradise
Ticket to Ride
From Source to Sea
Slow Trains to Venice
Slow Trains Around Spain
Park Life
Lost in the Lakes

ABOUT THE AUTHOR

Tom Chesshyre is the author of 12 travel books. He attended a state school and studied politics at Bristol University and newspaper journalism at City University. He worked on the travel desk of *The Times* for 21 years and now works freelance, contributing to the *Daily Mail*, *Mail on Sunday* and *The Critic*. He lives in Mortlake in London.

CONTENTS

Preface | 17

Chapter One | 29
London to Nuremberg in Germany, via Paris and Strasbourg
in France: Late nights, delights and strikes

Chapter Two | 65
Nuremberg to Budapest in Hungary, via Passau in Germany
and Bratislava in Slovakia: "Today, we are not working"

Chapter Three | 97
Budapest to Bucharest in Romania, via Timişoara:
Hungarian heavy metal, dictators and stag dos

Chapter Four | 131
Bucharest to Sofia in Bulgaria, via Ruse:
"Under communism Beatles not allowed"

Chapter Five | 165
Sofia to Istanbul in Turkey:
Bandits, spies and shish kebabs

Chapter Six | 199
Istanbul to Thessaloniki in Greece, via Kulata in Bulgaria:
Sleepers, gamblers, truckers and saints

Chapter Seven | 229
Thessaloniki to Naples in Italy, via Athens, Patras and Bari:
"We strive for a modern rail network"

Chapter Eight | 259
Naples to Visp in Switzerland, via Milan, Tirano,
Chur and Zermatt: Into the Alps

Chapter Nine | 295
Visp to Ghent in Belgium, via Dole in France, Luxembourg
and Waterloo in Belgium: Let the random rule

Chapter Ten | 323
Ghent to London, via Rotterdam in the Netherlands
and the Hook of Holland: Slow trains home

Afterword | 337

Acknowledgements | 343

Trains Taken | 345

"*To travel by train is to see nature and human beings, towns and churches and rivers — in fact, to see life*"
Agatha Christie

"*Trains are nice*"
rail enthusiast on the *Bernina Express*, Switzerland

"*Change of scene, and absence of the necessity for thought, will restore the mental equilibrium*"
Jerome K. Jerome, *Three Men in a Boat*

In some instances, names of those encountered during the train journeys for this book have been altered.

PREFACE

It all began on a park bench on a sunny July afternoon near the ping-pong tables in London's Soho Square, eight months before going.

I was with my old friend Danny, and we were drinking Red Stripe lagers. We were on can number two, discussing this and that: life in general, the state of the planet. No great strides were being made on either topic naturally. Not that this mattered. It was warm. We had liquid refreshment. We were not in an office staring at screens. We were not at the mercy of emails requiring "action". We were two middle-aged blokes minding our own business sitting on a park bench.

Danny seemed a little preoccupied, though I didn't read much into that. After a while, however, he cleared his throat and asked a question.

"You know Interrail?"

He knew very well I "knew Interrail": I had written a travel book about the popular European rail passes, *Slow Trains to Venice: A 4,000-Mile Adventure Across Europe*. This was what I did in between working as a travel hack (journalist) for various newspaper travel sections. I wrote, mainly, books about trains. I found this both relaxing and a good way of getting about, escaping to places I might never otherwise have gone: remote spots in Peru, the jungles of Sri Lanka, Australian deserts, the eerie (and captivating) Siberian tundra, the peculiar (and awful) badlands of North Korea, Iran, India, the foothills of the Himalayas, large swathes of Europe.

"Tickets are half price right now," Danny continued.

The Interrail passes, he said, were in a one-off flash sale to celebrate the fiftieth anniversary of the company's foundation.

Danny looked at me. He wore a fervent expression.

"Half price!" he said as a ping-pong ball sailed narrowly above our heads into some shrubs. Such avoidances were one of the downsides of our drinking location.

He straightened himself and regarded me once more. His face was full of zeal.

I replied that 50 per cent off was indeed reasonable – he had my attention on this point – even though the tickets were a downright bargain in the first place.

He resumed his "pitch".

"It will be life-changing! A month of living on the railway lines!" he said. "Freedom! Europe at our disposal! And cheap! We must not forget this: an excellent deal! We must take these chances! Grab them! So cheap! We are not getting any younger! It won't cost much! So cheap! Very very good value!" Danny, you may have noticed, had an eye for *good value*. "Let's do it! Come on, let's do it! We are simply not getting any younger! That is not happening! We are becoming old! We need to do this!"

And so on. Apologies for so many exclamation marks and repetitions. But that was how it was. He was adamant. Like a preacher at a pulpit in the American Deep South discussing the miracles of the Lord, except he was talking about going on a long series of trains in Europe, he was convinced of the urgency and importance of his thoughts on the matter.

His voice rose to a crescendo during his final declarations, causing a man wearing a purple velvet suit despite the warm day to turn our way. He had been sauntering by in a debonair manner and had overheard some of Danny's soliloquy.

He paused, eyeballed us, and said in an extremely deep and gravelly voice: "Yeah, man."

He seemed to agree.

Then he shimmied away beyond the ping-pong tables. Soho Square was full of such characters: a wonderful place, a let-your-hair-down place, a place where anything and everything seemed to go, and all the better for it. The perfect spot to dream dreams, to be whoever you wanted to be – conventional or unconventional. To drift. To scheme. To hatch plans on a sunny day… such as travel plans involving Interrail passes along railways in Europe. Train dreams.

The man in the purple velvet suit was right. Danny and I, with 100 years between us on the planet, needed to act. This was no time to be hanging around thinking: *we'll do it one day soon*. Danny was married with three children. His wife Clare, I was soon to discover over Red Stripe number three, had already given him the "green light" to go. I was childless, having fairly recently sadly-yet-amicably split from my long-term partner. I also had flexible work arrangements and could quite easily find time to get away. Somehow, and no one is ever, I suppose, quite sure exactly how and when it happens, we had well and truly entered the realm of "middle age". There was no escaping this fact nor pretending otherwise. We were beyond the point of no return regarding the matter. The logic of disappearing for a while on a whole load of trains (four weeks, we agreed, would do) suddenly seemed irrefutable.

Sure, Danny was concerned about teenage children being teenage children while absent, and how Clare would manage everything while he was gone, which was going to be on his mind, he admitted. Aside from those worries, the way ahead looked clear.

We were not, we knew, typical Interrailers.

We were not about to go to university or just leaving university on our way to "find ourselves" and cast the direction of our young lives ahead, our futures, our fates. Our young lives, futures and fates were both behind us and being played out. Though perhaps, if one thought youthful thoughts, a little bit of finding oneself remained possible.

On the park bench in Soho Square we there and then bought month-long Interrail tickets for the following April. Then we strolled to Stanfords, the extremely useful travel bookshop in Covent Garden, picked up two copies of *Rail Map Europe*, returned to the bench and idly began to choose a rough way ahead.

* * *

Yet we knew the destination.

A train journey to Istanbul had a classic feel.

Both the route to the edge of Asia... and its history.

When the *Orient Express* to Constantinople, as Istanbul was then known, began on 4 October 1883 it was a major event. Crowds had surged to Gare de l'Est in Paris for the 18:00 departure, while Georges Nagelmackers, the flamboyant and well-connected Belgian civil engineer behind the service (a prominent Belgian banker's son), entertained sponsors in top hats and directed government ministers to shiny carriages. Nagelmackers had been inspired by transcontinental train travel after a trip to America in 1869 during which he had admired the technology of new "bogies" providing extra suspension for a smoother ride utilized by the train impresario George Mortimer Pullman. This experience, being in the US when the highly symbolic "golden spike" was hammered onto the line connecting America from coast to coast at Promontory Summit in Utah on 10 May of that year, had infected him with "rail fever" and he astutely understood that long rail journeys, travelling in style, had a good chance of working back in Europe. Perhaps even better than in the States if he did it right. Nagelmackers had not been overly impressed by the interior designs of the American carriages in which he had ridden. They could, he believed, be much improved.

Using his banking and railway connections – his father had financed many of the early European lines – he set his plan in motion on his return. He had access to the European elites through his father, who was friends with King Leopold I, prince of Saxe-Coburg-Saalfeld and uncle of Queen Victoria, no less. People took notice of Georges Nagelmackers, born in 1845, a tall and solid-looking

Victorian stalwart with a big bushy beard. This was no hustler on the make with a get-rich-quick scheme that would ruin financial backers (though he himself had to shrug off early business associates hoping to leech off his name and wealth). But he was undoubtedly a player – and he knew how to get things done, helpfully and crucially having the means to do so.

Nagelmackers also understood good PR. He was a shrewd publicist, well ahead of his time in that area. The first journey on his Compagnie Internationale des Wagons-Lits service, the grandiloquent title designed to impress the impressionable, was a "freebie" for all passengers including some of Europe's most prominent journalists.

One of these was the characterful, bewhiskered and rather rotund Henri Opper de Blowitz, Paris correspondent for *The Times*, who had famously broken the news of the Treaty of Berlin, an agreement in the aftermath of the 1877–1878 Russian–Turkish war, having somehow got his hands on a copy before it was released to the public.

What a name, and what a write-up he was to give Compagnie Internationale des Wagons-Lits. Blowitz, who was nicknamed the "Prince of Journalists" and who enjoyed the finer things in life, was an immediate convert to fancy train travel: "The bright-white tablecloths and napkins, artistically and coquettishly folded by the sommeliers, the glittering glasses, the ruby red and topaz white wine, the crystal-clear water decanters and the silver capsules of the champagne bottles – they blind the eyes of the public both inside and outside", he wrote. "It must be said, during the entire trip from Paris to Bucharest the menus vie with each other in variety and sophistication – even if they are prepared in the microscopic galley at one end of the dining car."

Gush, gush, gush – he had clearly enormously enjoyed his junket, approving in particular that he could "shave at fifty miles an hour". This was thanks to the smoothness of the ride, which had not been possible on previous bone-shaking non-bogie trains.

A bogie, I should perhaps explain in more detail, is "an assembly of four or six wheels forming a pivoted support at either end of a railway coach, providing flexibility on curves" (so says *Collins English Dictionary*).

The correspondent from *Le Figaro* was of a similar mindset to Blowitz. He deemed the Burgundian chef in the dining car to be nothing less than a "genius". Of the journey itself, he said, referring to the return leg: "We made the trip from Constantinople to Paris in seventy-six hours instead of the usual one hundred and eleven, in perfect comfort and without the slightest fatigue", adding somewhat profoundly, perhaps after some ruby red or topaz white wine: "As progress rolls forward on wheels, the Earth seems to shrink."

Meanwhile, another happy passenger from the ranks of the press was Edmond About, a well-known French journalist and novelist, who declared of the inaugural ride: "I have never seen anything more remarkable than this odyssey." He was also impressed that "the magnificent refrigeration makes the freshest butter of Isigny [a place in Normandy] available throughout the whole journey, even when the train was roaring across the Hungarian Puszta, a thousand kilometres distant from France". Fresh Normandy butter being the way to a French travel reporter's heart, it would seem, or at least this one's.

The *Orient Express* was off to a very good start indeed and the sheer opulence of the ride – along with the eclectic backgrounds of its passengers – was of course to go on to inspire many films and novels, most famously Agatha Christie's *Murder on the Orient Express*, first published in 1934 during the train's early-twentieth-century heyday. It was the close confines and rich mix of classes (including those working on the trains, plus nannies and assistants), nationalities and personalities, so many "strangers brought together", that had caught Christie's eye. They slept together, dined together and could not "get away from one another". What could possibly go wrong?

As it happened, the first known murder on the *Orient Express* is believed to have occurred in 1935, a year later, when an ill-fated Romanian fashion designer, Maria Farcasanu, on her way from

Bucharest to Paris was pushed from a train window to her grisly death in central Austria after being robbed of a valuable silver-fox scarf, a gem-set platinum wristwatch and all her money (the equivalent of £450). It was a tragic event that gripped Europe for many months and seemed to have been plucked from Christie's pages. At the time, it was written up in headlines as "THE MURDER ON THE ORIENT EXPRESS" or "THE SILVER FOX MURDER". The perpetrator, Karl Strasser, a twenty-something Hungarian man, was eventually caught after an eagle-eyed Swiss policeman noticed a woman in his local church wearing the distinctive scarf, which she had attained from Strasser. After being arrested and admitting his crime, the Hungarian was jailed for life.

Yet despite all this intrigue, the train had come to represent the glamour of this golden age of rail travel attracting royalty, aristocrats, millionaire entrepreneurs (often with mistresses in adjoining compartments), ministers of state, spies, artists, actors and writers aplenty to the tracks. After World War Two, thanks to the advent of jet planes, all this naturally began to fade, and the *Orient Express* between Paris and Istanbul, towards its end known as the *Direct Orient Express*, was to continue falteringly until 1977 when it was cancelled for good. By then it had become a much-reduced version of Nagelmackers' original vision: little more than simple couchettes with bunks and not even enjoying a dining carriage.

Yet it was, at the time of our park bench summit, still possible to take an *"Orient Express"* train from Paris to Istanbul... with a big catch.

A trip faithfully retracing one of the old routes (there had been multiple ways to Constantinople over the years) covering five nights with three on board and two at plush hotels in Budapest and Bucharest was still offered for the eye-watering fare of £17,500 per passenger. This service was run once a year by a company named Belmond as the *"Venice Simplon-Orient-Express"* that catered for the very wealthy, of whom many seemed to be interested.

"Please note spaces are extremely limited on this popular route," the blurb read. "You need only glimpse its gleaming carriages and be greeted by the steward in his distinctive uniform to know that the most memorable journey of your life has begun... be wined and dined in meticulously restored 1920s dining cars, before raising sparkling toasts in Bar Car '3674'. Between plush cabins and palpable history, an astonishing journey awaits."

If you could afford it.

This was not cheap. This was not a bargain. This was not: *let's do it, we're not getting any younger, come on let's go.* Not for us at least.

Danny and I did, however, want to retrace the famous route, slowly and in a manner that was distinctly less ostentatious (but considerably better value).

This was where Interrail's month-long unlimited travel covering 33 European countries kicked in. These passes worked out at 2 per cent of the cost of the *Venice Simplon-Orient-Express*, and would allow us to make things up as we went along (deciding where we went day by day), avoiding having to sit next to the same people in the dining carriage each day (in those trains we were to take that had any), or having to worry about dressing up in finery either. The train's famous mantra was after all: "You can never overdress on the *Orient Express*".

Much better our way. Cheaper, too.

* * *

In *Slow Trains to Venice*, the tracks had wound across France, Belgium, Germany and Poland to Lviv and Odessa in Ukraine, before circling back through the Balkans to *La Serenissima*, the nickname for Venice that translates as "Most Serene One".

Serene it was indeed at the end, though the journey this time would not touch on the easternmost point of that previous backwards "C" of a route. That journey had taken me into what was to become a deadly conflict zone and had already had its borders breached, in Crimea, when I went in 2018. It had been an extremely odd sensation back then to have entered an invaded territory on a train holiday begun in a leafy London suburb. This time Ukraine was out of bounds being well into its full-blown war with Russia, even if the trains would meander very close to the troubled country in Romania.

As with the rides for *Slow Trains to Venice*, however, I had a modus operandi, one that suited both Danny and me.

This approach was simply to see where the tracks happened to lead on the way to the "goal" of Istanbul, to let serendipity reign and allow whims and fancies to take hold, timetables permitting. Attached to this freewheeling line of action was a park bench agreement to ban strict planning using the internet. This was a no-no. There would be no pressure to see the sights as prescribed by *If you only have 24 hours in XXX* guides. We would witness what we happened to witness, hear what we happened to hear, meet who we happened to meet, going wherever we pleased whether it was an officially pronounced tourist sight or not, taking a step away from the world of little screens attached to devices in our pockets.

Frankly and bluntly, the internet could f*** off for a while. Without any laws (as yet) preventing us from doing so, we would do what we preferred technology-wise. And what we preferred was to be lazy, if that was the right word, regarding online matters. Very lazy. Though perhaps "detached" or "disinterested" or "unwired" was more like it. In which case, we would be very detached, very disinterested and very unwired. We wanted to see, hear, smell, touch and taste what lay ahead. To use our senses, not fidget with tapping fingers, heads bowed to gadgets that we could just as well fixate our attention upon in our front rooms.

That said, we were aware that, even though we might be thinking such grand thoughts, the World Wide Web would be there deviously tempting us back (let's face it, we would probably succumb within a day or two). That said again, at least we would establish from the outset a back-to-basics, old-fashioned, unfashionable attitude, even if we knew only too well that this was Luddite, largely pointless and we would fail in the endeavour.

Frankly and bluntly once again, we knew deep down we didn't stand much of a (insert multiple swear words) chance with really leaving the world of little screens totally behind.

There was another consideration, for me at least.

Travelling with someone else on a long train ride was new territory. I had always before tried to follow a rather general idea about going solo on such trips espoused by Paul Theroux, the unofficial "godfather" of modern train writing. In *The Old Patagonian Express*, his colourful book about journeying from Massachusetts through South America, Theroux once wrote in a flourish of fancy: "Travel is a vanishing act, a solitary trip down a pinched line of geography to oblivion." A travel book, he said, allowed "the loner [to bounce] back bigger than life to tell the story of his experiment with space".

This had always seemed to make a lot of sense, with the word "solitary" and emphasis on being alone standing out: and, anyway, who in their right mind would turn down, if the opportunity arose, an "experiment with space"?

That had always sounded good. I also understood where he was coming from: heading off alone down the tracks was always like entering another universe, another *space* with a tantalizing sense of the possibility at least of *oblivion*: the opportunity to visit a parallel world (down parallel tracks). Or it could be if you let it.

On this trip, though, I would be in no *vanishing act*. I would be with one of my best pals who I had first met in college in my early twenties and travelled across the United States with by car for an article for a newspaper. Since then, I had been on many other international jaunts including to Bordeaux for another travel book *Ticket to Ride* and Cologne for *Tales from the Fast Trains*.

Or I would be with him from the start at least.

A week after our Soho Square summit Danny phoned.

"I really think I should only go for two weeks, max," he said. "Really, max. It's not fair on Clare. There's too much going on with the kids."

So he had bought a half-price pass and was only intending to use half of it: not such a glorious saving after all (but perhaps a better deal for Clare).

It meant that *Slow Trains to Istanbul... And Back* was to become a story of two halves: two middle-aged men on some trains, if you like (putting in plainly), during the first half to Istanbul, followed by a second half comprising Theroux's "solitary trip down a pinched line of geography to oblivion" returning home to Britain.

As much as I was looking forward to the camaraderie going to Turkey, which I was greatly, this journey alone into the unknown, whatever that might encompass, had a certain appeal.

We reserved seats on Eurostar. Not such a slow train at the start.

We booked a hotel in the Latin Quarter in Paris on Rue du Pot de Fer, the street where George Orwell had lived while working as a restaurant *plongeur* (washer-up) in the late 1920s when researching his classic book about poverty *Down and Out in Paris and London*. We were both big Orwell fans and wanted to indulge our shared interest. This was, after all, to be a trip all about indulgence: of trains and where they might take us.

We met for more park bench summits with our copies of *Rail Map Europe*. We drank more cans of lager on the park benches near the ping-pong tables, perhaps appearing to onlookers as down-and-outs ourselves, particularly unhinged ones at that with our increasingly tatty maps marked with a hopeless mess of vigorously scrawled circles around certain cities and towns.

Then one late-March morning at 8 a.m. we arrived at St Pancras International with backpacks, Danny's considerably smaller than mine.

This extreme minimalist approach to packing light seemed to come from a long-seated displeasure with paying anything more than the very minimum under-seat charge for cabin baggage on low-cost airline flights. He had adopted this method of travelling light for trains in Europe although I had pointed out prior to departure that he need not do so as trains were quite different.

He had not listened.

We passed through security into the cavernous, crowded St Pancras International departure lounge.

Europe awaited via an escalator on the tracks above.

Paris had been in flames the day before. Rubbish was piled high in the streets. Refuse workers were striking. Train drivers were striking (fortunately pausing the day before our departure). Everyone seemed to be striking. President Emmanuel Macron's favourite restaurant had been attacked by firebombs. His plans to increase pension ages by two years to 64, normal for most places in Europe, had Paris and much of the rest of the nation up in arms. The French would have to work two years more than usual, just like everyone else. It was unacceptable and not to be taken lying down.

Revolution was in the air.

Bring it on!

We showed our passports at immigration and headed for the "premier lounge", swiftly discovering our "premier passes", for which we had forked out extra on the first journey as a celebration of departure, did not allow entry to the "premier business lounge". Only "business premier passes" gave you that, said a woman on the door.

We cursed a bit between ourselves and went to Pret a Manger for a coffee.

We were on our way.

CHAPTER ONE

LONDON TO NUREMBERG IN GERMANY, VIA PARIS AND STRASBOURG IN FRANCE

LATE NIGHTS, DELIGHTS AND STRIKES

Clare, Danny's wife, texted him while we were in Pret a Manger. "Have you already started drinking in the lounge? I would be if I was you." We were not, of course, in the lounge, but it was a nice thought.

This message seemed to trigger a reaction in Danny, who was prone to making grand statements of intent and sometimes even keeping to them. "I'm not going to hold back on this trip. I'm going to be very louche," he said, as we ascended an escalator to platform five and entered our premier carriage. He seemed to enjoy the sound of the word "louche" and repeated it as though simply wallowing in it: "Yes, louche, *louche*." He had taken to the word. It appeared he had every intention of becoming a modern-day Henri Opper de Blowitz of *The Times* on the 10:26 to Paris Gare du Nord due in at 1.50 p.m.

He looked around.

"This is good," he said. "This is the life. Let's make the most of it. Where's the champagne? Let's get started!"

There was, however, for the time being, no champagne. We settled into grey seats in carriage two, which had a burgundy carpet and a pleasantly quiet *premier carriage* quality about it with staff who frequently referred to you as "sir".

I had picked up an armful of the day's papers at St Pancras International station to get a feel for the state of the world as we left on this park bench-inspired journey of discovery along the tracks of Europe. Before the premier carriage service began, I dipped into them.

They made chaotic reading. The front page of the *Daily Mail* was railing against eco-warriors and eco-minded lawyers: "FURY AT WOKE BARRISTERS REFUSING TO PROSECUTE ECO WARRIORS". The *i* newspaper was all about household concerns: "NO TAX CUTS IN 2023 AS INTEREST RATE CLIMBS TO 14-YEAR HIGH". *The Guardian* reported that: "ATHLETICS BANS TRANS WOMEN FROM SPORT". *The Daily Telegraph* announced: "LABOUR PLOTS TAX RAID ON SAVINGS AND INVESTMENTS". *The Times* offered up: "COFFEE DRINKERS

1,000 STEPS AHEAD OF THE REST", explaining that people who drank a lot of coffee were statistically proven to walk further than other people (unsurprisingly perhaps with all that caffeine). Meanwhile, the *Daily Star* asked, rather alarmingly: "HAVE KILLER MACHINES TAKEN OVER THE WORLD?" All about the dangers presented by artificial intelligence.

Eco-warriors, woke barristers, interest rate rises, transgender controversies, Labour Party tax raids, the benefits of coffee, and killer machines threatening the human race… plenty was going on.

As it still was in our destination, although this was rather tucked away. A short story inside *Metro* shone light on recent events the previous day in Paris and elsewhere in France. Water cannons had been deployed against protestors against Macron's pension-age rise in the city of Rennes in Brittany while similar activists had "blockaded train stations and Charles de Gaulle Airport in Paris".

We were about to go to one of those very stations, though no one in the premier carriage seemed particularly perturbed. Least of all, us. We were, as previously mentioned, curious to see this new revolutionary France.

Recent public service pay strikes were raging across the Continent, not just in our destination. Trouble was brewing in Germany and Italy too, said the *Metro* report, though the foreign pages in the other papers focused more on the war in Ukraine with dreadful headlines on arbitrary detentions, torture, rape and cases of summary executions of prisoners of war both by Russian and Ukrainian forces reported by the United Nations.

It was into this Europe that we headed along the tracks – no hiding from the sobering reality of that.

As the 10:26 moved away, an announcement over the speaker system said that French customs officials were on board "if you would like to make any declarations after Britain's departure from the EU".

Then a drinks trolley came by. That was the reality as far as the premier carriage was concerned. We did not fight it.

"Ah OK good. Let's get down to business," said Danny. We ordered glasses of Côtes du Rhône, in the seeming absence of champagne, and shortly afterwards entered the Channel Tunnel, where we were served cold chicken with coleslaw and chocolate cake. We ate the cold chicken and chocolate cake and drank our Côtes du Rhônes. Then we ordered more Côtes du Rhônes, which were included in the ticket price.

"If this was a really decent service they would be bringing a cheese platter now," said Danny, who had already assumed full Blowitz mode.

He began to have a postprandial snooze and I looked about the carriage.

A woman across the aisle appeared to be an actress learning a script. She left her seat for a while and I read a snippet of the highlighted text on her fold-down table: *What makes you think I would be angry? I think it would be difficult for you to have a romantic young woman,* were the lines she was learning.

You always seem to encounter artistic types in Eurostar "premier". The last time I had been on board I had been sitting next to a dance music group from Belgium that was celebrating some sort of record deal.

The actress returned and glanced our way as though suspicious I had been reading her script (which I obviously had). Then she sprayed her hands with a lavender hand sanitizer and began mouthing her lines again.

We exited the Channel Tunnel, shimmering and gently pulsating across sun-patched fields. The sky was inky with shafts of light breaking through as though trouble was rumbling in the heavens. Plough marks in wide farmland twisted in mesmerizing lines. Electricity pylons hung low like chains of paper clips on the horizon. Silhouettes of church spires slipped by. French cows munched French grass, not bothering to look up at the Eurostar as it paced along. Maybe they were used to it by now (Eurostar had been running since 1994 after all).

Across the way, a row ahead, a woman in a black top was speaking to a woman in a pink top.

Black top: "If they want to promote it, that's what they should be doing. We need feedback."

Pink top: "My position is that we need resources."

Black top, seemingly ignoring the need for resources: "People have copied this phrase *self-feedback*."

Pink top, uncertainly: "Yes. Really?"

Black top: "Yes, *self-feedback*. I wrote that in my report."

Pink top, apparently junior to "black top" and appearing to have grasped what was going on: "Yes, *self-feedback*." She paused. "It's very useful. It's brilliant actually as you're not just saying it, you're doing it."

She had lost me here.

Black top, abruptly but clearly pleased: "Yes! Oh yes!"

The subject changed to TV shows.

Black top: "I don't think I'm going to bother with the whole *Bake Off* thing."

Pink top: "Hmm."

Black top: "I mean I like *Bake Off*, but you have to commit."

Pink top: "Hmm, yes, hmm."

With that, they both returned to their laptops.

Bake Off, for whatever reason, had closed down the conversation. I suppose you either liked the programme about baking cakes a lot or you didn't care one way or another.

Such was the excitement on board the 10:26 to Paris Gare du Nord.

An unexpected, but pleasurable, silence ensued, accompanied by the pleasant hum of the train and a comforting whistling sound.

So it went for some time before customs officials in navy-blue uniforms with handcuffs attached to their belts jingled down the aisle: guns in holsters, crew cuts, *DOUANE* (CUSTOMS) written on their badges. They regarded Danny and me with disapproving eyes. On the one hand, we did not appear to represent a major threat to the stability of France. On the other, we were not, with our backpacks and empty bottles of Côtes du Rhône, exactly ideal visitors either.

A message flashed up on the screen ahead telling us that the record-breaking speed of a French train during a commercial service was 334.7 kph, or 207.97 mph. At that rate all the way we would be in Istanbul in 6.63 hours.

Soon afterwards we disembarked in the French capital.

Vive la révolution!
Paris, France

Eurostar had arrived five minutes early. We gathered our thoughts. It was not far to Rue du Pot de Fer from Gare du Nord, so we decided to walk, after looking briefly around the cacophony and mess of the station (which I had never much liked).

"When I was eighteen, I remember arriving at Gare du Nord and everyone was trying to fleece us," were Danny's thoughts on the station, looking about. It did not appear to be an especially sensible place to turn your back on your luggage 33 years on. Outside, furtive characters lurked by the taxi ranks watching passengers (us) from the 10:26 spill out on to the streets, perhaps taxi drivers, perhaps not. Shambolic figures in shabby clothing wandered by looking lost and desperate, some shivering and anxious, maybe in need of a fix. Hard-eyed guys wearing hooded tops and baseball caps stood at corners as traffic squealed and honked by as though it was perfectly natural to do so for extended periods while calmly assessing the environs and thinking whatever thoughts they may have been thinking. First impressions? Not quite the image portrayed by the local tourist board in its bright and breezy "*Paris: Je T'Aime*" advertising campaigns, perhaps.

Even if you have arrived by Eurostar many times before, the culture shock of Paris always strikes. You have entered a train in a Gothic

British station with WHSmith newsagents selling *The Daily Telegraph* and *The Times*, a statue of the oh-so-English poet Sir John Betjeman, a couple of pubs serving real ales, Boots and a Fortnum & Mason shop. You have been deposited in a thriving and edgy multicultural city (not that London is not one too) where another language is being spoken and everything is subtly, and not so subtly, different. Travel north on a similar-length journey from London, say to Liverpool, and it would not be quite like this.

"You can't do this in America," said Danny.

He was right. You could not take a train for a couple of hours from New York City or Washington, D.C. to the capital of France.

Despite its edginess, it was hard to deny Gare du Nord one thing. While the concourse inside was cramped and usually in a state of bedlam, the façade of Gare du Nord was as splendid as ever with its high arched windows, Corinthian columns and neat rows of crowned figurines clutching shields and swords representing international destinations from the mid-nineteenth century: Warsaw, Brussels, Berlin and Cologne, as well as French stops at Amiens, Arras, Lille and Rouen. Greek gods with bushy beards – Hercules, Zeus, Hermes – gazed down from circular panels and the sense of grandeur of the early railway days seemed to come flooding back (the station in its current form was completed in 1866, before the *Orient Express* was even a twinkle in Nagelmackers' eyes).

We set off for Rue du Pot de Fer.

This involved following a busy boulevard lined with kebab shops – "Restaurant Turquoise Istanbul" and, amusingly, "Partistanbul" – as well as various fly posters in favour of the recent protests against pension reforms: *"DÉFENDONS NOS RETRAITES!"* ("DEFEND OUR PENSIONS!"). Another feature of this walk was unmissable: great heaps of uncollected rubbish along the pavements, the result of the refuge collectors' strike. Spring in Paris had an unmistakeable pong.

This boulevard led to Place de la République, where yet more evidence of the strikers' protests was to be found. At its centre, red communist flags hung from the statue of Marianne, symbol of the French republic, where someone had daubed an anarchist sign and written: *"MORT AU CAPITAL"* and *"MORT AU ROI"* ("DEATH TO CAPITALISM" and "DEATH TO THE KING", not that France had one anymore).

Posters depicting President Macron lay scattered about, showing him with two faces superimposed (i.e., two-faced) saying: *"C'EST PAS BIENTOT FINI. CE PROJEEEEEEEEEEEEET!"* ("IT IS NOT OVER. THE PROJECT!"). This seemed to be an ironic statement, referring to the *projet* to cut the pension age. More graffiti on the monument said: *"POUR NOS RETRAITES, EN GRÈVE. ET ON RECONDUIT!"* ("FOR OUR PENSIONS, ON STRIKE. AND WE CONTINUE!").

There were no actual protestors about. Maybe they were taking the day off: on strike from striking. This was, it must be admitted – though this may be deemed deeply inappropriate, voyeuristic, generally awful and abominable (and so on) – somewhat disappointing. Having seen so much on the news, we had been hoping to spot some marauding French protestors. Where were all the marauding French protestors?

Just one or two would have done, to add a bit of "ambiance". But there were none. We continued past the Hôtel de Ville, crossed the river Seine and found our hotel on the edge of Rue du Pot de Fer, checking into a tiny chamber that cost more than two separate rooms at our next intended stop-off: Strasbourg – which we had already agreed upon on our park bench. The room rates in Paris were shocking.

The lift at the hotel was the size of an old-fashioned phone box. The room was not much bigger, even smaller than it looked on the website. For a while, we rested on narrow twin beds watching a news bulletin about the protests the previous day, saying nothing. Anti-pension-change demonstrators had smashed the windows of a McDonald's somewhere not far away; dramatic films showed groups of masked figures bashing away as though attempting to break in to purloin Big Macs.

"What has pension reform got to do with McDonald's?" asked Danny, squinting at the screen. "They should leave the golden arches alone, it's good value family food."

Again, he did have a point, though whether he was likely to raise it with any French protestors wielding cudgels in anger at pro-capitalist Egg McMuffin and Happy Meal displays was open to doubt.

Anyway, the streets were totally deserted, protestor-wise. The façades of popular fast-food chains seemed safe for the night.

* * *

We ventured out to explore George Orwell's old neighbourhood.

We did this in a businesslike manner – we had reserved seats on the 12:52 to Strasbourg the next day, so there was not much dithering time. We had planned a couple of stops ahead from Paris to Strasbourg and on to Nuremberg to get the trains rolling. From Nuremberg, however, anywhere was possible.

When I say "businesslike", it was more a matter of: *we went to a couple of old Orwell haunts*. Before coming, I had looked into where he had spent his time in Paris (the only such forward planning for the trip). We did not just want to arrive in the French capital and go to some bars – although that, to lay our cards on the table, was part of the plan, too.

When Orwell was in the French capital in 1928–1929 he was employed in a variety of jobs, most memorably, as previously mentioned, as a *plongeur*, the lowest restaurant position, but one from which he could observe waiters siphoning off wine, other thefts, petty grievances and the many complicated layers of French restaurant authority. Back then, this area of the Latin Quarter had been distinctly working class. It was not that way anymore. The narrow streets were teeming with smart bistros, cafés, cocktail bars and pricey hotels. Well-dressed young professionals and students roamed the lanes in between all the great piles of rubbish, looking as chic and Parisian as possible given the temporary surroundings.

Once again, not a single protestor was in sight. A sushi restaurant on a corner close to the hotel was almost buried beneath a pile of old bin liners and boxes, yet it was open and modish clientele were strolling in for chopstick dinners as if the small mountain of waste did not exist.

They did not look like anarchists hell-bent on bringing down the French state. They looked like what they were: stylish sushi-eaters intent on devouring raw fish in a convivial Japanese dining spot, albeit one almost enveloped in trash. You had to admire the Parisians' blasé attitude to the meltdown of their capital city. Pictures on the news earlier had shown some café-goers calmly finishing off coffees as streets had been set ablaze the previous day.

Orwell – who understood revolutions (*Animal Farm*) and with his "Big Brother is watching you" (*Nineteen Eighty-Four*) seemed ahead of the game so far as keeping them under control was concerned – had himself arrived in Paris by train and soon gravitated towards the Latin Quarter. In *Down and Out in Paris and London* he disguises Rue du Pot de Fer as Rue du Coq d'Or and the story begins with a scene describing local residents hurling insults at one another across the tiny lane in a "variegated chorus of yells".

"It was a very narrow street – a ravine of tall, leprous houses, lurching towards one another in queer attitudes, as though they had all been frozen in the act of collapse", he wrote. "All the houses were hotels and packed to the tiles with lodgers, mostly Poles, Arabs and Italians. At the foot of the hotels were tiny bistros, where you could be drunk for the equivalent of a shilling. On Saturday nights about a third of the male population of the quarter was drunk. There was fighting over women, and the Arab navvies who lived in the cheapest hotels used to conduct mysterious feuds, and fight them out with chairs and occasionally revolvers."

Back then, it had been a rough and ready district with grotty rooms in which many shared beds, one worker finishing a night shift to take the place of another who went off on a day shift.

Squadrons of the Republican Guard, part of the French National Gendarmerie, had patrolled the neighbourhood keeping an eye on matters.

In the spirit of not-just-going-straight-to-a-bar, we found Orwell's old lodgings at number six Rue du Pot de Fer, where the young writer, aged 25, had all his money stolen shortly before returning to Britain (and going to live with his parents in Suffolk for a while in not such down-and-out conditions). There was no plaque on the wall to mention that one of the most renowned authors of the twentieth century had lived there during one of the most formative periods of his life as apparently the owners did not want to attract attention to their nondescript grimy grey building.

On the ground floor number six was not so grey and grimy, however. It had become home to a hookah-pipe joint named Planet-Chicha, where France was playing football against the Netherlands on a television. And it was perhaps the smokiest room in Paris. We sat at a low-slung table opposite a man with gold-tinted shades, a Gucci manbag and Nike trainers accompanied by a woman wearing heavy make-up and a tan mackintosh, also with a Gucci handbag. They did not appear to be anti-capitalist, anti-pension-reformer anarchists taking a break. Though you never knew, maybe this was how anti-capitalist, anti-pension-reformer anarchists dressed and relaxed during their "time off".

The couple were smoking a hookah pipe. Everyone was smoking hookah pipes. We ordered a hookah pipe to spend a little time in this Orwell hang-out that had changed so much; during Orwell's stay, it had been a dingy bar where low-wage workers came to drown their sorrows. The tobacco tasted pleasantly of apple and mint, and when the waiter came over to check if the hookah pipe was to our liking, I asked about the writer.

"I don't know him," he replied. "I don't know anything about him at all." It was as though he was being questioned by a policeman about a local crime and he definitely did not want to be involved.

Our next "Orwell tourism" involved a bar on Rue Mouffetard, lit up by neon red lights and close to where Orwell's aunt had lived with one of the movers and shakers of the mainly forgotten Esperanto language, where there is now a Carrefour supermarket on Rue Lacépède. We had bought bottles of mineral water for the hotel at Orwell's Carrefour and were the only customers at this rather cool drinking hole playing indie rock music with plastic bags with bottles of mineral water.

We ordered two large beers and toasted Orwell, Danny even quoting him as he did so: "To Orwell! To freedom! If liberty means anything at all it means the right to tell people what they do not want to hear!"

He said this quite loudly. In the absence of any Parisians doing so, we were creating our own revolution. The bartender, overhearing the pronouncements and seeming to appreciate their anti-system sentiments, said: "Yeah, man," in the manner of the passer-by with the purple velvet suit in Soho Square.

Orwell was living on in the neighbourhood of Rue du Pot de Fer.

"Rubbish, decay and very sophisticated people," said Danny, referring to Paris and the Latin Quarter. "That's a very sexy sophistication when you think of it. It's the end of days, but it's not vagabonds in the streets. It's a very sophisticated people."

We continued in this vein for some time – happily talking a great deal of nonsense, that is – and returned clutching our Carrefour plastic bags to the hotel past midnight.

"It's enjoyable, isn't it? Watching the fields pass by. Peaceful"
Paris to Strasbourg

Clinking, crashing, clanking, smashing and beeping (of reversing municipal vehicles) were the prelude to the next day.

Paris was being tidied up.

The rubbish collectors were back in action, strike over, and Rue du Pot de Fer and its environs were almost disappointingly being cleared of these last vestiges of "uprising". The sushi restaurant on the corner was visible once again. It was a sunny morning in the Latin Quarter. We headed in the direction of Gare de l'Est, not long afterwards arriving at the tubular exterior of the Centre Pompidou outside of which a group of real-life French protestors was milling about. These were not anti-pension-reform demonstrators, however. They were campaigning peacefully against the construction of salmon farms. That said, they were actual Parisians on the streets with grievances, even if they were far from marauding while expressing them: polite Parisian protestors, gentle and charming, even.

"Zee ecology! It ees 'orrible for zee fish!" said Alina, one of the group. "It ees just zee huge multinational companies, they are behind all of this! Another lobby! Just another lobby! These farms, they manipulate our needs and wants... it ees ecological disaster! 'Orrible! So 'orrible for zee fish!"

We discussed this for a while with Alina, who was originally from Ukraine but had moved to France many years ago before joining the anti-salmon-farm movement. Then Danny and I made our way past a dozen riot police vehicles to the station. Trouble was clearly expected somewhere in Paris later in the day. Not that we would see it. We appeared to have timed our visit perfectly so far as law and order on the streets on the French capital was concerned.

As we neared Gare de l'Est, Danny, who must have been dwelling on the matter, said: "If you banned salmon farms, how could you afford salmon? If you banned the farms, only the rich could eat it."

Mulling this over, we entered the station.

* * *

Gare de l'Est was called Gare de Strasbourg in 1883 when the inaugural *Orient Express* steamed off with its fancy newfangled bogies in the direction of Istanbul. The main section of the station, despite expansions on the sides over the years, could not have changed much since then. An ornate stone façade with hoop-shaped doorways flanked by more Corinthian columns had the look of a (very large) summer house on a country estate. Palm trees grew in big pots in a tidy row on the roof above the doorways beneath a long, wide A-shaped roof and beside a striking stone sculpture of two naked maidens by a clock. Not as showy as Gare du Nord, but a fine setting nevertheless for the departure of Nagelmackers, Henri Opper de Blowitz and co. on the original freebie ride.

The station was much quieter than Gare du Nord, with just a handful of people by the entrance. Inside was a wide concourse with a curved roof with a shopping mall with escalators to a lower level. We bought coffees from a McDonald's that was not being attacked by anti-pension-reformers and were asked by a tall, thin American with a scraggly beard: "What day is it today, man? Friday? Saturday?"

We told him it was Saturday.

"Oh, OK, OK, man," he said as though we had been pressurizing him in some way by providing this requested information.

The thin, scraggly American shuffled away still looking quite confused. Perhaps he was about to ask someone else what day it was just to double-check. Or maybe something else was on his mind. Watching him depart you might have felt quite sorry for him. He did not cut a particularly heroic figure. However, that said, you got the distinct impression he was secretly enjoying himself very much indeed.

We boarded the 12:52 TGV to Strasbourg, the first stop-off for Nagelmackers' pioneering enterprise back on 4 October 1883.

On that razzamatazz day, the platforms heaving with onlookers, the train had departed in the evening with a series of hoots and the lucky passengers were soon treated to their first gourmet meal served by the well-regarded Burgundian chef in the elegant dining car with its gas chandeliers, swirly, gilt-edged marquetry and waiters wearing white gloves. This had proved to be such a hit, fine wines flowing freely between Paris and the eastern French city (and "not a drop spilt", said Blowitz, approvingly), that many members of the press had missed an electric light display at Strasbourg station.

Strasbourg had been the proud first station in Europe to have such lighting and this was the big deal, an "event". But the reporters slept through it in their compartments (much to the upset of local officials) and one of the journalists, Edmond About (the fussy butter eater), was only able to say that they "looked very well" in his report, based on second-hand observations from someone who had actually managed to stay up.

Like the Eurostar, the 12:52 was not a slow train. TGV, after all, stood for *Train à Grande Vitesse* (fast train), but it had seemed the most sensible option; silly to go any slower, just for the sake of it. We would be getting to Istanbul slowly one way or another, with some very leisurely trains indeed to come.

The TGV was undoubtedly fast, capable of 199 mph in commercial use (one special locomotive had touched 357.2 mph in a test run in 2007), and also a very fine train. The inside was smart and modern, the seats a natty lilac/orange and wide with legroom. The walls were deep purple. The tables were large. This was in standard class, which was good enough for us. In first class it must have been the lap of luxury.

We were soon zipping beyond the graffiti and tower blocks of the *banlieue* (suburbs) of Paris, firing into a countryside of hazy fields with low green crops. A milky grey sky flooded the landscape with milky grey light. A tip-tap of laptops emanated from nearby seats. Villages appeared and disappeared, little islands of cream stone and terracotta roofs amid the greenery.

I went to the dining carriage to buy more coffees, where a flamboyant man in a red bow tie served the drinks and told me the menu was created by a French celebrity chef named Thierry Marx, who had restaurants "mainly in Paris and Lyons" including one at the Eiffel Tower. He was so enthusiastic about Thierry Marx that I bought a quinoa salad with vegetables, olive oil and sesame seeds created by Thierry Marx. I returned to my seat and Danny said: "It's enjoyable, isn't it? Watching the fields pass by. Peaceful."

Reserving the seats had cost an extra ten euros. This was how it worked with Interrail passes: on certain routes reservations of around this amount were required, which was annoying but necessary if you wanted somewhere to sit (and avoid a fine). The conductor checked our Quick Response (QR) codes. He also scanned similar QR codes for our passes. For these to work, you needed to have activated/ booked the correct train on the Eurail app, which handled Interrail passes and had proved a test of the limits of our middle-aged minds at first, though we had eventually got it. Mark Smith, the legendary train guru behind the popular railway website Seat61.com, said the app was "easy to use, well-written and works well". This was high praise indeed from such a guru and made us feel a little hopeless on the technological front. The app had taken some conquering and each time a conductor accepted our QR codes we were flooded by a sense of relief mixed with disbelief, combined with a pathetic-yet-undeniable pride we had not messed it all up.

Generally, though, the app was an exceedingly good thing – much better than the paper version used during *Slow Trains to Venice* five years earlier – and it was simply a blessing that such passes existed at all. Interrail had clearly come a long way of late, as it had over its 50 illustrious years.

To begin at the beginning, the multi-journey passes were launched in 1972 by the International Union of Railways, formed after World War One with the aim of standardizing global rail networks. The point of the passes had been to encourage train excursions among the under-21s, who were cut off from travelling around Europe by high ticket prices. Back then, Interrail tickets had cost £27.50 for unlimited journeys for a month – the equivalent of about £360 in the mid-2020s – and they were such a hit in their first year, with almost 90,000 passes sold, they were continued and marketed more widely.

Fortunately, Interrail had kept going ever since, despite fierce competition from low-cost airlines and after being taken over by Eurail, a Dutch-based company, in 2001 (hence the slightly confusing name with the Eurail app). Even more fortunately, since just before the takeover, in 1998, all ages had been allowed to buy them, with higher prices for older travellers although discounted senior fares existed. While there had been 21 participating countries in 1972, over the years this number had crept up steadily to 33, with the cheapest tickets available these days for those under the age of 27.

There you had it. Interrail passes were an exceedingly good thing, too. They had helped young people to see Europe and broaden their minds for quite a long time, and they had been allowing older folk to attempt the same since around the turn of the century.

Thinking these thoughts, we settled in as the train scudded across more long sections of hazy, flat French countryside.

It was indeed peaceful. We admired snaking rivers and silver birch forests and possibly, it must be admitted in the interests of accuracy, even allowed our eyes to close every now and then in the tradition of passengers on the early *Orient Express* voyage on this route. The smooth metallic motion... the comfortable lilac and orange seats... the sense of setting off in the vague direction of the east and not having much idea where to go and no one advising us on the matter: all these sensations combined for what we both agreed was a highly satisfactory second ride.

The TGV entered the suburbs of Strasbourg, in the French region of Alsace, close to the German border.

There were warehouses, a FedEx depot, furniture shops, a Nissan car showroom and many higgledy-piggledy allotments, followed by a tantalizing glimpse of the famous local cathedral's spire. We pulled into Strasbourg station and exited into a ticket hall with high stained-glass windows, bas-reliefs celebrating tradespeople from the late nineteenth century and a modern façade with a conservatory-style atrium shaped like an enormous slug. We had reached destination number two.

Gothic glamour, EU rules and a game of darts
Strasbourg

Danny had been to Strasbourg before (I hadn't). We strode forward into the old town bathed in vapoury sunshine, crossing a wide square in the direction of the cathedral. This was reached via lanes of half-timbered medieval buildings and across a very old stone bridge. Strasbourg is remarkable in that it survived destruction in World War Two despite its location in such a key strategic spot between France and Germany, and you cannot fail but immediately like the city. As we strolled along, though, Danny was in a reflective mood.

"I remember the last time I came here," he said. "I remember talking to my father by phone. Chelsea had just won a game one–nil and we talked about that." They were both Chelsea fans. "A month later he had died." Danny paused and said: "We've got to make the most of life and do these things while we can."

He was referring to crossing Europe by train and "travel" generally, just like back on Soho Square (but this time not with his usual fighting talk). My father was still with me, though suffering sadly from Parkinson's, a dreadful disease. His state, and my mother's failing health too, had been much on my mind before the trip.

On this somewhat sombre note we followed lanes with many half-timbered town houses that seemed to lean towards one another as though "frozen in the act of collapse" as Orwell had said of Rue du Pot de Fer. They had a German style that was more solid in structure and distinct from the ornate architecture of Paris. We crossed Place Gutenberg with its prominent statue of Johannes Gutenberg, the inventor of the printing press, who had lived for some time in Strasbourg in the fifteenth century.

Then we reached Strasbourg's amazing Gothic cathedral, and our mouths fell open, Danny reacting just the same as me despite having visited previously.

There it rose, undeniable in its magnificence: a champion for a millennium (first erected in 1015), shooting up towards the canopy of hovering clouds at the end of the lane, its red sandstone façade blocking the way with stained-glass windows as intricate as butterfly wings. Parapets and carved panels fought for space with clustered columns, arches and figurines depicting angels and saints, pilgrims and priests, roaring lions (seemingly just to add a bit of medieval drama). Gargoyles with tortured visages stared down alongside disciples bearing gifts and everyday folk with wonderfully realistic faces offering worship, some smirking, some gurning, some looking pensive.

The German playwright and poet Johann Wolfgang von Goethe (1749–1832) once described the cathedral, with which he was smitten, as a "sublimely towering, wide-spreading tree of God" – which got it in one – while the French playwright Victor Hugo (1802–1885) said the cathedral was a "gigantic and delicate marvel", spot on, too.

Going inside was almost unnecessary, though we did and were blown away once again by the sheer scale of the building: the extravagant Gothic OTT look of it all, with the thin streams of coloured light drifting down from the stained-glass windows, the faint hush of voices echoing in the cavernous space above.

Strasbourg cathedral is enough of a reason to stop by on a train on the way to Istanbul.

Outside again, it was quiet on the streets with a youthful feel; the city, population about three hundred thousand, has one of France's best universities. Few signs of the stirrings of discontent over pension reforms were evident, just a few posters announcing that

"CAPITALISME BROYEUR DE VIES – 2 ANS DE PLUS C'EST NON" ("LIFE-CRUSHING CAPITALISM – TWO MORE YEARS IS A NO") and a handful of bored-looking riot police wearing body armour near a bridge close to Hotel Roses, where we were staying.

At Hotel Roses, Danny got into a conversation with the manager, Kalil.

"We are looking for an inexpensive place to eat," he said. Danny was still in full budget mode.

Kalil looked at us, getting our measure. A glint in his eye suggested that this assessment had immediately ascertained we were not aiming for anything remotely in the region of "expensive".

"These ones round here are not expensive," replied Kalil, cutting to the chase and pointing at a tourist map. Kalil wore a checked shirt and jeans and seemed as though he might be about to attend a barbecue rather than run a hotel. He was a down-to-earth Frenchman and knew his guests. "Do not go to the big restaurants," he said, pointing at the map. "Do not go to the restaurants by the cathedral. Go to the ones here." He indicated another place.

"So they are *inexpensive?*" said Danny, repeating the adjective as though trying to make absolutely certain that he had not been misheard and was not about to dine inadvertently at any *expensive* restaurants due to a language mix-up.

"Yes, though that depends on what you mean," said Kalil, looking squarely at Danny, and adding in a deadpan manner: "For zero euros, it is not possible to eat a meal."

Danny looked squarely at Kalil, assessing this joke. Then he laughed. The pair were getting on just fine.

Kalil switched subject to Britain's new King Charles. The king had just cancelled a state visit to France because of the social unrest. More than four hundred and fifty people had been arrested in Paris the day before we arrived, and four hundred police officers injured (making our attempted voyeurism even more reprehensible). The decision to postpone the visit had been made on the day of our arrival. It would have been King Charles' first trip abroad since becoming monarch. President Macron had considered it prudent Charles delayed coming, stating that it made "common sense" and that "it would have been hateful... to have attempted to maintain the trip with the risk of incidents".

In response to this, a far-left leader named Jean-Luc Mélenchon had said: "The reunion of the kings in Versailles has been disrupted by the popular disproval [sic]. The British know that Darmanin is rubbish at guaranteeing security." Gérald Darmanin was France's minister of the interior.

In response to *this*, President Macron had denied that he was losing control of France, saying: "I really don't think that's the case. The pension reforms continue their democratic process. Parliament is still functioning. We continue to move forward, we cannot grind to a halt."

Kalil, however, was far from sad that King Charles had postponed. He was not a supporter. "Unfortunately, we will see your King Charles eventually. We always liked Diana here." By "we", Kalil was talking about the French nation. "Does Charles think he can personally do something good for the English nation: *how are you everybody?* It will not bring us any money." By "us", Kalil was talking about the French nation. He was dismissive of King Charles and his belief that he could somewhat single-handedly help Britain's economic position by just turning up and doing king-like regal things. He waved a hand with a French flourish as though to see off King Charles.

He switched subject again, telling us that he had once worked in London. "In London, people like *to live*. To really *live!*" he said. "I like beer. People go to pubs in London. In pubs in London, there is life!"

Kalil, a man of many opinions, discussed the chances of Arsenal "doing the double" that season, winning both the Premier League and the FA Cup: "This year: I think it is the double. I am Arsenal." Regarding the prospects at Chelsea, he stated: "They have some problems now. This American owner... in football of course you need money, but I think he should go back to baseball." Chelsea

Football Club's owner, Todd Boehly, was also co-owner of the Los Angeles Dodgers.

Danny, Kalil and I discussed this further for a while.

* * *

Afterwards, Danny and I split up, arranging to reconvene later at a pub with a darts board and "good beer", according to Kalil.

Before then I wanted to visit the European Parliament. Danny did not want to do this. So I walked what turned out to be a longer distance than expected north-east across Strasbourg to the European Parliament, arriving at a metal and glass structure that was home to the politicians of the 27 European Union member states, with flags of each outside to prove it. The building looked a bit like an airport car park, with a gateway and a driveway into the middle. It was 5.01 p.m. when I arrived. A determined security guard on the gate would not let me in as last visitors were allowed at 5 p.m. even though tourists could stay until 6 p.m. I said something along the lines of *please, I'll be out in twenty minutes.*

"It is not possible," he said.

"Surely it's OK, I'm just sixty seconds over," I replied.

"It is not possible," the guard repeated.

"Come on, what's the harm?"

The security guard did not appreciate this pleading. He made a blowing-out sound with his mouth and turned away.

European rules, about which many people had many opinions, were kicking in at the place where they were invented.

I sat for a moment at a nearby public bench.

Sharing this bench was a man named Cleement, aged in his late twenties from Nanjing in China, who was studying for a PhD in civil engineering at the local university. He too had been denied entry by the security guard, who had blocked him for failing to have his passport on him.

Had I not caught the 12:52 to Strasbourg and been barred from the European Parliament, I reflected, it was safe to say I would never have met Cleement from Nanjing. He was a nice chap. In the absence of Danny discussing the imperatives of making the most of life before middle age crumbled into old age – and in need of a rest after rushing to make it before the 5 p.m. European Parliament closing time – Cleement and I chatted for a while.

"Last time they let me in without ID," he said. "But in France, it depends on who you get." By that he meant whoever was overseeing rules and whether they might be relaxed. "My girlfriend is in there now." He pointed to the European Parliament. "I feel very unhappy as I came with my girlfriend to show her this place."

Cleement, a train lover himself ("TGV, I like, so quick, so smooth"), was talkative. He said he enjoyed the "academic atmosphere" of Strasbourg and that the "city is very beautiful. A fantastic city. A very international city at the frontier of France and Germany."

Then he began to talk about China.

"Recently in China… a little bit of democracy," he said. "But it has decreased. So I don't really know now." He had been in Europe studying for more than four years. "I can see that some policies are not right in China. This I can say: not right."

He looked quite down about the situation back home.

"Would you be able to tell me that if you lived in China?" I asked.

"Maybe," he replied. "If *I* say that: nothing. But if you are *big celebrity*: very big problem. If you have influence on social media: very big problem. Most people don't say anything. The government, it controls social media. It see something it does not like, it delete it."

He looked even more down.

"Are your relatives happy in China?"

"In China, some people might feel like they are comfortable. But you see, a lot of people in China have not been abroad. So they do not have an example to compare. So they think that the government of China is the best," was his reply.

It sounded as though going back after his PhD in civil engineering was going to be quite a culture shock.

All this time, the security guard had been regarding us talking a few feet away behind his fence. He did not appear to approve of this impromptu camaraderie among those he had just barred entry. Not that we cared. I shook hands with Cleement, wished him luck, waved at the "key master" of the European Parliament (many of the tourists were still inside, so he had to hang around to let them out), and walked round the corner to see the office of the Council of Europe.

The United Kingdom was still a member of the Council of Europe, even though it had so spectacularly left the European Union to "take back control" of the country after the Brexit vote of 2016.

A Union Jack was fluttering outside the large concrete building along with those of the other 46 member states. This Council had been established after World War Two to promote democracy, human rights and the rule of law, acting as a separate entity to the European Union. A striking, symbolic statue entitled "*DROITS DE L'HOMME*" depicting figures huddled together in solidarity was on the front lawn. Shortly beyond was a pavement of stars mentioning that Barack Obama had visited Strasbourg in 2003, Ernest Bevin in 1949, and Charles de Gaulle in 1962, among many others. A little further on was the gleaming UFO-like European Court of Human Rights (ECHR) – to which the United Kingdom also still adhered, somewhat shakily. I say "shakily" as Britain's then home secretary, Suella Braverman, had been suggesting leaving the jurisdiction of the court so a scheme to send immigrants to Rwanda – which the ECHR had been blocking – could be given legal approval in Britain.

As well as having a lovely cathedral, Strasbourg was at the heart of what it meant to be European and you got that straight away wandering around this north-east "European admin" part of the city, the very location of which on the French–German border seemed to place Strasbourg firmly in the centre of the continent.

I walked back to find Danny, played darts with Danny, drank beers with Danny, and went to another bar/restaurant with Danny, only to be told by a wild-eyed waiter that "we are serving food but we do not have any plates right now" (the kitchen had run out of clean crockery, the first time either of us had ever been given this excuse for not getting a table at a restaurant). Around the corner, however, we landed on our feet at the wonderful little Shahi Mahal restaurant. Chicken jalfrezi curries: first-rate. Red wine: excellent. Jovial Strasbourg chatter: plenty of it.

Pleasingly inexpensive, too. Both Henri Opper de Blowitz (rapidly becoming our unofficial patron saint and "sounding board" of sorts when it came to judging whether we liked somewhere: *What would de Blowitz think?*) and budget-savvy Kalil of Hotel Roses would surely have approved.

"You put the milk in!"
Strasbourg to Nuremberg, Germany

So went our time in Strasbourg. As you may have detected, there was going to be something of a random quality to our pit stops along the line to Istanbul. But that was the way we always knew it was going to be and it suited us just fine.

We had an early start for Nuremberg.

The 08:46 would reach Stuttgart by 10.05 p.m. After this the 10:37 would spin onwards to Nuremberg arriving at 1.20 p.m., assuming there were no delays. The first service, run by Deutsche Bahn, the German national operator, was an ICE (Intercity Express) fast train. The second was a regional service operated by NVBW (Nahverkehrsgesellschaft Baden-Württemberg). *Nahverkehrsgesellschaft* translated as "local transport company". Going in a straight line between the cities would be 185 miles. The dog-leg journey via a place called Karlsruhe meant it would be longer and we would effectively cover the distance at an average speed of 41 mph.

We had chosen Nuremberg as we wanted to see its infamous Nazi parade grounds as well as the courtroom where the Nuremberg trials had been held. I had recently read a brilliant book, *East West Street* by Philippe Sands, about the prosecutors who came up with the terms "genocide" and "crimes against humanity" to ensure Nazi leaders saw justice at the courtroom, and it had piqued my interest

An Interrail trip allows such indulgences, as I have said (if anyone could really call Nuremberg an indulgence).

First, we arrived early at Strasbourg station and sat in the slug-like "conservatory" part of the station.

"It's like turning a new page every day," said Danny, referring to the journey. "Each day is like starting anew."

He had clearly, very quickly, caught the Interrail train travel bug (having never been Interrailing before).

Waiting at a bench for the 08:46, we read the BBC online news.

I shall not pretend otherwise: keeping off the internet was already (so early on) proving a step too far for us. As I had anticipated, we were clearly weak early-twenty-first-century people, no matter our park bench manifesto on the matter.

One story of the day stood out. The main news was that Vladimir Putin, Russia's president, had begun stationing tactical nuclear weapons in Belarus, yet another escalation of the war in Ukraine. Volodymyr Zelensky, Ukraine's president, had reacted by calling for an emergency United Nations Security Council meeting. This move to relocate the nuclear weapons had been declared "dangerous" and "irresponsible" by NATO, the BBC reported.

There we were messing around on trains while nuclear missiles were being shuffled about not so far away (the border with Belarus was 600 miles or so from Nuremberg).

We found our seats on the sleek grey-and-red ICE train and slid out of Strasbourg heading for country number three.

Shortly afterwards, I went to the dining car and had a puzzling conversation with the attendant.

This was how it went.

Me, the only customer in the dining car: "*Je voudrais deux Americanos, un avec lait, s'il vous plait.*" (I would like two Americano coffees, one with milk).

Assistant (expressionless, in English): "You want one Americano and one café au lait?"

Me (in English this time): "Two Americanos – one with milk in it, please."

Assistant (even colder eyes): "So two Americanos and one café au lait."

Me: "No, two Americanos, one of those with milk in it."

Assistant (frostier than ever, and abruptly): "You put the milk in!"

She pointed to some milk cartons on the counter.

This was how an Americano with milk as opposed to a café au lait was served in the dining carriage of Deutsche Bahn ICE.

Me, slightly more coldly myself: "Great."

The assistant glared at me in a manner that suggested she was unlikely to add me to her Christmas card list.

I held her gaze and asked: "Are you OK?"

Assistant: "Maybe I did not sleep so well."

The assistant handed over two filter coffees that were not Americanos and then took them back when I pointed this out and made Americanos, adding once again, in case I had forgotten perhaps: "*You* put the milk in!"

I returned to my seat, gave Danny his Americano with milk and explained the coffee stand-off, to which he said drily: "First the man at the gate at the European Parliament and now this."

The train scudded by industrial scenery and an impressive set of garden sheds with satellite dishes poking up from their roofs and neat little deck-like terraces with barbecues at allotments on the outskirts of Karlsruhe. Then it passed an IKEA warehouse and a Bosch factory and arrived at Stuttgart, a very dull station that appeared in the middle of major works judging by all the scaffolding.

* * *

The 10:37 to Nuremberg left a few minutes late, juddering slowly onwards beneath a silvery-grey sky.

An announcement informed us no fewer than five times in German and English that *this train does not stop between Stuttgart and Backnang because of reconstructions between these stations.* With this message reverberating, we passed graffiti repeatedly announcing: "KATS", "DENK", "RABID", "EGO" and "637" – the graffiti artists behind these pronouncements had clearly achieved local dominance of the railways of this stretch of German industrial heartland (presumably at a great cost in spray paint).

After a while, the city's suburbs, outer warehouses, graffiti and electricity plants fell away and we entered a silver birch forest. This did not last long. We paused briefly at Backnang station. We stopped for longer at Oppenweiler station. We passed piles of timber and several scrapyards. Then the train left this industrial area, very briefly, weaving between small, misty hills as though we were in the middle of nowhere. Then more timber and scrapyards emerged followed by another Bosch factory.

Inside the carriage a large man with a tattooed forehead and a t-shirt celebrating the rapper Tupac Shakur with the message "LEGENDS LIVE FOREVER" sat opposite us with his partner and a baby. They said not a word although the man would occasionally emit "*aargh*" as though in some pain. There was a strong temptation to try and make out what the tattoos on the large man's forehead said (or represented). But instinct suggested that staring too much was not a great idea.

The train swayed and tilted. Wind and solar farms came and went. It was an industrious, if not entirely industrial, landscape. Things seemed always to be going on, even in the forests, where all the trees, at least quite a few of them, appeared soon to be cut down. Where else did all the wood come from in all the timber yards?

As we were pulling into Nuremberg, some Americans we had not noticed rose further down the carriage and stopped near us by the door, talking about a storm that had hit the United States just before they had flown to Germany.

"Four inches of rain in an hour. Winds. Tornadoes. This climate sheeeet is goin' crazy," said a wiry elderly man.

Danny said they were better off away from all of that and the elderly man said: "You're goddamn right, sheeeet."

The woman he was with nodded with agreement. The dull grey southern German weather was an improvement on dodging tornadoes in Midwest USA, though they had come across another problem in Germany.

"Now we've got plane strikes," she said. "We were meant to meet up with our friends in Berlin but we can't because of the plane strikes. Goddamn plane strikes!"

Danny and I had known nothing about these strikes. Because of them, the couple would be stranded in Nuremberg for a day. But they didn't seem to mind too much.

"Sheeeet, things could be worse," said the elderly man.

Danny and I chatted to them for a bit as the train drew to a halt in Nuremberg. They seemed a nice pair.

"One of the weirdest places I've ever been"
Nuremberg

From near our modern chain hotel not far from the extremely grand station (more of which later) the number 36 bus went straight to the old Nazi rally grounds, curving round a high red-stone wall enclosing the old town.

It arrived at a stop near an enormous, ugly, horseshoe-shaped building. We had reached the edge of Dutzendteich lake, beside which were the Nuremberg Nazi Party rally grounds, where Adolf Hitler had ranted many times to crowds of up to 700,000 supporters between 1933 and 1938, setting out the 1935 Nuremberg Race Laws that became the legal foundation of the Holocaust.

Visiting made for an indelible experience and for some time Danny and I said very little to each other as we tried to get our heads round the place.

It was, quite rightly, not an overly promoted tourism destination. No hype. No grand signs at the entrance. No souvenir shops. A small map laid out the basics: the location of the Congress Hall (the big horseshoe-shaped building), the "main areas of the rally grounds" and the "Zeppelin Field/Grandstand", where Ferdinand von Zeppelin landed his strange aircraft in 1909 and Hitler often spoke. Close by was a small building where you could buy tickets to enter the Documentation Center of the Nazi Party Rally Grounds, in a wing of the Congress Hall.

We visited the latter, which from the middle looked like a Roman amphitheatre on a partially completed, warped scale. Had it ever been finished, the hall could have held 50,000 people, a similar capacity to Rome's Colosseum, which had been the architects' inspiration. It was a desolate place. No effort had been made, again quite rightly, to improve or restore the site. It was just *there*: the giant towering semicircle of damp-looking walls rising to 130 feet. The overriding feeling was *help, get us out of here.*

This construction was no Colosseum, just a colossal failure. This was why local authorities had kept it, as a symbol of the defeat of National Socialism in Germany.

Danny and I went to the Documentation Center, where we learned that Hitler had attracted such large crowds in Nuremberg as the National Socialists had strong local support. Anti-Semitic factions had been active for many years, coming to prominence in the 1920s.

The dictator had picked his parading spot with all this in mind. Before the first Nazi rally in 1933 the anti-Semitic atmosphere had already reached such a fever pitch locally that more than half of Nuremberg's Jewish population had left. Later on, more than two thousand local Jews were sent to concentration camps from the parade ground, where they had been gathered. It is believed 52 survived.

A truly chilling spot.

Then, Danny and I, almost stunned into silence, went to Zeppelin Field.

This had been a particularly important parade ground for the National Socialists. Nothing much had been done to the area. The parade route, the terraces and the grandstand, where visitors could stand at the spot Hitler gave his infamous addresses, had been left untouched, looking weather-worn more than seventy years on. Behind the grandstand, a giant marble swastika had once existed, but it had been blown up by Allied forces on 22 April 1945 (captured in a brilliant old newsreel that can be found on the website of the United States Holocaust Memorial Museum).

We went to the lake, where a solitary hot dog stall stood near a jetty where odd flamingo-shaped pedalos could be rented, and Danny said: "This is one of the weirdest places I've ever been."

It was extremely strange; hard to get your head round. Disturbing. Unsettling. Unnerving. And yes: just plain weird.

We returned to the city centre and went to the courtroom where the Nuremberg Trials were held in 1945–1946.

The wooden-panelled Courtroom 600 had hardly changed since 1945 when Hermann Göring (creator of the Gestapo secret police), Joachim von Ribbentrop (Hitler's foreign minister), Hans Frank (in charge of Poland, overseeing the concentration camps) and nine others received the death sentence. Ten other defendants including Rudolf Hess (Hitler's deputy for some time) and Albert Speer (architect of the Nuremberg parade grounds) were issued prison sentences from ten years to life. Speer's sentence was 20 years. Hess, a life-timer, died in prison aged 93 in 1987, when both Danny and I were aged 16, doing our GCSEs.

You could stand in the courtroom, visit the press room and explore the museum rooms learning all about the landmark trial. Inside the latter, you could spend hours and any visit by its nature depended on which bits you had time to see. One section I happened upon described how the defendants behaved in court on hearing their judgements. The reaction of Göring, as related by the prison psychologist Gustave Gilbert, was instructive of the repentance of the head of the Gestapo as he railed against (and ranted about) those who had handed in senior Nazis to face trial and those who had been disloyal to Hitler: "I don't give a damn if I get executed, or drown, or crash in a plane, or drink myself to death! But there is still a matter of honour in this damn life! Assassination attempt on Hitler! Ugh! I could have sunk through the floor. And do you think I would have handed Himmler over to the enemy, guilty as he was? Dammit, I would have liquidated the bastard myself! Or if there was to have been any trial, a German court should have sentenced him! Would Americans think of handing over their criminals to us to sentence?"

A deadening sense of evil, along with a sweet validation of justice, hung in the air at Courtroom 600.

* * *

After all of that, it was time for a beer.

This was easily done in Bavaria.

The centre of Nuremberg inside the old town walls was strange and slightly soulless, with many structures rebuilt since the war, and almost deserted streets. Where was everyone? We popped into the King's Arms pub to see what a German King's Arms pub was like. This was what we found: England playing Ukraine at football (nil–nil) and a British man at a bar with just a couple of other drinkers droning on about how he would "like to get shit-faced but my wife won't let me get shit-faced". So: quite similar to at least some King's Arms pubs back home, no doubt.

We did not hang around to find out whether the British man or his wife got their way.

Instead, we walked down a lane and played darts at an old-fashioned beer hall with beams and solid wooden tables and a sign outside depicting – how can one put this in the 2020s? – an extremely buxom woman in a low-cut dirndl traditional dress. Inside, however, no such women were serving beer, though there were a few more people in this watering hole, mainly men playing darts at a row of dartboards (the game seemed all the rage in Nuremberg). There was a simple pleasure to be had joining the Bavarian darts players for a while. A camaraderie in the "arrows". We were easily pleased middle-aged Interrail tourists.

Then we found a neighbourhood of beer halls, with similar adverts as the previous beer hall. Finally, we had found everyone! The beer halls in this neighbourhood were much larger with more beams and more solid wooden tables and waitresses who *were* dressed as earlier described; the clichés of southern Germany alive and kicking, oompah music even playing. It was jolly and it was raucous and for a while I thought to myself: *we really are tourist suckers; we really should be digging harder to experience an unclichéd account of a night in Nuremberg beyond the tourist trap beer halls, how have we descended to this, so soon?*

The only thing was that this "clichéd" night out seemed to be a regular night out in Nuremberg. No cliché, if you thought about it: just reality. We ate our sausages and drank our beer delivered by the waitresses in dirndl costumes. The beer was fresh and frothy. The sausages pleasingly juicy and seasoned nicely with herbs. We toasted our good fortune at living this southern German cliché dream, the only slight annoyance being two American businesspeople drinking frothy beers on a solid wooden table next to us who were loudly discussing how "I'm not going to allow Marjorie to squeeze me out of small sales… I expect a leadership challenge… *we* are the proper kings… we need a hit list [of colleagues to subdue]… don't worry about him, he'll retire soon…" And so on. Couldn't they have found somewhere else to hatch their office subterfuge? And do it a bit more quietly? Though beer hall intrigue in southern Germany was no new thing, we supposed. All part of the (frankly extremely enjoyable) cliché, you might say.

Then we returned to Hotel Park Inn, where we took the lift to our rooms and Danny said: "Hold on, what's this?"

A piece of paper had been stuck on the lift wall while we had been out. It said: "Information for our Guests… due to a mega strike, no subways, streetcars, trains and buses will run throughout Germany from 00.01 to midnight and some airports will be closed". The message suggested calling taxis to get wherever you wanted to go and concluded with: "If you have any questions, our reception team is always happy to help! Wishing you a colourful stay, Your hotel management."

This sobered us up pretty sharpish.

We went back to the lobby. We were meant to take a train to Passau, still in Germany but right on the border with Austria, in the morning. We had had no idea about the *train* strike. All we had heard about was the *plane* strike mentioned by the nice elderly couple when we were pulling into Nuremberg station.

The curly-haired receptionist looked at us with kind eyes as though observing two curious English lunatics who had not been following German industrial affairs closely enough. Which we had not been. We thought we had seen the back of industrial troubles in France.

"Did you not know? It was announced a week ago," she said.

We had missed this announcement and evidently planned our visit to Germany to coincide with a rare widespread national strike.

She gave us another of her earlier looks: we were, after all, just another couple of middle-aged tourists who had drunk a few beers in the beer halls and did not have a clue. *We* were the clichés to her.

Like the notice had mentioned in the lift, she suggested we try a taxi. Then, when we explained that long-distance taxis did not fit in with our understanding of "good value" (as established on our park bench), she recommended a company we had never heard of called BlaBlaCar that offered cheap rates for shared rides in cars. "It is useful. It is usually safe. I never heard anything terrible about it. All you have to do is log on and search." She regarded us as though considering the chances of us working out BlaBlaCar pretty low.

Miraculously, however, within ten minutes we were booked, for a small fee, to travel in a BMW Series 5 with "tan leather seats" driven by a man named Roman (rating 4.9 out of 5 on BlaBlaCar). He looked like a suave fellow in his profile picture. We were, BlaBlaCar instructed, to meet him at a Shell petrol station on the edge of Nuremberg at 1.50 p.m. the next day.

The receptionist appeared surprised, even startled, that we had actually managed this feat of online endeavour. We were, too.

An unusual "train" day lay ahead… involving no trains whatsoever.

CHAPTER TWO

NUREMBERG TO BUDAPEST IN HUNGARY, VIA PASSAU IN GERMANY AND BRATISLAVA IN SLOVAKIA

"TODAY, WE ARE NOT WORKING"

Whistles and the thump of dance music emanated from Frauentorgraben street.

This was the one that led to Nuremberg station. Nosiness about what a German train station would be like during a German rail strike (presumably rather eerie) had made me drag Danny away from the hotel for breakfast at the station; he had seemed to want to have a bit of a lie-in but did not appear too bothered to be accompanying me for this slightly unusual act of devotion to the train journey. Before meeting the BlaBlaCar we had time to kill. We could return to the hotel for bags later.

As we left Hotel Park Inn, however, we heard a cacophony. Curious, we went in the direction of the racket, not thinking much of it, perhaps a funfair was taking place. But as we arrived at Frauentorgraben, we realized we were about to join a march of several thousand irate German rail workers.

We may not have encountered many French protestors, but we had stumbled on quite a few Germans having their voices heard.

Our German rail workers' strike timing was exquisite, if that is quite the right expression. We had arrived precisely the moment the lead vehicle of the protest was passing, speakers booming dance music. We fell into step with the disgruntled German rail employees on what was the "biggest strike for decades" according to the local television channel that morning.

Danny was beside me in the column of marchers.

"The West is in crisis," he declared solemnly. "And this is part of it."

He seemed in a serious mood, perhaps due to having had his lie-in cut short to witness striking German train employees.

He peeled away to the pavement to take snaps and I continued with the main column. They were chanting: "*Zusammen geht mehr!*" ("Together is more!"). Many wore fluorescent jackets. Some had beer bottles sticking out of back pockets. A few were already drinking beer. Police escorts both preceded and followed the protestors. Some police were also by the side of the street disdainfully inspecting us. There were no confrontations, however. People who usually took public transport to work walked by smiling benignly. A poll of the German public had found 55 per cent of people supported the strikes, said the earlier TV report.

I began talking to my neighbour, a man named Markus.

I asked what was going on.

He replied somewhat obviously: "Today, we are not working."

"Why are you on strike?" I asked.

"Because of work conditions and poor payment. During Covid we worked very hard to keep everything going. We are here on the streets for the transport system. We are also here on the streets for the hospitals. For all the public offices. We are here for all. For all the things to do with electricity and power and health and education and transport and traffic," he said.

Markus was in his early thirties, bright-eyed and welcoming. "It is especially difficult now for those who do not get much money, everything is more expensive," he said.

What did the union want?

"Ten point five per cent," he said.

This was the officially requested pay rise. The inflation rate was 7 per cent, somewhat confusingly. The unions wanted more than the inflation rate, however, to make up for previous low pay rises against inflation. They were not getting it. Hence the strike.

The unions involved were Eisenbahn- und Verkehrsgewerkschaft (the "railway and transport" union) and ver.di (a shortening of Vereinte Dienstleistungsgewerkschaft, the "united services" union). When not yelling "Together is more!" the strikers were also sometimes chanting *"Heute ist kein Arbeitstag!"* ("Today is not a working day!") and *"Heute ist Streiktag!"* ("Today is a strike day!"). The songs being played included a tune called "Schüsse in die Luft" ("Shots in the Air") by Kraftklub, "Move Your Body" by Öwnboss & Sevek and "Seven Nation Army" by DJ Fluke. So there was a revolutionary musical theme of sorts.

The strikers arrived at the grand, somewhat austere-looking neo-Baroque station.

As we did so, curving round to head into the city centre, a few startled station drunks became animated. There they had been quietly contemplating things with their bottles, with the whole empty station to themselves for once, and suddenly several thousand chanting and whistling unionists had arrived.

Having quickly assessed the situation, a little blearily, they began cheering on the marchers, patting them on their backs and yelling approvingly. Nothing so tremendously uplifting had ever happened round the station so early on a Monday morning before, their surprised looks seemed to suggest. A gnarled man with a beacon-red face roared to the heavens and lifted his arms as though in a state of ecstasy.

A party atmosphere had broken out. The protestor mix was about 60–40 male–female and it was a celebratory affair despite the underlying concern of low pay.

The strikers were waving banners that said: "*SCHAFFEN WIR FRANZÖSISCHE VERHÄLTNISSE, ALLE IN DER STREIK*" ("LET'S CREATE FRENCH CONDITIONS, ALL ON STRIKE") and "*WIR LASSEN DIE ZÜGE NICHT GERNE LEER STEHEN, ABER WIR WOLLEN EIN FAIRES ANGEBOT*" ("WE DON'T LIKE TO LET THE TRAINS STAND EMPTY, BUT WE WANT A FAIR OFFER").

Danny and I followed them round a bit more. It was eye-opening to see European strikers up close and personal. They seemed dug in and ready for a long, hard fight. They were also, as though overcome by gallows humour, enjoying themselves, if only for the march.

There was a problem they faced, however.

That problem was that German public opinion regarding the standard of trains in the country (if not the current strike) was extremely low and had been for some time.

Analysts blamed underinvestment in Deutsche Bahn for many years. An unwieldy, complicated rail network featuring multiple hubs also added to difficulties and delays when work needed to be conducted; Germany had 20,753 miles of track compared to a mere 10,018 miles in the UK and 18,580 in France. Deutsche Bahn faced a "chronic crisis", according to the German Federal Audit Office. The situation had become so dire that badly delayed trains travelling into Switzerland were being blocked entry into major cities by Swiss rail authorities, who were instructing drivers to stop at earlier stations to allow passengers on to rail replacement buses. Officials did not want endless tardy German trains messing up schedules on their lines.

It had all become so bad that, in Germany, *zugwitze* (train jokes) had become something of a craze. For example:

Ticket inspector: "May I see the ticket for your child?"

Woman with toddler: "I don't have one."

Ticket inspector: "Why is this?"

Woman with toddler: "I was pregnant when I began waiting for this train."

Even the Swedish wonder-environmentalist Greta Thunberg, a big railway fan as trains are estimated to be a six-times greener way of getting about than planes, was down on Deutsche Bahn, implying she had had no seat on a service through Germany back from a climate protest in Italy in 2019. At the time, a picture of her on social media had showed Thunberg slumped on the floor in a carriage corridor. "Traveling on overcrowded trains through Germany. And I'm finally on my way home!" she had written to accompany the photograph.

This, however, had led to a spat. Deutsche Bahn, stung by the criticism, had responded by issuing a statement for Thunberg: "It would have been even nicer if you had also reported how friendly and competently you were looked after by our team at your seat in first class."

Touché!

Funnily, I had always found Deutsche Bahn quite good.

Maybe I had just always been lucky.

Anyway, one way or another, the German rail strikers appeared to have an image issue on their hands.

Danny and I went for breakfast at the somewhat austere, neo-Baroque, echoingly empty station, where the departure boards simply said "*STREIK*". Then we returned to the hotel past a closed café with a notice by the door that said in English "IF YOU ARE RACIST, PUTIN, TRUMP, SEXIST, HOMOPHOBIC OR AN ARSEHOLE, DON'T COME IN" (no one could if it didn't open in the morning, we observed), and tramped across Nuremberg amid snow flurries, which had just begun, to the Shell garage.

At the garage we sat on a wall waiting for Roman and his BMW Series 5.

Danny was in a contemplative, if rather cynical, mood. Regarding the strikers, he said: "They reminded me of Peter Sellers in the film *I'm All Right Jack* when he's leading a trade union and they have the slogan: *More pay, less work!* That's at the heart of most industrial disputes."

Not one of the most nuanced of interpretations, perhaps (but admittedly amusing).

Regarding the trouble the strike was causing to our slow trains to Istanbul, however, he said: "If it's a smooth journey all the way, what's the point? You might as well go on a Saga Holiday. Don't freak out if something goes wrong. Just roll with it."

He had, it seemed, quickly converted to the realities of a long, early-twenty-first-century journey on a series of trains round Europe.

One of those realities being: *the trains don't always run when you want them to.*

Blah blah car
Nuremberg to Passau

Taking to the roads was humiliating yet necessary.

Roman arrived in his dark grey BMW Series 5 looking as suave as his BlaBlaCar picture: slicked-back hair, casual but expensive-looking clothing and a manner that was both languid and purposeful. He was tall and beanpole thin, aged in his mid-thirties, working as a "lead sales specialist" for a British pressure-sensor company based in Leicester in the UK, a little light questioning revealed (journalistic habit – aka, being very nosy – being my usual habit). He was driving to Austria, to Vienna and Graz, to do some pressure-sensor business and was picking up another BlaBlaCar passenger along the way. He was often moving about on such trips and took passengers for the company they provided on the road, not the money, he said.

The BMW Series 5 purred into life and we rolled out of Nuremberg in comfortable tan leather seats.

Roman, it transpired, was a big BlaBlaCar car-share, carpool man. So much so, he had met his wife on one.

"I started using BlaBlaCar as a passenger when I was in my teenage years," he said.

The French company, which we had never heard of before, had been created in 2006 and now had more than 100 million members and its very name came from the propensity, or not, of drivers to provide chit-chat.

"At the beginning it was not as organized as now. Now it is not so wild. Now it is safer and much more organized. Back in the old days, you might have four people squashed in the back, unable to use the seat belts. You could have a driver smoking all the way," said Roman.

Passengers were now able to check whether drivers were smokers. Safety, seat belts and so on had become a major priority.

Roman's best BlaBlaCar drive had been ten years ago when he hit it off with another passenger, his wife-to-be, who had happened to need a place to stay that night. Things had "worked out", Roman said: "We got together."

As he told us this, we joined an autobahn with no speed restrictions and began purring along at 100 mph. So far as the scenery was concerned, this comprised the sides of other vehicles and countryside greenery whizzing by. Nowhere near as good as being on a train.

Roman liked Leicester. "I do go there sometimes yes," he said. "There are a lot of Indian food dishes. I do like that. I like the area there. I usually stay at a small countryside hotel. I enjoy the pubs, of course."

Roman also liked Passau, our destination by the German border with Austria next to where three rivers converged: the Inn, the Ilz and the Danube.

"Definitely nice," he said. "Quite a small place."

He paused as he swiftly overtook a series of lorries that had been blocking us. Roman's languid style did not extend to his driving.

He continued of Passau: "Each year, you know, there can be quite high water levels. Each year this can be an issue."

Passau, which had a population of 50,000, was so flood-prone it was against the law to have bedrooms in basements in some parts of the city, he said.

Roman began to tell us about a problem that sometimes cropped up when immigrants attempting to reach northern Europe used BlaBlaCar. Drivers on the website preferred debit/credit card payments in advance, but immigrants often did not have these, just cash. This meant some drivers faced taking people who might not have the money to pay or did not turn up. Roman, however, had recently given a lift to an Iranian, who could pay, and transported him several hundred miles to Nuremberg.

"This Iranian he asked me: *is there really no speed limit in Germany?* I said: *yes*. I said I was going one hundred miles per hour, this is just a standard speed. The Iranian seemed very surprised by this." Roman paused to consider the autobahn's lack of speed limit. "It is not really rational, but Germans simply love autobahns, this crazy side of life. Every few years politicians try to set a speed limit, but it is too emotional for German people."

He talked about pressure sensors for a while. "Airplanes, power plants, many industries need pressure sensors," he said. "To measure water levels and weight of water." It was a growing area of business, but Britain's departure from the European Union meant "issues, a lot of problems with shipping to Europe. It's just not as easy as it used to be without Brexit. We have opened a service centre in France. Now we are not always shipping to Leicester."

We stopped in Regensburg, about halfway, where we collected the other passenger.

She was a twenty-something Chinese student wearing a pink outfit and brandishing long pink nails. She had been visiting her boyfriend who worked in IT in Regensburg. On learning about our travels, she said, before saying anything else, that we should eat at a place called Ratskeller in Passau.

"You must go to Ratskeller!" she said with absolute certainty. She repeated for emphasis: "Ratskeller!"

We said we would go to Ratskeller.

She looked very pleased.

She was from Guangzhou in China, close to Hong Kong, and was studying at the University of Passau. We never got what she was studying, nor what her boyfriend did, nor even her name such was her rapid-fire delivery.

She began to talk about a young pop singer from Hong Kong named Jackson Wang, who had recently defended the Chinese regime while on stage at a concert in London. This had resulted in widespread criticism as he had failed to mention the plight of the mistreated Uyghur community in Xinjiang in north-west China.

"One month ago, Jackson Wang said that it is OK in China, a good place," she told us, sounding suddenly impassioned. "Well, it is OK! It is good place! But Jackson Wang was attacked in the media." She spat out the word "media". She continued: "The media says a lot of horrible things about China, especially the BBC. It is wrong! The BBC is wrong!"

She went quiet for a while. Danny and I looked at each other: we had not quite expected this outburst.

Then she began to talk about Beijing: "It's begun again."

"What has?" Danny asked.

"The smog! It's back! It's horrible! There are no trees and the sand and smoke just blow through to Beijing."

She swivelled round and regarded us somewhat fiercely from the front passenger seat as though the smog was somehow our, or perhaps the BBC's, fault, before switching demeanour and gesticulating casually with handfuls of pink nails seemingly to suggest of the smog in Beijing: *oh, but this is just life.*

We sped at great speed into Passau, where we all got out by the front of trainless Passau station, said our goodbyes and thanked Roman, who looked at us languidly, suavely and purposefully, before hopping back into his BMW and revving away.

We had successfully negotiated the effects of a German train strike, having even taken part in one.

Not bad for a day's Interrailing.

Three rivers, Hitler's near miss and a karaoke evening
Passau

At the tourist information centre by Passau station, we asked the tourist information officer about what to see in the little border city. Her reply was surprising and succinct: "It has the biggest church organ in the world. It is quite outstanding."

This was at St Stephen's Cathedral.

"There is also a marker by the river showing the highest ever level of the floods," she said, suggesting we take a look at this marker. "We always have floods, and this is also outstanding."

As though by way of explanation as to why there were so many outstanding floods, the tourist officer explained: "You see, we have three rivers." She paused, before adding almost as an afterthought: "And we have a castle." She paused once more, considering this. "But everyone has a castle. It is not an outstanding castle."

She was an honest tourist information officer fond of the word "outstanding". She added that Passau had been a Roman city and "we had Celts here". Furthermore: "We have a white sausage called *Leberkäse*."

We asked what *Leberkäse* comprised.

"It's all the bits they can't use of an animal. It is outstanding." Presumably this meant the "bits" that could not be sold elsewhere after a carcass had been butchered.

"I'm a vegan, this is not something I like," she added.

With this briefing we set forth by foot across Passau into its old town following a narrow cobbled lane up a hill to a grand pink church, a fancy hat shop, a guns-and-knives shop and the Baroque cupola-topped towers of St Stephen's. Our lodging, the 24-7 Apartment Passau, was opposite and it was extremely good value once again (two rooms for half the Paris price). We keyed in a code and ascended a twisting staircase arriving at a new "hostel-style venue for grown-ups" with modern double rooms, a pool table, a kitchen, and shared bathrooms. My room had exposed beams, a New York warehouse apartment style and a river Danube view.

Not bad at all for this extremely good value price, which had Danny's full approval.

Our passage in Passau went thus. First, a game of pool accompanied by beers at 24-7 Apartment Passau. Next, an ascent to the non-outstanding castle, which was really quite imposing and eye-catching and even *outstanding* (no matter what the tourist information person had said). From the castle, you could see the fine Baroque city spread out below, squeezed between all the rivers, seemingly perilous and vulnerable on its narrow headland. We gazed out for some time simply admiring the steeples and the tight web of cobbled lanes and the terracotta rooftops in the evening chill. Hazel-yellow light enveloped the Danube as the sun was setting: it was a lovely, mellow spot.

From pamphlets distributed by the tourist information officer we had learned that Passau had long been a place of human settlement.

The Romans had come when Passau was known as Batavis. In the fifth century, St Severinus had founded a monastery. In 1552 the important Peace of Passau was signed during the period of Charles V, the Holy Roman Emperor, which was to be a forerunner to the even more important Augsburg Settlement allowing rulers in Europe to choose between Roman Catholicism or Lutheranism. This was considered a key moment in what would eventually result in European sovereign states.

Much later on in Passau's history, however, somewhat surprisingly for us so soon after taking in Nuremberg (and *not* mentioned in the tourist office information): Adolf Hitler had been brought up in Passau from the age of three to five (in 1892–1894).

During this time, the future Nazi Party leader was believed to have almost died, if many accounts of the period are to be trusted. The word-of-mouth story goes that Hitler fell into the fast-flowing icy currents of the river Inn when aged four and was rescued by a boy named Johann Kuehberger; an article in the *Donau Zeitung* newspaper of 1894 describing a "young fellow" slipping into the river and being saved by a passer-by seems to match this timing. The reason Hitler is understood never to have spoken of the matter is because Kuehberger went on to become a priest and this had not aligned with the Führer's position on religion (which he despised). Of his time in Passau, Hitler was only ever to refer to enjoying playing cowboys and Indians by its many riverbanks: not that a priest-to-be had played some part in keeping him on the planet.

Somewhere down there Hitler had been saved. Not such a lovely, mellow thought.

Danny and I returned down a winding path to the bridge across the river Danube and the city centre.

We examined the old (very high) flood marks of yesteryear. A great part of Passau's centre had been underwater in 1501, while the next most calamitous year was 2013, when the Danube had risen about a foot lower, and 2002 had seen another bad one. We couldn't find our BlaBlaCar companion's Ratskeller so we ate beef stews at a beer hall named Altes Bräuhaus at a table with red dahlias in vases of old beer bottles next to a table of people playing cards for coins beneath a vaulted ceiling. Then we shiveringly ventured out into the narrow lanes. It had suddenly become extremely cold, and not quite knowing where we were going, our feet took us along a lane to the Shamrock Irish Pub, where a karaoke evening was in full flow.

This turned out to be quite unexpectedly brilliant. What was impressive was that though this was a Monday in late March, the Shamrock Irish Pub was packed to the rafters with all ages from grandparents to those only just of drinking age. A wonderful sense of community spirit was alive, people letting their hair down and having great fun: who gave a damn if it was a Monday night in late March (nothing to do with St Patrick's Day, it seemed) and extremely cold?

At this juncture, however, Danny received a text and suddenly seemed immediately stressed out. He left the main bar and went to deal with a domestic issue on his phone while I drank a beer and watched a succession of performers sing Annie Lennox, Shakira, Oasis and Amy Winehouse songs. The highlight was a south-eastern German man's version of "The Real Slim Shady" by the American rapper Eminem. He went for every rattle-gun lyric, barely managing to keep up, stumbling badly from time to time but continuing with impressive gusto. Bravo to the Bavarian rapper!

Danny had returned by this stage, having dealt with matters at home. We listened to some entertaining Bavarian versions of James Brown, David Bowie, the Arctic Monkeys and the Spice Girls – and, with the lyrics of the Spice Girls' catchy "Wannabe" reverberating, sung by a trio of gutsy twenty-somethings having the time of their lives on a frozen Monday night near Germany's border with Austria, we paced back through the chill to 24-7 Apartment Passau.

All things considered, an excellent time in Passau: a pleasant stroll to the castle, a good view of the three rivers and the city squeezed between them from above, a fine dinner and agreeable Bavarian-Irish karaoke evening.

We were also just glad really, it must be conceded, to have reached there and not to have been stuck in Nuremberg. We were making yet more progress eastwards, if perhaps not as we had quite imagined.

"We are descending to new lows"
Passau to Bratislava in Slovakia, via Vienna in Austria

In the morning, snow blanketed the rooftops of Passau and the hill leading up to the castle. A blissful silence had descended. All was quiet, white, gentle and peaceful, an occasional barge floating by on the Danube.

We went to the station. This was long and apricot-coloured and looked like a nineteenth-century army barracks, featuring rows of arched windows tapering along the façade, a newsagent, a café and a pair of pigeons that had got the knack of the automatic sliding doors. These pigeons would trigger the doors to open, look around for crumbs in a somewhat haughty manner and trigger the doors to exit. This they would repeat every few minutes. Evolution in action: twenty-first-century-style.

We bought sandwiches from a burly café owner from Rome, of whom Danny asked whether he supported Roma or Lazio, the two local football teams. This triggered an outburst.

"There is only one team in Rome!" said the burly café owner. "Roma! Roma is Rome! Rome is Roma!" He was a blaze of passion about the matter.

Danny and the burly café owner discussed the merits of Francesco Totti, a legendary former Roma striker. Then they considered in some detail the tactics and personality of José Mourinho, the volatile Roma manager.

And as we boarded the 10:26 Deutsche Bahn ICE train to Vienna, Danny said: "Football: it's a great way to communicate with men around the world. The everyman will know a lot about football, the players, the tactics – from *The Sun* or whatever. It's an excellent form of communication."

The 10:26 train pulled away.

A train again, finally: it was good to feel the motion of the tracks after an absence caused by the German rail strike.

This one had snazzy purple seats with white cushion headrests and was soon speeding across a blur of flat green farmland marked by giant barns and broken by silver birch woodland.

Our four-person table seats had another occupant, a tiny man whom we had seen earlier on the freezing platform stuffing a great number of bananas and Marlboro cigarette packets into an enormous backpack that must have weighed a similar total to the tiny man. Maybe he was a smuggler but had not been informed about the European single market. Maybe prices for bananas and Marlboro cigarettes were just a bit lower in Germany than in Austria or wherever he was eventually heading. He wore a green beanie, chewed gum incessantly, and from time to time furtively consulted a pair of mobiles he had placed on the table in front of him.

For a while the train followed the Danube. A lemon-coloured palace on a hill came and went, disappearing without giving us a chance to consider it properly. The Deutsche Bahn ICE was zipping along at 100 mph (it could be tricky sometimes to find a slow train in Germany). Crows occupied treetops, their nests like blobs of ink amid the faint green buds of spring. We pulled into Wels station, where the "smuggler" disembarked with his bag of bananas and Marlboros. Then we pulled away from Wels station and, soon after, snow-topped mountains arose to the right after which the train stopped at Linz station, close to a large graveyard and a strange office tower block with blue-tinted windows.

Danny and I were (all digital discipline cast aside) busy on the internet.

We booked a private room with several beds in the Patio Hostel in Bratislava. This was extremely cheap – and this time it was me trying to keep down costs.

"Where will this end?" mused Danny. "A park bench?"

Where it began, to be fair.

He did not, however, seem that bothered by the idea of the room in the hostel, given its excellent value.

We proceeded into a series of tunnels as Danny expanded his thoughts on budget travel, of which he had many.

"I must admit I feel a bit ashamed of myself going so low," he said, before pausing and adding: "But f*** it. It'll be an experience."

Meanwhile, I was clicking away to reserve seats for Bratislava to Budapest on the trusty Eurail app. While I was preoccupied doing so (silently cursing a feature that kept sending me back to an opening page), the train slowed down, stopped, and Danny yelled: "We're here!"

We disembarked at speed. We looked around. Then we realized we were not "here", as in the main station in Vienna. We were "here", as in a station named Wien Meidling, not the main station of Vienna, Wien Hauptbahnhof. Having not been on a train for a whole day, we seemed to have forgotten how to catch them properly and let them take us to the correct destination.

An icy wind blew across the platforms as we waited for the next train.

It began to snow once again.

The new train turned up quickly enough though and we arrived at a large, modern station that we actually wanted to arrive at – where the first passengers of the *Orient Express* had been greeted (at some length) by the national anthems of France, Germany, Austria, Hungary, Romania, Bulgaria and Turkey played by the Imperial Guards of the Austro-Hungarian Empire in 1883 and treated to a slap-up meal at the station's restaurant. Our experience involved grabbing a sandwich at a busy concourse and soon after boarding a lurid lime-green and yellow VOR train to Bratislava, the 13:45, due in at 2.44 p.m. We had decided not to stay in Austria's capital simply because we had both been there before (very enjoyable: the Baroque architecture, the cake-and-coffee cafés, the old Ferris wheel, the markets, the waltzes, the nights at the opera... all of that) and wondered what went on in Slovakia's capital. It was only a short distance away, about 40 miles.

VOR stood for Verkehrsverbund Ost-Region and was Austrian owned. We settled into lurid lime-green and yellow seats – this VOR train had a citrusy look, both inside and out – and watched as we rolled towards Slovakia passing sidings with wagons designed to carry coal and liquids and then a series of level crossings, industrial zones and warehouses, before traversing into flat countryside with wind farms and grain silos. Stops were made at stations with names such as Gramatneusiedl, Bruck, Parndorf and Gattendorf before large, ugly, grey communist-era tower blocks arose and the train drew into its destination, Bratislava-Petržalka station, right next to a huge estate of yet more large, ugly, grey communist-era tower blocks.

We had arrived in Eastern Europe.

* * *

Bratislava-Petržalka station matched its surroundings. It too was large, ugly and grey, redeemed only slightly inside by some potted plants in the atrium. Aside from those it was almost uniformly depressing and dystopian-looking. A haggard man staggered by across the ticket hall clutching a bottle of wine, seeming to symbolize what large, ugly grey surroundings might lead you to. We followed him for a while at the start of what turned out to be a 45-minute walk northwards heading for a bridge across the Danube. We had not arrived at the main central station. This was probably another error on our behalf (our second such "train mistake" of the day).

Through the large, ugly, windswept grey communist-era tower blocks we went. A gang of youths was drinking beer and larking about. They observed us – two middle-aged backpackers clearly not natives of Slovakia's capital – but did not seem particularly interested. Danny was taking no chances, however.

"I'm going to put my hat on to make me look poorer," he declared. He put on a grey beanie.

This immediately produced a less savoury look, although whether poorer or not it was difficult to judge.

Over the long, windy bridge we continued with a view of a massive, stately whitewashed castle with four terracotta-topped corner towers. While this massive, stately whitewashed castle was undoubtedly "impressive" it somehow managed to be a decidedly dull-looking massive castle. When we later looked it up online (yet again failing shamefully on the pronounced online-detox front), we found it had been completed in 1964, squarely during communist years, although an original castle at the site had dated from the ninth century. So, it was a communist-era-improved, whitewashed medieval castle.

Walkways on the far side of the bridge led to an industrial area and warehouse outlets, a footbridge over a major road and a space-age-style tower with a UFO-shaped chamber at the top featuring mirrored-glass windows. The streets were quiet and grim communist-era shopping malls and civic buildings were clustered all about, although the ornate columns and balustrades and busts of famous former performers at the old Slovak National Theatre did provide a break from the monotony.

The Patio Hostel was dour and uninviting though, like so much else, a concrete block that looked like a low-security prison.

Inside we were given a key by a scraggly-haired man with an unkempt beard who had the manner of a distracted poet. We asked about a bowl of earplugs on the reception counter. The scraggly-haired poet explained it could sometimes be noisy at night in the hostel (noise caused by other guests). "They are also in your room," he said – more earplugs. Danny said nothing on this subject, he was soaking it all in, looking pensive. We went to the room. It was a pale grey box with four single beds with earplugs on the pillows. Danny said nothing once more, although I sensed he had quite a lot to say.

A champion of budget prices, he was not necessarily always a fan of the reality of frugality.

We stepped out into the grim communist-era streets of Bratislava. I bought a one-euro jumper from a second-hand clothes shop and put it on; the temperature was hovering around zero. Breaking his silence as I handed over my one-euro coin, Danny said: "We are descending to new lows."

A bit beyond the one-euro second-hand clothes shop was a distinguished turn-of-the-twentieth-century building with arched entrances and windows that looked like an old train station.

"Looks like an old train station," I said.

"You and your f***ing train stations," said Danny. "I have higher things that I am looking for."

He did not explain what these higher things were.

He seemed generally aggrieved about Bratislava.

Anyway, the building turned out to be an old market hall, not a station. Yet the streets beyond were a surprising delight. Neoclassical bell towers arose. Pleasant squares were lined by neoclassical town houses, each around four storeys high and either cream or pistachio-hued, in many subtle variations, forming elegant patchworks of façades redolent of better pre-communist times. Narrow lanes twisting every which way led to more graceful buildings painted saffron, salmon-pink and shades of pale pastel blue. The pavements of these narrow lanes, and many mysterious alleys, were cobbled. Cosy-looking, candlelit basement establishments tucked away here and there offered beer and goulash. The oppression of the grimmer suburbs of Slovakia's capital faded away as we wandered onwards.

Further on down the pleasant lanes, we came to the Devil's Gogo Dance Club. This was bang in the heart of Slovakia's capital, down an alley about equidistant between the presidential palace and St Martin's Cathedral. We did not go in the Devil's Gogo Dance Club, although we could not help speculating on what went on inside a place with a name like that and even looked it up on the internet at an almost empty nearby pub with long, bare wooden tables. This was purely out of nosiness, or you might say, prurience. Several mentions of Devil's Gogo Dance Club sprang up. It appeared to be a famous place, in certain circles. One website, named Red-light-district.co, deemed it to be "very good". Stagdoin.com considered it as being among the "best activities" in Bratislava. Meanwhile, Lustscanner.com summed up its thoughts on the venue thus: "Wonderful women. American film party. Sinful doses of adrenaline." Quite what the "American film party" was all about was not clear. The club, so far as we could establish, did not have its own website.

We were in the mood for a night out, as usual. But not at Devil's Gogo Dance Club or the bar with no people and long wooden tables. Danny's online research led to the Bukowski Late Night Drink Bar.

This was close to the old market hall I had thought might be an old train station.

Inside, it was dimly lit with neoclassical architecture, a mezzanine and a buzz of fervid conversation as though a revolution was in the offing, or simply as though everyone had already had quite a few drinks. With another internet search – we had by this stage given up any pretence of travelling without the accompaniment of little computers telling us everything in our pockets – we learned that Charles Bukowski (1920–1994) was an American poet/writer, born in Germany, whom *Time* magazine once described as a "laureate of American lowlife" as much of his subject matter touched on hard drinking, the drudgery of low-paid work and thorny relations with women.

Apparently, quite randomly it would seem or perhaps these themes simply touched something in the psyche of the people of Bratislava, Bukowski was a local hero.

He was, we were rapidly discovering, an extremely famous poet/ writer who neither of us, to our shame, had heard of before. He had lived in his adopted city of Los Angeles and had penned a column in the little-read newspaper *Open City* entitled *Notes of a Dirty Old Man*. Among his books were *Tales of Ordinary Madness, Love is a Dog from*

Hell and *The Pleasures of the Damned*, a posthumous poetry collection. The singer Leonard Cohen, another artist with an alternative edge, once said of him: "He brought everyone down to earth, even the angels."

Bukowski was so well thought of in Bratislava that a bar had been named after him, though nothing racy or sordid or particularly lowlife was going on, just a lot of people nattering away with drinks in a slightly rebellious-seeming manner: groups of friends and office colleagues (judging by attire).

We ordered beers from a barmaid from Odessa in Ukraine who was living in Bratislava and studying for an online management degree from her university in Odessa while waiting for the war to end. She preferred Odessa to Bratislava and seemed homesick with an unsurprisingly sad streak, given what was happening in her country, despite the lively surroundings of the Bukowski Late Night Drink Bar. We chatted to her for a while at the bar (finding out all this about her, which she seemed more than happy to divulge) and then drank our beers on stools in a corner in a middle-aged manner minding our own business and returned to our box-like four-bed private room at the Patio Hostel, whereupon Danny declared: "It's good to rough it once in a while. This is that once. We've been there, done that."

Fortunately, the earplugs, which we did not bother wearing, were unnecessary that night.

"Just a couple of old soaks on a train"
Bratislava to Budapest, Hungary

Bratislava's main station was in the opposite direction to Bratislava-Petržalka station, about a half-hour walk north across cracked paving stones scattered with broken glass. There were tattoo parlours. There were slot machine arcades. There were food kiosks serving *hot dogy* and *bagety*. There was graffiti that read: "ANTIFA AREA: NO COPS, NO NAZIS".

This graffiti was showing solidarity with the worldwide "Antifa" movement, whose name comes from the first letters of *anti-fascist*. It was on a wall of the Heydukova Street Synagogue, the only synagogue in Bratislava, just behind the hostel. This was a striking building with a pale pink façade lined with a row of squared-off columns. A plaque said the modernist structure dated from 1926. Repairs were underway so the entrance was blocked, but a side alley led to a walled back garden, where black-and-white pictures depicted members of the pre-World War Two Jewish population of Bratislava.

Of the city's estimated 15,000 Jewish population in the early 1940s – 12 per cent of the city's then total – only around 3,500 survived and it is believed that more than 60,000 Slovakian Jews were murdered in the Holocaust. Many of those in Bratislava were sent to the death camp at Auschwitz. Of those taken to the camps in the first round-ups in 1942 perhaps 300 survived the war, among them Alfred Wetzler and Walter Rosenberg, who importantly provided some of the first accounts of Auschwitz. Some local Jews had avoided the concentration camps, managing to escape across the border to Hungary before 1942. Others had survived in hiding.

One of the most prominent survivors of the Holocaust from Bratislava was Ivan Otto Schwarz, born in the city but who was sent by his parents, accompanied by his sister, to Wales in 1939 as part of the Kindertransport programme to escape as anti-Semitism rose. Schwartz, aged 16, promptly joined the British Army and was posted in 1941 to the Czechoslovak Defence Force, later serving as an airman in the 311 (Czechoslovak) Bomber Squadron RAF, which was to sink the German blockade runner *Alsterufer* as it carried important bomb-making cargo in the Bay of Biscay in December 1943. After the war, Schwarz returned to Slovakia but did not feel comfortable in a political atmosphere in which anti-Semitism still festered. Horrid showdowns had occurred at houses once owned by Jews that had been taken by others during the war when survivors returned. Schwarz went back to live in England in 1946, set up successful engineering and machinery companies, lived in London as a British citizen and died in 2018 at the age of 94.

A photograph on the synagogue garden's back wall shows Schwarz, who rose to the rank of major general, meeting Queen Elizabeth II and the Duke of Edinburgh. Information about his remarkable life is outlined on an information board beside this picture.

* * *

Bratislava station was yet another grim communist-era affair.

Buses revved outside and a chaotic central concourse was cluttered with small kiosk-cafés serving almost identical sandwiches and snacks. Destinations on the departure board flickered: Žilina, Komárno, Hamburg and Banská Bystrica. Many trains were running late. Our train was running late, a good 15 minutes.

It was a cramped, busy ticket hall that was distinguished by a long communist mural above the departure board depicting dramatic figures with angular faces and bodies. A story appeared to unfold as you looked at this mural from left to right. It began with war, then the trauma of the aftermath of war, then society coming together with hospitals, schools and universities being built under a new, stronger collective society. These images led to a final section in which seemingly wise men were looking back at what had happened in the rest of the mural as though proud of society having come through its troubles and having collectively acted to strengthen state institutions. The seemingly wise men appeared to be the architects for the latter and figures that the mural's artist believed should be trusted. That was how I read it at least. Perhaps this interpretation was completely wrong.

We boarded the 09:57 to Budapest, a grimy blue-grey train with "CD" (initials of the Czech train operator České dráhy) on the locomotive, compartments of six seats and a gruff inspector who wordlessly checked our passes. The interior decoration was in orange and blue swirls. Grey curtains with a circular pattern swayed as the train moved off. Smoked-glass mirrors above the seats gave the compartment a late-night cocktail bar feel. The overall effect was smart and somehow optimistic, as though we had travelled back to the 1970s or 1980s, but not in a bad way. Over the speaker system, an American voice drawled in English: "This train is twenty minutes delayed due to construction work on the track." It must have been a robotic recording. Unlikely that České dráhy was recruiting from across the Atlantic.

The grey tower blocks of Bratislava were soon behind us and we rolled into farmland with long, ploughed fields.

A stubble of green crops poked through these fields, and the occasional rabbit scampered off in fright at the passing of the 09:57 to Budapest. A profusion of bushes with white blossom prettily lined the tracks. Storks' nests clung to the top of old telegraph poles, substantial constructions that must have taken some effort to build twig by twig. The sun had come out and the old train was rumbling, bumping and creaking along. It was relaxing in the compartment, which we had entirely to ourselves.

"Ah, this is the way," said Danny, pleased to have put Slovakia's capital behind us. "This is how it should be. Now we are living our best life!"

He paused. He was sounding quite euphoric. "We should do something like this each year," he added. "We're not getting any younger."

Back to his old Soho Square soliloquy, which was never too far away.

Were we plunging into some sort of midlife train crisis? Quite possibly. Not that we minded much about that. Let the midlife train crisis happen! It was simply too enjoyable messing about on trains to allow too much introspection. Suffice to say, we had adopted a *make the most of it whatever* approach.

In this spirit, at around 11.30 a.m. we went to the dining carriage.

This was simply fantastic: smart black leather chairs, crisp white tablecloths, table lamps, and a waiter with an alert manner and impeccable English wearing a waistcoat, starched white shirt and red tie. We had vowed not to drink today, but in Bukowski-style swiftly succumbed and ordered two small bottles of Merlot.

"We're just a couple of old soaks on a train," said Danny, taking his first sip.

We also ordered pork slices with polenta (me) and roasted pork with spinach and bacon (Danny). Both were excellent. The few other diners had left and we had the carriage to ourselves: a private carriage to Budapest.

The train was rolling along a wide, muddy-looking section of the Danube.

Mark, the waiter, came and joined us for a bit.

He had a rosy complexion, blue eyes and short cropped hair. He had taken off his tie and looked worn out.

"I'm on the long shift," he said. "It's five a.m. to midnight, about twenty hours for eight days in a row, then I get eight days off."

The train had begun in Prague in the morning, and he was on day three of his eight-day pattern: "You see me in five days, I'm like zombie."

Mark told us how he had once been to London and had had to make two train changes from Hampstead just to reach the city centre. This he considered, as a train man, ridiculous.

He had also found London too busy.

"What is the population?" he asked.

"About eight and a half million," replied Danny.

"The whole of the Czech Republic: eleven million," he said, as though London was mind-bogglingly big.

With that, Mark, looking exhausted already three days into his eight-day shift, went back to the kitchen.

Somewhere around a place called Szob, the train crossed into Hungary, our fifth country.

We began to consider what to do in Budapest.

The city was famous for its spas. Danny launched into a tirade about the overrated standing of spas in general: "Too much hassle, they're just glorified swimming pools. I don't want to see fat old men in a hot tub if it costs me thirty euros. I don't want to get flip-flops, a cap, trunks and all the crap and carry it all the way to Istanbul."

We had just read in a guidebook that flip-flops and a cap seemed to be required and that entry was 30 euros.

So ended our Budapest spa thoughts (anyway, I'd been to a very good one already during writing *Slow Trains to Venice*).

The dining carriage was at the rear of the train and there was a view through a doorway at the end to the back of the tracks. After checking this out, the train came to a halt in a cavernous terminus: Budapest Nyugati station.

* * *

Nyugati was like a giant bird's cage. It was built with great sheets of glass and iron beams by Gustave Eiffel, no less, and was once one of Europe's grand stations receiving the likes of Emperor Franz Joseph and his wife Empress Elisabeth during the height of the Austro-Hungarian Empire (1867–1918). Its Art Nouveau interior had then been the epitome of fashionable taste and would have been appreciated by early passengers on *Orient Express* trains heading from Strasbourg to Vienna, Budapest and beyond.

On our visit, shafts of light filtered through dirty-looking skylights way above and an imposing but grimy glass wall by the entrance.

We located the temporary ticket office – works were going on across the station, which was in the middle of much-needed renovations – and inquired about ticket reservations, required on top of the passes for our next planned stop, Subotica, just over the border in Serbia. I'd had my eye on Subotica as it was the scene of the denouement of Graham Greene's early novel *Stamboul Train*.

During this curious thriller about travelling on the *Orient Express* from Ostend in Belgium to Istanbul, referred to by its old variant "Stamboul", the protagonists include a wanted communist leader, a lesbian journalist, a businessman trading in currants, a dancer (whom the businessman seduces and sleeps with in his compartment), a murdering thief and a travel writer (possibly based on J. B. Priestley of *English Journey* fame). Each becomes entangled with intrigue along the way and events come to a head at the Serbian border city, where Greene has the train delayed and the communist, the dancer and the murderer arrested, before the trio attempt to escape. The book was published in 1932, two years ahead of Agatha Christie's more famous *Murder on the Orient Express,* and has a dreamlike, disturbing quality.

Graham Greene being one of my favourite writers, I had been curious about Subotica.

An attendant wearing gold-framed glasses at the "International Ticket Desk" in the temporary ticket office simply said: "No."

She paused and looked at me. I do think train ticket office attendants take at least a small amount of secret pleasure when telling you a route is impossible, perhaps simply because it means no further discussion on the matter can be had.

"No," she repeated. "You cannot go."

"Why?" I asked.

"There are no trains. None at all. No trains. Every operation to Serbia is cancelled," she replied. Work was being carried out to improve the tracks.

"When will the trains re-start?" I asked.

"I do not know," she said. "Hopefully next year."

She was quite friendly about all of this, even if somewhat enjoying being the bearer of bad news (I suspected).

"Are you British?" she asked. We said we were. "It is common. Every day a couple of Brits. You used to be able to make a booking all the way to Istanbul from here."

This was not possible anymore. She seemed secretly pleased, I also suspected, about this.

She paused and returned to Serbia's closed train line, which was clearly causing consternation. "We really do not know when the reparations will be complete," she said in a tone of: *Serbia is Serbia and Serbia does what Serbia wants.*

She suggested trying Timișoara in Romania instead. From Timișoara it would be easy to reach Bucharest by sleeper train. From there, we were thinking of going to a remote city named Ruse by the Danube in Bulgaria (part of the 1883 *Orient Express* route), followed by Sofia, Bulgaria's capital, and a further sleeper train to Istanbul. All rough plans.

We went to a corner of the temporary ticket office to assess the visiting potential of Timișoara. To do this, of course, we took out our mobiles and tapped away, the Hungarian international ticket attendant watching us, with no other customers about.

An article in *Time* magazine explained that the western-Romanian city had installed the first street lighting in Europe in 1884. This, although interesting up to a point, was not in itself enough to convince us to go. Another claim to fame was that Timișoara was where the protests had begun against the communist dictator Nicolae Ceaușescu in 1989, leading to his toppling. This was more like it, especially as there was a Revolution Museum covering the events of 1989 and a Communist Consumers Museum in an apartment from that era that showed what life was like back then.

Timișoara also happened to be one of the official European Capitals of Culture the year we were travelling (though main events would be later in the summer). Remarkable, really: we had stumbled upon a *capital of culture.*

Finally, there was a pub with the unlikely western-Romanian name of The Scotland Yard, described by Restaurantguru.com as being "a cozy establishment offering a delightful mix of Romanian and international cuisine… a must-visit eatery". Who in their right mind would turn down the must-visit Scotland Yard pub in Timișoara?

This research was conducted in a matter of moments.

We did not need reservations for the tickets for Timișoara, where the plan was to spend the day in the city after catching a morning train. Then we would leave Timișoara in the evening on a sleeper for Bucharest, Romania's capital, which did require reservations. We booked these from the attendant wearing gold-framed glasses at the "International Ticket Desk" in the temporary ticket office, who had been extremely helpful in a matter-of-fact way.

* * *

Past kebab shops, gold-trading shops, sex shops and Bill's Pub, along a wide boulevard busy with old-fashioned mustard-yellow and white trams and a stream of traffic, we arrived at our good little business-traveller-style hotel: the Central Hotel 21. We had two rooms with brown carpets, televisions and en-suite shower rooms. Everything was neat and tidy. Our hostel days were over.

We rested for a while in our luxurious business-traveller rooms with brown carpets.

Before exploring Hungary's capital, I checked the news back home.

It had been a busy day. The popular comedian Paul O'Grady had died and the reaction to his passing from his friend Camilla, the queen consort, was the main story on the BBC. She was "deeply saddened". Another item was all about King Charles III going on a state visit to Germany (still too risky for him in France, but OK in Germany). He was to attend a banquet in Berlin in the evening, along with Camilla, who was gamely tagging along. Tomorrow the couple would be visiting a renewable energy plant in Hamburg.

"MIGRANTS TO BE HOUSED ON CRUISE SHIPS AND BARGES", screamed the front page of the *Daily Mail*, which highlighted the high cost of paying for the housing of recently arrived immigrants in hotels. The bill of £6 million a day was a "farce", the paper said.

The Guardian covered news of the sports presenter and former England football captain Gary Lineker, who had won a battle with HM Revenue & Customs over a massive tax bill. Meanwhile, *The Times* ran a story about a new portrait of King Charles III painted by the artist Alastair Barford, in which the new king wears a quizzical expression, a pink tie and a pinstripe suit.

Celebs, royals, more royals, immigration worries, more celebs, and more royals again… British news was like that of no other country.

In Europe, things were slightly different.

Hungary was, after all, a nation that bordered a major war that might, some believed, lead to World War Three. Its controversial right-wing leader, Viktor Orbán, was considered by many to be Russia's closest friend within the European Union. Hungary's border with Ukraine stretches 85 miles and it refused to provide arms to support its neighbour, nor would it allow military provisions to the beleaguered nation traverse its territory.

We were travelling by train through a country that favoured the "other side".

What was it like on the streets of the capital of what was, some might say, *the enemy*?

CHAPTER THREE

BUDAPEST TO BUCHAREST IN ROMANIA, VIA TIMIȘOARA

HUNGARIAN HEAVY METAL, DICTATORS AND STAG DOS

Quite normal, was the answer.

Having crossed off thoughts of visiting one of Budapest's famous spas, we set about seeing Hungary's capital in an afternoon and an evening.

The astute reader may possibly have detected by now that Danny and I were not your typical sightseers.

We were not ticking off attractions in an orderly manner: *city done*. Neither were we even vaguely attempting to "know" the essence of places properly and authoritatively in the manner of Grand Tourists of earlier centuries or modern-day social analyst/historians able to assimilate all and draw authoritative conclusions. Such matters were beyond our skill sets. We were often not even in cities for a full day; all those *24 hours in…* guides were, frankly, wasted on us. We were not really guidebook people at all, even though I had one: a (heavy) *Lonely Planet*. We had a slightly different approach to travel that might be summed up thus: *make it up as you go along, use your wits as well as they may happen to serve you, follow what catches your interest, often get things wrong, have a drink* (I will not pretend we did not do quite a lot of that), *and move on, take another train down the line*. We were managing this quite happily – the odd messed-up journey (into Vienna and Bratislava) or complete train network shutdown aside.

This said, after our rest in our luxurious little business-traveller-style hotel, we returned to the wide boulevard leading to Budapest Nyugati station where we entered a metro station named Blaha Lujza. We were heading for Kossuth Lajos, the station for Hungary's famously big and said-to-be impressive parliament (often ranked among the most impressive parliaments in the world in impressive parliament lists), a short ride of three stops away. We wanted to *do some tourism like normal tourists*.

The sight we wanted to see also of course happened to be where Russia's closest friend in the European Union, Viktor Orbán, hung out. To find it, we took my *Lonely Planet* guidebook. We would follow what it had to say, planning afterwards to walk along the Danube and visit a place called the Great Market Hall and a "ruin bar" named Szimpla Kert. "Ruin bars" were in the Jewish quarter of the city in formerly derelict buildings left unoccupied after the Holocaust. They had become a major attraction and I had been to some of them before when writing *Slow Trains to Venice*. Danny wanted to see the ruin bars, too, and Szimpla Kert was the biggest and most famous of the lot.

We had (temporarily) become well-organized holidaymakers, although you might also say that we were simply going for a riverside walk followed by a drink.

Which would be accurate, too.

A little bit of politics, poppyseed strudels and disco balls
Budapest

The walls of Blaha Lujza underground station were plastered with abstract modern art featuring city landmarks as well as adverts for home improvement companies, electric toothbrushes and the 1960s and 1970s British heavy metal group Deep Purple, which was conducting a European revival tour with a visit to Budapest Arena. The band was pictured wearing shades, leather jackets and inscrutable expressions, all of them that is aside from the lead singer Ian Gillan, who looked rather pleased with himself in a crisp white shirt.

This advert caught Danny's attention.

"Look at them, they're wrecks," he said.

They did have a certain ageing rocker demeanour.

Danny paused and considered his previous statement and corrected himself.

"Then again, I'd do that if I was them," he said: i.e., milk their fame for all it was worth for as long as they could. "Why not? Good on 'em."

This observation made, a wide red-and-grey train rolled into Blaha Lujza. We boarded it and rolled smoothly beneath Budapest, shortly arriving at Kossuth Lajos, where we were met by an unusual bronze statue of a man with a dog on the platform. This was Tiresias, the blind prophet from Greek mythology. The Budapest metro, the second oldest in Europe after the London Underground, was well decorated with a slightly left-field, off-the-wall look, and the trains (at least the one we went on) were clean and seemed to run on time.

Up an escalator we went, soon gazing upon Hungary's huge neo-Gothic parliament. It really was massive, reminiscent of the Houses of Parliament at Westminster, but much larger and somehow different in aspect.

The difference was hard to pinpoint at first, but after a while it was obvious: *everything was all just a little bit too perfect.*

Too pristine. Too well organized. Too neat. Too grand, in-your-face, imposing and downright majestic. Too *look at me, look at me* for democracy.

And some had been questioning that of late in Hungary. Democracy, that is.

Widespread accusations of electoral fraud in recent elections involving intimidation, vote buying, tampering of postal votes and voting software irregularities had been made. It was believed by many, including the influential lobbying group Unlock Democracy Europe, that this string of anomalies had directly contributed to the two-thirds "supermajority" of the country's Fidesz party. By reaching this magic number, the party had unlocked a constitutional ability to take greater control of the judiciary and media.

This opportunity had been seized. The legal system had been severely undermined by slippery changes that favoured Orbán, whose control had been cemented by appointing the godmother of his eldest child as head of the National Office for the Judiciary as well as by packing courts with sympathetic judges. Meanwhile, press freedom had come under attack with many media outlets being bought by oligarchs close to the prime minister. Reporters Without Borders, the international lobbying group for journalists, estimated that Orbán's

Fidesz ruling party had seized control of 80 per cent of the media, crucially including the main public broadcasting channel, which it described as having become a "propaganda organ".

Quite aside from all of this, Orbán's Hungary had witnessed the recent introduction of a controversial new law banning LGBTQ+ people from featuring on children's television shows or in educational material, while the "promotion" of homosexuality and gender reassignment had been prohibited. The country's largest bookseller, Libri, had been fined for selling certain titles involving same-sex parents and for the "improper display" of other books with LGBTQ+ characters. Libri had begun wrapping such books in plastic for fear of further penalties.

A whole new term had been invented for Orbán's version of running matters: *illiberal democracy*. It was not meant to be flattering.

We looked up at the ever-so-perfect HQ of Hungary's legislature.

The turrets, walls, arched windows and domes of Hungary's parliament were scrubbed spotlessly clean. Not a grimy mark in sight. Not a single damp patch. Not a blemish. Windows gleamed. Turrets struck up towards the heavens looking recently restored and much as they must have the day the parliament was inaugurated in 1904, after 19 years of construction involving more than 100,000 workers and 40 million bricks. The giant structure featured no fewer than 365 towers, one for each day of the year, and 691 rooms. A copper-coloured Renaissance-style dome soared above, dominating the cityscape. Everywhere you looked, everything was in absolute order and just so: grand and spotless and perfect. No wonder it is considered by some to be the world's "most spectacular parliament building". That phrase was often bandied about.

The gardens and lawns in the square facing the legislature were carefully clipped, not a blade of grass out of place, not a scrap of litter in sight. Policemen with batons sauntered by in starched uniforms that looked brand new. These patrolmen were all male. They were all over six feet. They all had crew cuts and upright postures. They looked alert, on-the-ball, ready to leap into action. Other such policemen patrolled in pairs across the wide square. There were quite a few of them. The seat of power of Russia's closest friend in the European Union was clearly well guarded. The overall effect made an obvious statement: *I am in charge, better not try anything round here.*

Near the front of the parliament building, close to the river Danube we came to an unusual underground memorial. It was free to enter and was dedicated to the events of 25 October 1956 that took place at Kossuth Square.

You accessed the memorial via a tunnel with a ramp lined by steel walls potted with bullet holes, presumably from 1956. Inside, displays explained what happened on 25 October of that year when Hungary had risen to protest the Soviet Union's control of the country. Soviet tanks had rolled across the streets and troops had indiscriminately opened fire that day. It was a bloody event with an estimated one thousand people killed leaving a deep-seated local hatred of the Soviet Union.

Displays within the strange memorial, which comprised a series of intertwining underground passages, explained how the uprising had unfolded as well as offering background to the unrest during that period. The lead-up to 25 October 1956 had seen Hungarians watch on as Austria declared neutrality against the Soviets in 1955. Locals had also seen how Poland had negotiated for fewer Soviet troops earlier in 1956. Both actions had acted to weaken the Warsaw Pact of Soviet-influenced nations, which included Albania, Bulgaria, Czechoslovakia, East Germany, Hungary, Poland and Romania.

The Soviet Union, though, was still going strong, yet to be reduced to the house of cards it became in 1989 with the fall of the Berlin Wall, the Velvet Revolution in Czechoslovakia, the rise of Solidarity in Poland and fall of Ceauşescu in Romania – all in that year. In March 1989, Hungary itself had been quick off the mark among the protests against the Soviet Union, holding mass demonstrations and, later in May, dismantling 150 miles of barbed wire along its Austrian border. This had been deemed by many to be the first (literal) chink in the Iron Curtain.

So what happened at Kossuth Square in 1956 is key to understanding Hungary's national identity. Its fightback against the totalitarianism of the Soviet Union had found expression at the square and laid the foundation stones for eventually escaping the clasp of Moscow. All of which made the country's current leader's decision to cosy up to the Kremlin even odder, and more distasteful, to many.

A little bit of politics. Why not? Taking trains across Europe doesn't mean you have to wear blinkers to the world beyond the carriage windows.

We went for a walk along the Danube.

Buskers were playing violins and guitars, poignant tunes resonating across the eddying mud-brown water. Artists on little wooden stools offered to draw caricatures. Tourists and locals sat outside bars drinking wine and beer in the sunshine. More mustard-yellow and white trams rattled by. It was relaxed and congenial. Thoughts of rigged elections, judicial meddling and assaults on press freedom seemed a long way away.

Beyond the elegant swoop of the Széchenyi Chain Bridge linking the Buda and Pest sides of the city (we were on the eastern bank, Pest), we arrived at the Great Market Hall.

The entrance of this hall had an owlish appearance, with circular windows and tufty towers. Inside was a cacophony of commerce with a jamboree of stalls cluttering the main floors and a mezzanine. You could buy just about anything: coconut- and pistachio-flavoured chocolates, dried sausages, honey and jams, traditional Hungarian ceramics, dolls, scarves, shot glasses marked "Budapest", bottles of firewater to fill the shot glasses, lighters, magnets, key chains, t-shirts, hoodies and just about any souvenir you could dream of in a terrific tumble of colourful little stalls in rows connected by narrow walkways beneath a high cast-iron and glass roof.

The hall dated from 1896 when five local markets had been joined together and was almost 400 feet long: reminiscent of Nyugati station.

Danny and I ate cherry and poppyseed strudels from a kiosk at the centre of the hall. Then Danny and I went to a courtyard with walls plastered in graffiti at Szimpla Kert and sat among a cool hipster crowd comprised of youngsters (mainly), the middle-agers (quite a few) and folk in their seventies and eighties (a few) too. We all sat round listening to a cool hipster acoustic guitarist playing Massive Attack and Oasis songs while drinking cool hipster beers in the cool hipster setting.

Buddhist figures gazed down serenely. A disco ball glittered. A pair of skis dangled from a rafter. Neon pink and purple lights ran along railings and twisted round potted plants. There was clutter. There was chatter. The cool hipster acoustic guitarist finished his gig. We listened to a cool hipster Hungarian heavy metal band. It was a very noisy, highly energetic cool hipster Hungarian heavy metal band and we could not understand a single word.

We returned to our little business-traveller-style hotel.

Our sightseeing in Hungary's capital was complete.

"Don't forget to say: beautiful country!"
Budapest to Timişoara, Romania

Ahead lay 24 hours of movement.

First up: catch the metro to Budapest Keleti station for the 07:10 to Timişoara, due to arrive at 1.34 p.m.

This involved rising early, walking back to Blaha Lujza metro station and promptly making friends with the station drunk. He was a bald man with electric-blue eyes that shone out from a face so filthy he was tricky to age. He could have been in his thirties. He might have been in his sixties. He was going up the escalator and extremely unstable on his feet. As we glided downwards, he turned to us and growled something that we took not to translate as *Welcome to Budapest, dear foreigners.* Then he cackled and repeated his message once more.

Then he cackled again. Then he beat his fist on the escalator a few times as though to reinforce whatever he had to say.

"Just like Orbán: a simple-minded thug," said Danny.

We gave him a smile and a thumbs up, which seemed to infuriate him further.

Shortly afterwards we caught a metro train a couple of stops and arrived at Keleti station ("Eastern station").

Like Nyugati station ("Western station"), Keleti was another grand dame from the 1880s with a towering façade of columns and figurines including prominent statues of the Scottish engineer James Watt and the early English railway legend George Stephenson. We bought breakfast sandwiches from an almost comically stony-faced kiosk attendant. We located platform one, which was a long way from the station entrance, and we boarded the 07:10, a two-tone blue-and-grey train with "EUROFINA" written on the locomotive and bright green-and-red seats along with grey curtains adorned with a locomotive motif and the letters "CFR", the logo of Romanian State Railways.

The sun was rising in a blaze of blood orange down the tracks as the train juddered away and a conductor wearing a baseball cap at a jaunty angle checked the Interrail passes on our phones.

"It's amazing," said Danny, of the passes. "Every time they work."

We were yet to get over this.

Budapest's outskirts were marked by a small forest of smokestacks and cooling towers and grim, tightly packed apartment blocks similar to the ones in Slovakia. After these faded away, pancake-flat farmland soon came into view with electricity pylons beside the tracks and high white fluffy clouds. Some of the stations we passed looked incredibly run-down: weeds growing out of platforms and half-derelict crumbling sheds. Yet more flat farmland followed, green and red tractors dragging ploughs and trailing clouds of dust above the plains. Long, low chicken sheds popped up every now and then (far from "free-range", or so they appeared). Shrubs with white blossom lined the railway, which seemed common in these Central European parts.

"It's like a film on loop," said Danny, gazing out at the horizon, happily hypnotized by the subtle shift of scenery.

Watching long stretches of Hungarian countryside could have this effect.

On the original *Orient Express* on this stretch, the distinguished passengers had been entertained by a jolly band of Gypsy musicians that one of the journalists, Edmond About, declared to have "the devil in their fingertips… they play with marvellous brilliance" and the much-admired Burgundian chef – the one who was keeping About's beloved Normandy butter so fresh during the journey – sang along to a fine rendition of "La Marseillaise". This party had begun at a station platform where the performers had unexpectedly leapt on board as the train moved away, playing tunes in the dining carriage where the younger male passengers duly danced with the "amiable Viennese women a dance of all the devils". Passengers including these "amiable Viennese women" occasionally boarded along the way to experience the wonders of the new train, especially the cooking of the renowned chef.

Things were not quite as lively on the 07:10 to Timişoara.

I went to the slightly different dining carriage and got chatting to Lily.

Lily was an *ospatar*, Romanian for "waiter". She ran proceedings in the dining carriage, standing behind a red lacquer counter with a few crisp packets, peanuts, small wine bottles and liquor miniatures, each with an orange sticker showing the price marked in black pen. The counter was set out as though offering prizes at a village fete raffle. A menu listed a dozen different types of sandwiches were also to be had, most featuring "smoked pork loin" with various slightly different combinations of vegetable fillings. This menu was typed in small print on two grubby pieces of A4 stuck to a column. In place of prominence on the red lacquer counter was a large old-fashioned calculator.

Lily was diminutive with protuberant hazel eyes, a gold necklace embellished with the word "Sweet", a spattering of English and a cheerful disposition.

I asked for two coffees and how she preferred to be paid: in cash or by card.

"I like money all the time," she replied. There was no card machine.

She would accept Hungarian forints; I had no Romanian leu. She made the coffees and told me that she was from Curtea de Argeş, in the southern Carpathian Mountains in central Romania, where the last king of Romania, Michael I, was buried in his home town. He had died in 2017 in Switzerland, and his body had been transported back. The last king of Romania had been forced to abdicate in 1947 and, after the fall of Ceauşescu in 1989, had tried unsuccessfully to stage a comeback. The king was dead, and royalty no longer existed in Romania.

Lily had lived in Britain for a while.

"I go and I stay in London for six month and for three years in Guildford," she said. "I work for Amazon. Deliveries. It was very difficult. In one van I would do twenty stops in eight hours. Very hard. Most of deliveries Croydon. Also, Rochester in Kent. Traffic OK, most times, but not always. Very difficult for me. Very hard."

Did she like English culture?

"It is OK," she said.

She did not sound, or look, especially enthusiastic about English culture.

What did she like best?

Lily strained for something to say in reply. "What about English pubs?" I asked as a prompt.

"Yeah, OK," she said.

Why had she returned? Though perhaps that was obvious.

"I had two children at home," she said. "Now they are twelve and seven."

"Did you go to England to make money?"

"Yes."

"Were you successful?"

"No."

"Why was that?"

"The company that took me over," she said – the one that had arranged employment and visas. "They take my money."

"Everything?"

"Yes, everything," she said.

She handed over the coffees with a shrug. What happened had happened. Now she was working for Romanian State Railways and her Amazon delivery days in Croydon were long over. Emigration had not paid the bills.

I returned to the green-and-red carriage, gave Danny his coffee and picked up *The Mystery of the Blue Train*, published in 1928 by Agatha Christie, which I had begun in Budapest the day before. Seeing as we were on such a train, this reading material seemed especially appropriate.

The plot is all about the three largest rubies in the world, once worn by Catherine the Great, and how their secret sale brings misery to all those concerned as a nefarious cast of characters attempts to get their greedy hands on them. A murder takes place on *Le Train Bleu* between Paris and the French Riviera. The daughter of a wealthy American businessman has been strangled in her compartment. The rubies have vanished. The dapper Belgian detective Hercule Poirot, in retirement, happens to be on board. He has been saying to those who have asked that his occupation is simply to "enjoy the world" now that he no longer works, but he cannot help himself and with the assistance of another passenger, a woman wearing a "mauvy pink dress", begins to solve the murder. The estranged and emotionally detached husband of the daughter of the wealthy American businessman appears to be the prime suspect, especially as he is in line for the inheritance and has flippantly and heartlessly stated: "You shouldn't die on a train. I believe it causes all sorts of legal and international complications and gives the train an excuse for being even later than usual."

But is he really the murderer? Surely, that would be too pat.

Our blue (and grey) train passed through Kétegyháza in south-eastern Hungary, where mounds of earth and concrete pipes were piled by a crumbling old station house. A little beyond Kétegyháza, farms with strangely bulbous cattle materialized, as did a succession of peculiar metallic water towers shaped like olives attached to cocktail sticks.

At a place called Lőkösháza at around 10.50 a.m., three Hungarian border control officers stamped our passports, and we entered Romania.

"Do you think it looks any different?" I asked Danny – any different in Romania than it did in Hungary.

"A little shabbier," he replied, speaking of Romania.

The view outside did seem almost immediately less inviting: the state of the buildings (crumbling a bit more than they had been on the other side of the border, with peeling paint and dirtier walls), the condition of the streets (more potholed, narrower), the look of the housing estates (less inviting, more human factory-like). Or perhaps that was just my imagination.

The horn blew. Romanian border control officers stamped our passports at Curtici station. We were exiting the Schengen free-travel zone, which includes all European Union members except for Romania, Bulgaria, Cyprus and Ireland, although it includes non-EU members Norway, Iceland, Liechtenstein and Switzerland.

The officers ambled away.

Shortly afterwards, I fell into conversation with a man named Dr Jasko, who was sitting across the aisle.

Dr Jasko was a retired geologist who once specialized in petroleum, bauxite and iron mines. He was in his late seventies and on his way to attend a petroleum, bauxite and iron mining conference in the town of Reşiţa, further down the line after Timişoara. He maintained an interest in the field despite no longer working in it. He was born in Budapest and had a Hungarian wife though he lived in Watford "at the end of the Metropolitan line", after having previously resided in Glasgow, where he had moved many decades ago due to work connected to North Sea oil.

He wore a checked shirt and had a neat grey moustache, smiling blue eyes and an amiable, avuncular manner. He was reading a novel entitled *Drei Männer im Schnee* (*Three Men in the Snow*) by the German writer Erich Kästner, 1899–1974, a comedy about a millionaire who pretends to be poor as he wishes to understand what it's like, resulting in a series of twists and turns; a bit like *Down and Out in Paris and London*, without Orwell's real roughing it. We discussed *Three Men in the Snow* for a while.

Dr Jasko was a loquacious retired geologist. Timișoara, he said, had become the biggest industrial city in Romania thanks to iron mines in the region. When he was in Glasgow, Dr Jasko had worked for the British National Oil Corporation (BNOC), a body that was set up by the Labour government in 1975 to spread the benefits of oil profits to the state – like the highly successful Equinor business operating to this day in Norway – but this was privatized under the Conservative Party rule of Margaret Thatcher in 1982 and eventually bought by BP (British Petroleum). He said that BNOC had "got into trouble" when the oil price had dipped below $10 a barrel and one morning there had been "white envelopes on our desks: half went, half stayed, the pubs of Glasgow had big business that day".

Dr Jasko had weathered the storm, and still looked chipper about this corporate survival so many years on.

His face dropped a bit, however, when we began to talk trains. Dr Jasko had missed the train from Budapest Keleti station to his conference yesterday as he had made a mistake with the time difference from the UK and arrived a couple of minutes before the train was due to depart but could not reach it in time as platform one was so far from the entrance. This miscalculation had made him a day late.

"Trains used to go from the main hall," he said. "I would never imagine they would not go from the main hall."

He seemed peeved about this, but only temporarily.

He turned to pre-1989 days. During the time of Ceauşescu there had been "clandestine" movements of people (spies) along the line we were travelling on, Dr Jasko said: "When Ceauşescu was at his most rabid, Hungarian authorities would not actually be helping with this, but they would shut their eyes. Then Ceauşescu became even more paranoid and started to create a siege economy. He was taken by surprise by the fall of the communist regimes in 1989, as they collapsed all around him. Then the revolution happened in Timişoara."

This had been triggered by an attempt to evict a local pastor in the Hungarian Reform Church named László Tőkés, Dr Jasko explained. He wrote his name in my notebook. Demonstrations in Timişoara on 17 December had led to police and soldiers firing on crowds, killing some. By 25 December, after attempting but failing to quell copycat anti-government protests in Bucharest, the Ceauşescus – Nicolae and his wife Elena – had been captured, tried on counts of genocide and illegal profiteering, and executed.

I was getting some of the story of the making of modern Romania thanks to a retired geologist who once specialized in petroleum, bauxite and iron mines on the 07:10 to Timişoara.

At this point, as though to prove his undying allegiance to petroleum, iron and bauxite mines, Dr Jasko took out a small mining axe from his luggage and waved the axe at me. He travelled with the small axe at all times for good luck.

This presentation and waving of the axe acted as a kind of farewell gesture. We shook hands, but then, as we did so, Dr Jasko asked: "Do you want to see an oil well?"

I said I did.

He pointed out of the window at a metal pump across a field.

"That is an oil well," he said – you never would have guessed, looking at the flimsy contraption. "Not much oil anymore. But it's still pumping. About a barrel a day I would say."

Dr Jasko looked momentarily sad, as though remembering the good old days when the oil pumps would deliver much more than that. But he was one of life's optimists and could not maintain being "down" for long. His face lit up at some private thought. He waved his mining axe once more as though this was quite normal among retired geologists who once specialized in petroleum, bauxite and iron mines. We shook hands again.

Then I returned to Danny.

Danny, I had noticed, had been watching our interactions with a growing mixture of disbelief and mild bemusement.

"Had a good chat with that old fellow you'd never met before?" he asked when I returned.

"Yes," I replied.

Danny looked at me in a manner that was tricky to interpret, though I gathered from his demeanour that, in his opinion, such encounters with previously unknown retired Hungarian geologists were perhaps not at the top of his to-do list on the 07:10 to Timişoara.

The train rolled onwards through the forests of western Romania.

Not long after, it pulled into Timişoara station, where a couple of forlorn figures were hunched by the weed-strewn track looking as though they had no better place to be. Probably, by the look of the bags of possessions by their feet, they did not.

Past this rather wretched (and sad) welcoming committee, we entered Timişoara station. The architecture inside was from communist times, but not quite as brash and flashy as in Bratislava. We walked past a "*BIROU MISCARE*" office, which we understood to be the complaints department, and entered a tunnel with a mosaic saying "*SOUVENIR DE SYRIE*", showing figures in headdresses that must be something to do with the Syrian immigration into the

European Union in 2015, before arriving at the "*CASA DE BILETE TRAFIC INTERNATIONAL SI INTERN*". There, we reserved seats on the 21:50 sleeper to Bucharest from a polite and efficient woman wearing a blue cardigan.

Timișoara station was notable for its communist-era artwork – colourful abstract works plus pieces capturing local scenes including monuments and churches – as well as a vending machine offering Romanian novels and books with titles such as *Learn English Grammar: 440 Exercises!* I had never seen such a machine before. Quite a good idea.

The station's other principal feature was the attendant at the luggage storage room in the basement. He wore a red beanie and was in a kiosk to the left as you arrived, although if you did not notice him at first and walked past, he would fire off a stream of invective in Romanian, gesticulating wildly and pointing at a list of rules and charges on a wall. You would then, before taking another step forward, pay various fees to store your luggage, which we had planned to leave so we could collect it later for the onward sleeper, and he would say in English: "Name! Name! Name! Two leu! Two leu! Two leu!"

He had clearly seen many people such as us and was not at all impressed by our slow uptake on the rules and charges. He had a bushy moustache and was clearly the boss of Timișoara station. On receiving the fees, however, his demeanour completely altered, and he smiled at us with a broad grin. He had only been messing around.

"To be fair," said Danny as we left. "He is probably equally rude to everyone. I quite like him."

* * *

There was a pleasure in knowing we only had a few hours in Timișoara.

There was no way we could see it comprehensively, just have a quick look about.

We left the communist-period, space-age-style station and crossed a road passing a high mosaic mural depicting heroic communist period workers next to a red flag. Shortly afterwards, we arrived at a large square, Union Square, flanked by damp neo-Baroque buildings with peeling paint, a mosque decorated with elaborate swirly patterns (Timişoara had been a key city during Ottoman times from 1552–1716) and a stripy Orthodox church. A sign said "2023" in honour of its European Capital of Culture status, next to a street gallery of laminated paintings depicting scenes of destruction from the war in Ukraine. It was at this square that the protests against Ceauşescu began, sparked partially by the attempt by authorities to quell the influence of László Tőkés.

This is what we did in Timişoara.

We ate barbecue chicken with pitta bread and salad that took a very long time to arrive served by a man wearing a t-shirt bearing the slogan "IT WAS EXQUISITE" at a café in a cobbled alley close to Union Square. We also drank two large beers at this café, having only expected to drink one (but ordering another as the food was taking so long). We visited the Communist Consumers Museum, a house with a clutter of old communist propaganda posters, vinyl records, radios, cutlery, crockery and all sorts of other dusty junk from the communist era (though the café was really quite nice). We walked past the "Super Jackpot Club", a woman offering "Free Bible Classes" and a restaurant called "Posh" on the way to Liberty Square. We discovered the Memorialul Revoluţiei museum was closed (which, to be honest, was a relief after already seeing the Communist Consumers Museum). We watched the sun set in a beautiful blaze of gold and orange beyond a fountain, a distinguished twin-towered church and a cluster of pink and aquamarine town houses at Liberty Square – the most pleasant bit of Timişoara. We decided not to go in the Scotland Yard pub as it looked too busy. We drank red wine and ate pizzas to accompany this red wine as an early dinner/snack in another cobbled alley where the swarthy pizzeria owner, named

Bodan, said: "Romania has bad roads and bad trains, but don't forget to say: beautiful country!"

Then we went to catch the 21:50 sleeper to Bucharest, due to arrive in Romania's capital at 8.06 a.m.

None of that fancy stuff
Timişoara to Bucharest

A gang wearing bandanas was huddled on the dimly lit platform at Timişoara station. "Dickensian," said Danny, looking around distastefully and adopting his occasional (though increasingly intermittent) Henri Opper de Blowitz manner of handling Eastern Europe. Blowitz was, for the time being, back.

He had put on his grey beanie once again in the belief that this offered some form of protection against the Romanian bandana-wearers and had positioned himself behind a column, obscuring himself, although not me, from the youths. A general scrum of people was milling about in the gloom. The sleeper to Bucharest, on its way from Budapest, seemed likely to be full.

We were due to travel in carriage two. A man clutching a bag full of beer bottles as though his life depended on this bag directed us to the back of the train when it arrived, and the crowds of train travellers scrambled on board. The conductor took our tickets and pointed down the carriage and we entered a compartment where every bunk was occupied. We returned to the conductor, who looked at our tickets again and said we were in the wrong carriage and that carriage two was at the front of the train.

So we disembarked and ran to carriage two whereupon we found the correct compartment, which had six bunks: three on each side. Danny and I had the two top bunks on the left-hand side. Danny took the top. I had the middle. The other passengers included a small child, aged about five, who was accompanied by what appeared to be his grandparents. The boy had three shaven stripes in his haircut, a little like the Adidas logo. This trio was taking up the limited floor space where they were in the middle of a feast involving multiple Tupperware pots and slices of quiche, breaded chicken, boiled eggs and grapes. Aside from them, a guy in his twenties with a beard and long hair occupied the top bunk on the right facing Danny. As the train moved off, we were handed sheets and pillows by another conductor.

Being in the middle bunk and with the feast below, their heads a foot or so away from me, I could not easily make my bed until the feast was finished. Everyone else's beds, including Danny's, had been sorted out. He had more room including a shelf to place his bag at the top, so had been able to tuck in the sheets and fix the pillow. I had positioned my backpack at the end of the bed, limiting the leg space, and was waiting for the feast to end, which it did after about half an hour, when I hopped down and made my own bunk.

We slid past sodium-lit streets. There was a smell of body odour. The carriage rattled, bounced and swayed. The grandmother, who had distinctive dyed red hair, showed me how to lock the door. I pulled down the blind. The lights were switched off. Someone coughed. Someone faintly snored. Someone made "another sound" (coming from the direction of the grandfather). The mattresses were lumpy and on mine two hinges connecting the bed to the wall dug into my side. The guy with long hair watched a film on a tablet. Then his phone rang and he whispered into it. Various devices occasionally bleeped: persistent little reminders of the digital world outside the 21:50 to Bucharest.

Danny said: "We've gone from the *Orient Express* to this."

Which was not quite true as we were never intending to take the £17,500 train, the special once-a-year service that called itself the *Venice Simplon-Orient-Express* (it was quite possible other private operators could come along offering similar style products, of course, there being no copyright on the name "Orient Express"). The real

Orient Express – or you might say the "people's" *Orient Express* – from Paris to Istanbul had finally ended in 1977, as previously stated, by which time it had become a shadow of the pre-war service.

But Danny was right in his general thoughts: the 21:50 sleeper from Timişoara to Bucharest was a far cry from the old glory days of Georges Nagelmackers and co. No silk sheets. No Cuban mahogany. No velvet curtains. A distinct lack of Art Deco embellishments by celebrated French designers such as René Prou, who had famously completed so many of the best *Orient Express* carriages during the train's heyday. Nothing by René Lalique, the equally famous jeweller and glassmaker from back then, either.

None of that fancy stuff on the 21:50 to Bucharest.

We all, after a while, fell asleep.

* * *

Then we all, after a while, woke up.

I rose at 7 a.m. and entered the corridor. The scenery through the grimy windows was two-tone: green and grey, a blend of fields of crops beneath a moody cloudy sky. Hulking grain silos emerged, then a rubbish dump, smokestacks, warehouses and derelict buildings on the edge of a small town. It was a mess. Almost all the way along, plastic bottles were scattered by the tracks. Sidings were occupied by wagons marked "MARFA" and "CFR" and the rusty wrecks of old passenger carriages. The grandmother left the compartment and sidled up to me holding forth a bottle of cold coffee, which she kindly offered as a morning gift to a compartment compatriot. I accepted and she smiled and said: "*Prost!*" She must have thought Danny and I were German: hence this *cheers*! How very nice of her. We were all getting along swimmingly on the 21:50 to Romania's capital (although later, looking up the word *prost* in Romanian, I found it translated as "dumbass", so perhaps I'd been getting the wrong end of the stick).

This seemed pretty unlikely, though, she was just too good-natured for that. She beamed at me as I drank my cold coffee bottle. Then the grandfather exited the compartment into the corridor too, drinking a similar cold coffee bottle and wearing a grey tracksuit and an "LA" cap. He nodded at me and we both drank our cold coffee bottles in silence as a series of oil pumps materialized close to the rails (recognizable thanks to Dr Jasko) and a hunched woman wearing a shawl and a sheepskin coat shuffled by leading a large brown-and-white dog, half curtseying as she passed.

It was soothing looking out as the scenery opened into Romanian countryside, even if it was interrupted at regular intervals by desolate post-industrial/industrial scenes. Despite the close quarters and early-on discomforts of the compartment, it had been a good night's sleep, the movement of the train almost therapeutic in a way that was hard to pin down. The thousand little sways, judders, jolts and rolls combining with the hums, whistles, clatters, clangs, clinks, squeaks and tap-tap-taps in a strangely satisfying manner. Who cared whether you had paid £17,500 or a few euros? Sleep was sleep. The carriages rattled for all classes.

The train passed simple abodes with corrugated metal roofs. A bird of prey perched on an electricity wire watching the 21:50 from Timişoara. A concrete water tower that looked a bit like a military watchtower emerged, then a large pile of rusting girders, a man in a fluorescent jacket chopping wood in a yard, a metal-framed bridge above a muddy river, a woodland with twisty trees, and a lake lined by tall oatmeal-coloured reeds. Smoke rose from a bonfire. We entered an industrial warehouse-land. Danny stepped into the corridor, as did the guy with the beard and the long hair who had been watching the film.

"Whatever the privations," Danny said. "You get a better sleep on a train than in business class on the way to New York. And you pay a lot more for a space on a plane. The sheets and the pillow were clean. I like it."

It had been his first experience of a sleeper.

The guy with the long hair turned out to be from Colombo in Sri Lanka. He was working at a pizzeria in Timişoara (not the one we had been to) and his name was Dinesh. He and six friends had emigrated to Romania a year ago. He worked 16-hour shifts at the pizzeria – two days on, two days off – and had a "good salary" although "not everything is good, not one hundred per cent, but not everything in life can be perfect".

After five years' work, he said he would be eligible for a Romanian passport; he was travelling to Bucharest to visit an office to extend his visa. He had not slept particularly well and seemed drowsy but was keen to talk about cricket.

"Do you like IPL?" Dinesh asked, rhetorically – Indian Premier League. "Your Joe Root: T20 best player."

T20 is a shortened "20 over" form of cricket, an "over" being a period of play within the game (for those who have no idea about it). Joe Root was a much-celebrated England batsman.

"I watch it all online. All the Sri Lankan guys in Timişoara watch it online," he said. "We've started playing here, too: the Sri Lankans and the Indians, we like to play. The Romanians watch us and wonder what the hell we are doing."

We had quite a long chat about IPL and cricket.

Then the train pulled into Bucharest Nord station.

"Hello, may I introduce myself, I am representing a massage parlour"
Bucharest

We said goodbye to Dinesh and lugged our rucksacks into a dusty concourse with a lovely old-fashioned timetable featuring a bewildering listing of destinations hand-painted on wooden slats coloured red, orange and blue. These were slotted into a wooden rack the size of a small house and there was something endearing about the contraption: its straightforward simplicity, no clicking on apps or waiting for new screens to flash up. Evocative-sounding destinations awaited down the line: Craiova, Târgoviște, Pitești, Suceava, Constanța, Urziceni. Looking up at the board, Romania seemed mind-boggling. What was life like in Târgoviște or Pitești? We would never know (at least not on this trip).

Light from skylights in the metal-framed roof filtered down on a row of adverts for "THE EUROPEAN YEAR OF RAIL 2021" (even though it was 2023). A newsagent near the old-fashioned board sold novels in English including Richard Osman's *The Thursday Murder Club* and Donna Tartt's *The Secret History*. A fug of smoke hung in the air. Passengers stood around waiting for trains, a large number of whom were smoking including one of the tallest men I had ever laid eyes on. He must have been well over seven feet. Taking a sleeper between Timișoara and Bucharest for him must have been a nightmare.

For breakfast, we ordered Sausage McMuffins and fries from a McDonald's next to the newsagent in the station's most prominent spot, which said something in a former communist country, even if communism was in the distant past – gone since 1989.

"God bless the golden arches," said Danny, who had demanded we dine there and who held many opinions about many matters, as you may have noticed, one of which being that McDonald's got a bad press and was an international dining institution to be cherished, as he had intimated back in Paris. Not that I minded. When it came down to it, much of our long-standing friendship could, you might say, come down to *making the most of things*, while also wanting to know about things that may not turn out to be important things, not worrying too much whether we missed things as they may not be important things, generally being sceptical of things (in particular expensive things previously unknown to us), and sharing a similar attitude towards fussing about things. And that attitude was perhaps best summed up thus: *what was the point in fussing about things?* All of this usually served us fairly well, allowing for a minimum of complications while in foreign lands.

The passengers on the 1883 *Orient Express* had been whisked away for a slap-up lunch and an audience with King Carol and Queen Elisabeth at their newly refurbished summer palace at this juncture on their journey to Istanbul. We would not be meeting the Romanian royalty (there was none anymore). Nor would there be any slap-up meals. We would be dining at the station McDonald's. Fine by me, even though it may not have been my first choice so far as *getting beneath the surface of Romanian culture* was concerned. But all of that could wait: Romanian culture could reveal itself in its no doubt many-layered, intriguing complexities later. Anyway, I quite liked Sausage McMuffins and fries: a perfect breakfast really after a night on a Romanian sleeper train. And anyway, too, this was the "culture" at Bucharest Nord station, you might argue. You could only play with the cards which you were dealt.

We began to eat our Sausage McMuffins, saying very little. Then, as we did so, a small girl in a grubby pink jumper came and begged for what we thought was food, holding out her hands but saying nothing. She cut a sad, plaintive figure. Tragic. Desperate. Lost. There we were, a little crotchety, perhaps, after a night on a Romanian sleeper train. And there she was: begging for her breakfast. Not quite knowing what to do, we gave her a bag of fries and watched as she then went round other tables, and more people offered food. We seemed to have done the right thing. By the end, she had a full tray.

Then we noticed her go outside and, not realizing she was being observed, unceremoniously drop all the food in a bin on the concourse.

It had been cash she was after – and she counted the few leu diners had given her. Sad… tragic… lost. And seemingly a station fixture.

No surprise, really. Poverty in Romania was rife, the country was one of the poorest in Europe. The annual GDP per capita on our visit was £12,466, according to the World Bank, which worked out at £34 a day. The country was suffering from a chronic brain drain of workers to other parts of the European Union. Since joining the EU in 2007, more than 3.4 million Romanians had fled the country (17 per cent of the population). On a worldwide scale, only Syria had experienced a greater exodus during that period, and an even more telling statistic was that the number of Romanians aged 15 to 29 was down 28 per cent from 4.86 million in 2008 to 3.52 million in 2016. The housing charity Habitat for Humanity estimated that of Romania's 19 million population, 5 million were living in poverty, and of those 1.5 million were children. Meanwhile 8.5 million people lived without showers, baths or running water (41 per cent), while 35 per cent of the nation's housing stock was in a "state of complete neglect and needs urgent repairs".

We re-entered the fuggy concourse.

Bucharest Nord station had complicated automated luggage storage lockers. We found these lockers in a side hall with fluorescent lighting and set about conquering them, not wanting to carry the backpacks around all day as check-in at the apartment we had found was 4 p.m. While we were cursing the lockers, a pair of twenty-something American backpackers came up and asked us how much the lockers cost. They were ten leu an hour (£1.75).

"Damn, that's expensive," said one of them, who looked a bit travel-worn and rough around the edges, probably from staying at the likes of the Patio Hostel in Bratislava for an extended period. "Two bucks, man. Damn!"

They turned away.

Although the Americans had backpacker-weary looks, it was clear they were well educated and from a good background, on a gap year both to "find themselves" and learn about Europe, rather like the Grand Tourists of the seventeenth and eighteenth centuries mentioned at the beginning of this chapter, without lackeys transporting possessions, of course. Future congressmen, perhaps, senators, even – who knew, maybe higher still. Nothing wrong with that. What a great way to get a better feeling for the world: breaking free and hitting the tracks. Maybe the guy back at Strasbourg station who had asked for the day of the week was in the same boat (or maybe not, in his instance). For the time being though, ten leu an hour was too much of a stretch for these "congressmen"-to-be.

We went to visit the Palace of the Parliament.

This was Nicolae Ceaușescu's old HQ, reached along a grim multi-lane road lined by austere government structures. Everything seemed austere. The façade of Bucharest Nord station, comprising six enormous columns aping ancient Greece in lead-grey stone, was austere. The multi-lane road was austere: too functional, too big for a city. Rain pelted down, adding to the austerity. Not much traffic passed by. Adverts featuring busty women promoting online betting opportunities were attached to austere apartment blocks. Bucharest seemed dirty, damp and down on its luck. Plaster façades crumbled. Tangles of electricity hung loosely here, there and everywhere. Former shops with windows boarded up with corrugated metal looked closed for good.

Then, across a park, austerity came to an abrupt end and grandiosity took over.

We had reached the Palace of the Parliament.

It was hideous. A huge concrete and marble neoclassical monstrosity loomed ahead, said to be the second largest administrative building in the world after the Pentagon. Countless windows and arches formed the façade, with wings of the ugly building tapering to each side.

Stone walls and metal railings encircled the large plot of land around the Palace of the Parliament. At a break in these by a driveway we came to what appeared to be an entrance gate. Tours were possible from there. This forbidding building was to be our only regular "tourism" in Bucharest, we had decided. At the gate, however, a notice headed "CHAMBER OF DEPUTIES – INTERNATIONAL CONFERENCE CENTRE" displayed a disappointing message:

"Tours are subject to availability. A prior booking is mandatory! [They] can only be made by phone, 24 hours prior to the visit." We had messed up. We had walked a long way down a grim multi-lane road lined by austere buildings just to stare at an ugly grandiose building in the rain.

Ignoring the rules, we continued up the driveway and entered a grandiose doorway that led to a wide grandiose reception, perhaps the width of a football pitch. White marble gleamed beneath fluorescent lights and a long cloakroom, perhaps a quarter of the length of a football pitch, was to the right. No one was there. So we went to the left and found a small gift shop selling "I LOVE TRANSYLVANIA" fridge magnets and decorative Palace of the Parliament spoons. This was next to a ticket booth and a short queue for a tour.

Trying our luck, we went up and asked the man at the booth if we could buy tickets. The attendant was in his thirties with ruffled dark hair and had an inscrutable manner, although a flicker in his expression suggested: *what have I got here?* We looked (and were) soaked from the downpour. We explained we were from London and had come by train. After this, he regarded us once again.

Of the state of us, he said: "You should feel at home. This is English weather."

Of how far we had travelled along the tracks: "That is a very long way."

Then he smiled and said, of the tickets: "No problem."

We had gatecrashed the Palace of the Parliament.

There was no one else in the queue. Danny asked for recommendations for restaurants in Bucharest, to which the attendant replied: "May I suggest two traditional restaurants, the Wheelbarrow and Manuc's Inn. I don't know any high-class restaurants."

To which, Danny replied: "Don't worry, we're not high class."

The attendant regarded us yet again and said: "You may want to go to the Mojo bar, association British football is played on the TVs there."

We chatted to the attendant for a while about Romanian emigration. He said: "Not all Romanians want to go to Britain to work." He paused. "But I want to go."

He handed over the ticket and took our leu, telling us as he did: "This is the biggest building in this part of Europe. Ceaușescu also had a villa to the north of the city…"

He cut himself short, looking over our shoulders. The tour was about to go. He indicated we had better hurry, or we would have to wait an hour.

What an excellent, extremely helpful ticket kiosk attendant at the Palace of the Parliament.

The tour took about an hour, led by a small, equally excellent guide with purple hair, a purple jumper and purple boots. After going through an airport-style security scanner, about thirty of us were directed up marble stairs to a long hall with a green-and-gold carpet.

"More than nine hectares were demolished to create this palace by Ceaușescu. I suppose you have heard of him?" she asked rhetorically.

The building, we learned, had 1,100 rooms, 2,800 chandeliers, 2,368,060 square feet of carpet, a width of 800 feet and a length of 885 feet and was the heaviest man-made structure on the planet at 4.1 million tonnes. More than thirty thousand people had to be moved from the area and a major Orthodox church was "completely demolished". As many as one hundred thousand Romanians had been involved in "Project Bucharest", with construction beginning in 1984, and lasting until Ceaușescu was deposed.

"In 1989," said the guide, who had a dry sense of humour. "I suppose you also might know, there was a revolution."

After that, a debate began about what to do with the hideous palace, said the guide. Some suggested turning it into a luxury hotel. Others felt that it should be demolished, though as the heaviest building on the planet that would have been more expensive than other options. The media mogul Rupert Murdoch had made a move to buy the palace (for one billion dollars), but this had been rejected. A scheme to turn it into a massive shopping mall did not come to fruition either. It had become home to three museums including the National Museum of Contemporary Art, as well as the Romanian legislature and the conference centre.

The purple guide led us through various halls glittering with gold decorations and chandeliers, down corridors like small airport runways flanked by marble-plated columns. There were special brass radiators. There were silk curtains from Transylvania. There were mahogany panels from the Democratic Republic of Congo. There were steps on a staircase designed to make Ceauşescu appear as tall as his wife Elena, who was slightly taller. There was a gaudy pink "Protocol Hall", with the colour chosen because "pink is said to be the diplomatic colour as you do not find it on anyone's flag". There was a final giant hall, with a balcony from which Ceauşescu had hoped to address military parades though the palace was not quite finished at the time of his death. Michael Jackson, however, had apparently taken to the balcony during a tour and said: "Hello, Bucharest, I love you!"

So ended the tour of the awful palace. We retrieved our bags from the station and found our two-bedroom "Lovely Loft Apartment" (booked online the day before). It was reached up a steep, narrow, uneven, creaky staircase past doorways of apartments that seemed to contain elderly residents judging by those we encountered. Inside though it was like stepping into the pages of an interior magazine, all designer lights and minimalism mixed with splashes of abstract art and bookshelves with carefully selected novels. The only problem was the heating did not work. A text to the owner received a reply that she would reset it; nobody had been staying the night before and the boiler must have clicked off.

Our night out in Bucharest was an unusual one.

It began in the old town at Mojo, where a gang of muscle-bound shaven-headed British thugs was dominating proceedings.

"If I'd wanted to hang out with British yobs, I'd have stayed in Britain," said Danny.

So we went to the Half Time bar next door, which was almost empty. We once again played darts. The darts had Union Jacks on their flights. We were getting better at the game, hitting doubles with more fluency (Danny won, so the "series" stood at one–all, after the game in Nuremberg). Afterwards we walked along the cobbled streets, which were heaving with revellers meandering between the endless neon-lit bars and busy little bistros; nothing like the grim streets by the station leading to the palace. It was Friday night and a party was on.

There was, however, an unmistakeable undercurrent of what you might simply call "activity". Within a few minutes of our stroll, a greasy little man on a corner sidled up to us: "Hello, you like ladies? Hey, hey, ladies? Nice ladies?"

We walked on by, and as we did he said: "You like naked boys?"

Not far on after the greasy little man, another street salesman, much smarter than the last one, he was even wearing a tie, approached.

"Hello," he said quite formally. "May I introduce myself. I am representing a massage parlour."

Bowing slightly, he handed us cards with the motto: "REAL HOT GIRLS IN OUR PARLOURS".

The man in the tie said: "Please feel free to call at your convenience."

He bowed slightly again. As we walked on, Danny said: "Wow, it was as though his next job will be a UN representative."

We stopped at a small bar with neon red lights that specialized in Ukrainian cherry wine. I had been to a bar selling the same brand in Lviv during *Slow Trains to Venice* and had enjoyed the drink. We stood at a high table facing the cobbled lane – there were no stools – and watched the debauchery pass by. It was a bit like William Hogarth's famous drawing of *Gin Lane* in London in 1751, except everyone was in designer clothes and no one was lolling about in the gutter. Not yet at least.

We continued our investigation of Bucharest nightlife.

The Paradise Club, beyond a bar named Sinners, was advertising "LIVE GIRLS NUDE". In the front window of the Paradise Club, a woman in a thong and high heels – virtually nude – was dancing seductively. A group of men with caps saying "BACHELOR PARTY" staggered by pausing to ogle the woman in the window. A group of women led by a woman wearing a sash saying "BRIDE TO BE" was yelping about something further down the lane. This seemed to be stag and hen central.

We entered an upmarket-looking restaurant/bar that had a mix of men and women, people chatting away, thinking that we had found a respectable watering hole amid all the madness. We ordered two expensive Heinekens, standing at the bar to drink them. Then "the ladies" arrived. In the space of about 30 minutes, enough time to finish the beers, no fewer than five pairs of women, each of them slightly different in appearance, came and loitered casually beside us, casting glances our way as though wishing to enter into conversation with us (two middle-aged blokes from Britain who had arrived on the 21:50 sleeper from Timişoara). Almost all were smoking, the preference being for thin cigarettes with gold tips and menthol aromas. Each glanced at the barman with quick looks communicating a message that appeared to be: *may I have a drink please?* They then received what seemed to be free shots from the barman, whose manner suggested he knew them. The ladies appeared to be connected to the establishment.

We kept ourselves to ourselves. The best word to describe the scenario really was: "awkward". And when we left, Danny said: "There was a shaven-headed guy on the far side of the bar who kept staring at me – the sort of guy who looked like he'd beat the shit out of you for fun. You couldn't see him from where you were. He kept looking over. If he'd done it once: fine. But he kept doing it, like he was a pimp or something."

Lots of things seemed to be going on in Bucharest's old town.

All that was left was to stop by at Mojo, where the yobs had left, for a final tipple. From upstairs though, what seemed like live music emanated. Which was how we found ourselves attending a very good karaoke night with high-quality singers who might well have gone far on *Romania's Got Talent* (such a television show did in fact exist). It was almost all locals: groups of extended families and friends. No seediness. No clandestine transactions. No pimp thugs staring at you. No gold-tipped menthol cigarettes. No hidden agenda. No UN officials-to-be bowing unctuously, presenting you with their cards. Just people having a good night out, high-quality Romanian karaoke-style. Even better quality than back at the Shamrock Irish Pub in Passau. What more could any long-distance train traveller want than that?

CHAPTER FOUR

BUCHAREST TO SOFIA IN BULGARIA, VIA RUSE

"UNDER COMMUNISM BEATLES NOT ALLOWED"

On our return from Mojo, the heating was still not working. In the morning, it was off, too. So was the hot water for the showers. We had cold showers and walked to the station to catch the 10:50 to Ruse in Bulgaria.

A few stragglers were out and about on the streets, leftovers from the night before, smoking and gesticulating and arguing about something on the square near "Lovely Loft Apartment". The streets were mainly empty save for a few cars with tinted windows driving fast. One of these had lime-green hubcaps and a skull and sheriff's badge emblem on the side saying: "LIVE WITHOUT LIMITS", while another showed the torso of a muscular figure with a skull's head saying: "NEVER BACK DOWN". Romania's capital was home to a few folk you would perhaps not want to rub up the wrong way.

No wonder Andrew Tate, the notorious Anglo-American kickboxer cum television personality, who once admitted he was "absolutely misogynist", had made his home in Romania, moving from Britain in 2017. In another interview, Tate had said of Romania that he liked "living in countries where corruption was accessible for everybody". Perhaps this attitude had led to his downfall, as the controversial figure – whose online persona was of concern among many regarding the effect it had on young males (he had almost 7 million followers on Twitter and was extremely influential among this group) – was under house arrest on charges of human trafficking, rape and forming an organized crime group to sexually exploit women. The eventual fate of Tate, aged 36, had yet to be decided.

What was clear though was that a new wave of anti-corruption politicians that had taken the helm in Romania had a huge job on their hands with organized crime. Fortunately, unlike in neighbouring Hungary, the country could "boast of a diverse, relatively pluralistic media landscape that produces hard-hitting public interest investigations", according to Reporters Without Borders, although pressure from shadowy media owners might "hamper the reality of information".

Lots of things seemed to be going on in Romania in general.

On a battered old banger
Bucharest to Ruse, Bulgaria

The 10:50 to Ruse, due in at 1.45 p.m., was a battered old banger covered in graffiti that blocked views from many of the windows, several of which were also shattered but not replaced and unlikely to pass "health and safety" back home. Narrow purple seats with their numbers written in pen on the walls were set in a formation of two across each side of the aisle and some parts of the carriages had raised sections. We sat at one of these in the front carriage, which was mainly empty, just a scattering of other passengers. Looking forward we could see the silhouette of the driver hunched at his chair directing the train, the door to the cab wide open. Again, unlikely to be allowed back home.

With a whistle – and a juddery start and abrupt stop – the train rattled cautiously into the suburbs of Bucharest beneath a pewter sky, passing wrecks of old carriages decomposing in forgotten sidings and a long wall of faded graffiti. A half-collapsed factory appeared on the left. On the right, a series of small abodes, perhaps where the factory workers once lived, were covered in vegetation as though slowly disappearing into the Romanian landscape. We traversed a wide section of what looked like potato fields. This, after the mess moving out of Bucharest Nord station, transformed into relaxing, pleasingly untouched scenery.

I went to check out the view from the driver's cab.

You were not allowed to step into the cab, but it was interesting to see the track ahead, two lines of steel with a metallic gleam tapering towards to a hazy horizon. The driver was young with a crew cut and pointy ears. He was positioned in the middle of the cab so that he was directly in the centre of the tracks, his right hand clutching the speed controller.

It was raining and the windscreen wiper was thudding slowly from side to side. The windscreen itself was badly smashed on the right as though rocks, or some other heavy objects, had struck. Spidery cracks emanated from a cluster of circular marks in the thick glass where these impacts had occurred. The worst damage had been covered by a fraying piece of plastic glued to the screen, presumably to keep out draughts and rain. Had the train been hit by a landslide in more mountainous parts? Or perhaps come under attack from youths chucking stones for fun? I didn't ask. I didn't want to distract the driver.

For a while I tried to put myself in the mind of a Romanian train driver on a remote regional line in charge of a chain of clapped-out old carriages splattered with graffiti. It was clearly a solitary existence. There he sat facing the long metal tracks for hours on end, pressing buttons, nudging the controller, while staring through a cracked windscreen. No left or right: impossible. Just forward down the line through the empty Romanian landscape, clicking across plains, rolling to the Black Sea or winding between mountains (when sent on routes further north in the country). Forty years, perhaps, till retirement. And how many miles during that? It must take a certain mindset.

The train pulled into Videle station on its dog-leg journey south to Ruse. A Romanian flag hung by the old red-brick station house outside of which a few half-broken plastic chairs were attached to the wall. A railway worker wearing a furry flap-eared hat – the flaps tied above his head, ready for colder weather – strode along the platform with his hands in his pockets. Two women with plastic bags awaited the train to Bucharest. Not much was going on in Videle.

Moving on past looming grain silos, where wagons stood by the track, the train rattled on once more to Giurgiu, a city on the river Danube facing Bulgaria on the far banks. We were catching up with the mighty river once again, last seen in Budapest.

Giurgiu, 40 miles south of Bucharest, had played an important part in the original *Orient Express* service back in 1883. Georges Nagelmackers, the soon-to-be famous Belgian civil engineer and early long-distance rail entrepreneur, had his eye on the city as he saw it as a key early link to Istanbul, allowing him to launch trips on his Compagnie Internationale des Wagons-Lits service from Paris to the "East". Before the line was laid to Giurgiu, the terminus from Paris was Vienna, reached via Munich. Nagelmackers had already begun train trips there with passengers departing from Paris Gare de l'Est at 18:30 and arriving the following day in Vienna at 11:20 p.m. However, when the way lay clear to the remote Romanian city on the Danube, he was quick to act. His plan was to ferry passengers across the Danube to Ruse in Bulgaria, where a rudimentary railway was already established to the port and seaside resort of Varna on the Black Sea – not an ideal arrangement as the train would travel through what some considered potential "bandit country" in Bulgaria (some passengers on the early trains, aware of this, had packed firearms). From there another ferry to Istanbul/Constantinople awaited. The entire journey time from Paris? Around 80 hours.

It had taken a couple of years more before the trip to Istanbul was possible entirely by trains, going via Vienna, Belgrade and Plovdiv. By 1889, the first direct trains began taking 67 hours and 35 minutes, and the *Orient Express* proper was up and running.

So travelling to Ruse was like following along the rail route of those very first passengers way back in October 1883.

The 10:50 rolled on through more potato fields. The driver with pointy ears hooted the horn. A line of trees rose on the horizon, looking like soldiers on a march. A ticket inspector with a burgundy tie and a blue jacket checked our passes, finally.

David, a twenty-something environmental student from Münster in Germany, was sitting two rows away. He wore tortoiseshell glasses and a hoodie that said "HURRICANE" and had his legs primly crossed as though he were an Oxford don about to address his students. His hair was purposely ruffled in an arty way and he had neatly trimmed "designer" stubble. He was laid-back and seemed secretly amused by something. He was a backpacker on an Interrailing trip, doing it on a tight budget.

"I always look for the very cheapest hostel," he said thoughtfully, in the manner of a professor discussing Marx's theory of historical materialism. "In Budapest: nine euros and breakfast was included. At this hostel, if I drink at the bar, they give me bread free. Some hostels are very bad: fifteen, twenty euros and not so good. Some are OK. This hostel was the best."

Danny and I were probably blowing five days of his expenditure every 24 hours and sometimes more (and we thought we were cheap). The Patio Hotel in Bratislava had been twenty-nine euros each, our personal low, which had almost broken us in terms of comfort, with its earplugs and bathroom down the hall. David was on a different level with his *nine euros* and *free bread*, as though he was some kind of Interrail frugality guru. Had we stumbled upon the cheapest rail traveller in Europe?

I expressed admiration for his good housekeeping along the tracks. He nonchalantly waved away the compliment in a manner that suggested *it is nothing, but you may learn*. The Oxford don of budget trains did not suffer from hubris but was quite self-assured.

David had already travelled around France, Spain and Portugal for a month, after which he had returned home to take two exams in environmental engineering, before embarking on six weeks that had already taken him to Prague, Vienna, the Austrian Alps, Ljubljana in Slovenia, Zagreb in Croatia, Budapest and Bucharest. He was heading for Sofia, Bulgaria's capital – Danny's and my intended stop after Ruse – followed by Istanbul and Athens. It was like a military operation, with every day carefully costed.

"Maybe if I have time and the weather is right, I want to climb Mount Olympus," he said. "It's two thousand nine hundred metres. It's the home of the Olympic gods."

He said this in an offhand yet slightly mysterious tone. He wanted to hike up to meet the Greek gods. Such an excursion also fit in with his budget, being free.

David was sitting by a window covered in graffiti but could just peek through, the colours of the paint creating an almost psychedelic effect, casting the landscape in strange shades of orange and purple.

He was an Interrail convert. "It feels like an adventure going by train. Not: *up in the sky and two hours later you're there*. I want to see the whole of nature."

By train, this was possible, and at a good price.

What did he want to do when he had finished his studies? The recent exams had been the last.

"I really don't know, maybe an environmental advisor," he said, looking momentarily worried about the reality that lay waiting at the end of his rail adventure. "Sometimes I'm like dreaming about what I can do in the future." While he was gazing out of the carriage windows. "An internship at a company, maybe."

"What kind of company?"

"Well, I don't know," he replied, as though surprised to have been asked.

David was not a fan of Bucharest. "I don't like the traffic," he said. "I don't like the restaurants. All the people say: *Come and eat here, come and eat here*. I was getting a little sick of that." He too had been approached by representatives of the massage parlours.

He switched back to his favourite topic.

"The hostel cost thirteen euros," he continued, almost wincing at the memory as "really it was not so good for thirteen euros".

This had been a black mark against Bucharest.

His firm favourite stop-off on the journey so far had been Budapest and the nine-euro hostel, which was where he had made a friend. "His name was Luke. He was from Canada," he said. "I went with him to have some wine in a ruin bar. We got back at midnight. We follow each other on Instagram now."

It may have been half a century since Interrail passes began, but they were still doing what they set out to achieve in the first place: letting young people explore the continent by trains at a cheap price. Older folk as well, in their newer format. Danny and I – by this stage of the trip, having conquered the Eurail app – were both in agreement that Interrail passes were all in all a Very Good Thing. Deep in Eastern Europe after departing St Pancras International some time ago, it was hard to get over the freedom they offered: *step out of your front door and go wherever the rails may lead* (no two journeys quite the same).

Our passports were gathered at Giurgiu Nord station.

This was an ornate affair with neoclassical arches, panels painted in pale pink and a lawn planted with an assortment of trees. The station had an evocative air of faded grandeur and for a moment it was possible to imagine the steam locomotive pulling in with the original *Orient Express* carriages in 1883 packed full of statesmen, businessmen and members of the press, so carefully selected by Nagelmackers, who had pulled off considerable feats of deal-making with Europe's various railways, including the Royal Romanian Railways on this leg, to have been granted permission to get his beloved train as far as Giurgiu.

The station on our visit had become run-down, or perhaps it had always been a little so. The nicest description that George Behrend, a train historian who specialized in the *Orient Express*, could make of Giurgiu as he understood the station to have been at the time the *Orient Express* had pulled in was of "some outlandish place in Roumania that nobody had ever heard of, where there was a steam ferry across the Danube". The first passengers, he says in his book *Grand European Expresses*, were not exactly enthralled.

They probably would not be much impressed by what we saw in the early twenty-first century either: grass on the station lawn growing in untidy clumps, peeling paint on the station wall, weeds sprouting by the track. A somnolent station dog with a curly tail rose from its position of slumber to observe the 10:50 from Bucharest. Its manner seemed to be asking a question of the train: *can you deliver me anything that might improve my day?* The dog after a minute or so of panting and regarding us with calculating-but-unexpecting eyes decided not. The hound returned to its former position, chin and solitary paw hanging over the edge of the platform. Just another train along the line.

It is worth pointing out here that not only had those early first passengers been less than impressed by the surroundings at Giurgiu and Ruse – although they had appreciated the accompaniment of no fewer than 20 bottles of wine "uncorked by Mr Nagelmackers' valet, borrowed from the Wagons-Lits cellar", as Edmond About put it, on the ferry across the Danube – they would have been noticing a sharp slowdown in the *Orient Express* in Romania, which had not really been living up to its "express" billing by this stage of the 1883 journey. The average speed across France and Germany had been about 45 mph, while in Hungary that had dipped to 30 mph, and in Romania to a lowly 20 mph, according to another rail historian, Christian Wolmar, in his book *Blood, Iron & Gold: How the Railways Transformed the World.*

On the first "express" on the route it really had been *slow trains to Istanbul.*

Danny set off on a rant.

"I mean what is this? Holding us up just for the sake of going into their poxy country. We should be checking their passports," he said.

It was just for effect – he didn't really mean it.

His stomach was speaking. He was champing at the bit for lunch overlooking the Danube having found a suitable restaurant online called the Terassa, right by the waterfront in Ruse.

"A nice lunch by the Danube, an expensive lunch, a superior lunch, a good lunch by the river," he said. The idea of this superior, expensive lunch, compared to our other previous less indulgent (cheap) lunches, seemed to have become rooted in his imagination and something of an obsession. A step up from breakfast at McDonald's. He had rediscovered his inner Henri Opper de Blowitz.

At times it almost felt as if this swaggering journalistic ghost from 1883 had joined us: two middle-aged men rattling about on some trains becoming three; Blowitz had been 58 when he had ridden the rails enjoying himself so much. *Two Middle-Aged Men in Some Trains* at these moments was turning into *Three Middle-Aged Men in Some Trains*, or at least two and one phantom on a freebie.

The wait for our superior, expensive lunch did not last long.

The train rattled on beyond a miserable series of mid-twentieth-century apartments and reached a metal-framed bridge across the ever-eddying Danube, more than half a mile across at this point with a milky sheen and not a single vessel. To the east, it was 80 miles to the Black Sea. To the north-west, about 650 miles to Budapest, or perhaps more given the river's meanderings.

Down below, ahead and to the right, was the port of Ruse with cranes rising like robotic giraffes. We passed smokestacks and a queue of lorries waiting for customs checks and an old wooden carriage that was so decrepit it looked as though it might collapse just from the reverberations of the 10:50 from Bucharest. More wretched apartment blocks arose on the other side of the river in Bulgaria, higher than the ones in Romania and not quite as worn down. A stern border guard in a stiff green uniform checked our passports and we arrived at Ruse station, disembarking from the old banger with its shattered windows and graffiti.

Stickers on a platform column, featuring a deranged-looking half human, half dog creature baring its teeth, bore the slogan: "RUSE OUTLAWS, 100 PER CENT HOOLIGANS".

"I'm putting on my poor hat," said Danny, swiftly. "Need to go down a few social classes."

He seemed generally wary of some parts of Central and Eastern Europe, although – aside perhaps from the muttering man on the Budapest underground – nobody had bothered us much. Not in the slightest really.

"Enjoy every Ruse minute!"
Ruse

Sometimes when you travel to out-of-the-way places by train, you get lucky and stumble upon an unexpected gem of a station. This is one of the joys of long railway trips.

On recent journeys I can think of the extraordinary mustard-coloured Indian-maharaja-style palace of Wrocław station in Poland (completely out of place in its Eastern European surroundings). Then there was the Gothic medieval revival extravagance of Maastricht station in the Netherlands (all stained-glass windows, high ceilings and beams as though you had entered some kind of cathedral of train). Meanwhile in north-west Spain, while researching my book *Slow Trains Around Spain,* the ornate, OTT Renaissance/neoclassical Zamora station had come as a total surprise, complete with its highly unusual Wild West-style bar.

Ruse station was another. Constructed during communist times, opened in 1955 just after the Danube Bridge in 1954, it was a grand, three-storey affair built in what has come to be known as "Socialist realism" design. This meant that everything was about five times larger than it needed to be and that slapdash copycat attempts had been made to emulate both classical and some random non-classical European architecture. While this may not sound exactly great, all these various touches seemed to have pulled together somehow at Ruse station by the simple fact it was so enormous, so muscle-bound in its approach, so in-your-face. The architects had clearly been working on the premise of *never mind the logic of the detail, just be dazzled by the sheer size.*

Inside the ticket hall, great Corinthian columns arose amid high-swooping arches and balconies with balustrades that might grace a garden terrace of a Tuscan villa. The ceiling appeared modelled on the hall of a Tudor-era English country house, or perhaps Hampton Court Palace, with indented rectangles in a symmetrical pattern. A peculiar, large brass chandelier of the type that you might find in a mosque hung low, as though added as an afterthought simply to fill the void of the space above. On this heavy-looking chandelier, instead of candles, Art Nouveau flutes with electrical bulbs poked upwards like long, thin tulips.

Outside, a 112-foot bell tower arose that would not have been out of place by the banks of the Grand Canal in Venice. Meanwhile, the station façade comprised yet more Corinthian columns, these ones shooting up the full three storeys and reminiscent of the Parthenon in Athens. Directly in front of these columns a subway beneath a road leading towards the city centre was decorated in an abstract mosaic depicting a metal-framed bridge with water rushing below. This was presumably in honour of the opening of the Danube Bridge.

In short it was a hotchpotch of a place: a very grand, somewhat ridiculous, yet also strangely wonderful Soviet hotchpotch. There was not much about it online when I later checked. However, a website devoted to the "Romanian-Bulgarian Cross-Border Area" named Audiotravelguide.ro was extremely positive concluding its review, somewhat briefly but to the point, with: "It should be noticed by any foreigner."

We were foreigners. We had noticed it.

Ruse station was clearly a collector's item of stations among those who care to collect such things (i.e., increasingly, people like me).

In a corner of the ticket hall was the "International Railticket Agency".

There we worked out how to reach Sofia the following day, after being reprimanded by a woman wearing a green cardigan in the booth. We had done something wrong. We did not know what. Anyway, we would be catching the 07:53 to Bulgaria's capital the next day, arriving at 2.43 p.m. all being well.

Ruse was a peculiar place.

We wanted to like it. But we were not sure we did.

It began like this: you walked down a long street flanked by a long run of cheerless apartment blocks sprouting satellite dishes. This street was home to no fewer than four slot machine centres and three sex shops. It led to a large square with a cluster of fountains, none of which worked. By the square was a courthouse with imitation Greek columns. There were also several elegant neo-Gothic and neo-Rococo buildings with stone carvings of maidens and august historical figures that looked as though they could do with a lick of paint. The most elaborate of these structures was known as the "Profit-Yielding Building", opened in 1901 with shops, a casino, a theatre and an art gallery.

By all accounts, around that time Ruse had been flourishing following Bulgaria's break from the Ottoman Empire in 1878 after its bloody uprising supported by the Russian Empire (which had been mindful back then of protecting Christian regional interests). Its position on the river Danube made it a key trading city, and soon Bulgaria's first cinema was to open (in 1911), as well as the first private bank and printing press. The railway to Varna on the Black Sea had begun in 1867, an important part of this "rise of Ruse".

The riverside city had been a big deal, even if the first *Orient Express* passengers passing through had been sniffy. The French reporter Edmond About was of the opinion that "the shovel and the broom will cause a sensation if they ever fancy to come" to its streets.

Danny and I were rapidly beginning to side with the Normandy-butter-loving reporter.

On the edge of the square with the fountains that were not working was a tiny tourist information centre. Inside, we asked the tourist information officer whether the centre was open. She had been chatting to a friend and the lights were dimly lit.

"Yes, what you want?" she asked, as though distracted.

We requested a map.

She handed one over. Then she gathered a clutch of booklets entitled *Enjoy Every Ruse Minute!*, *Guide: Architecture, Temples and Museums* and the *Business and Weekend Tourism Guide* – each one covering more or less the same material in subtly different ways.

Ruse was not only home to Bulgaria's first cinema but also to its first leather-processing factory, steam brewery, soap factory, knitting factory, insurance company, factory for iron rollers, bicycle factory, and "factory for blueing", apparently.

She looked at us as though that was that: job done.

But we were hanging around, trying to work out the map and the guides.

"Are you from a cruise ship?" she asked.

Cruise ships quite often stopped in Ruse.

We explained that we were not.

She looked at us a little suspiciously as though not sure whether to believe us. Satisfied she did, she appeared both pleased and relieved by this information. This relief seemed to come from the fact there would not be a sudden flood of tourists such as ourselves dropping by asking for maps and booklets.

After flicking through one of the latter, I said I was interested to see the house of the family of Elias Canetti (1905–1994), a locally born writer who had gone on to win the Nobel Prize for Literature for his sharply observed books about crowds. Canetti believed that most people are fearful of being touched by the unknown, tending to "avoid physical contact with anything strange", including unknown people, yet in crowds this fear dissipates creating a great sense of "relief" that might overflow spontaneously, especially where large numbers have gathered.

This, he believed, helped explain much of the early twentieth century, especially the rise of fascism. Canetti, who was Jewish, had lived an extraordinary life, falling into a tub of boiling water as a child and almost dying, moving to Manchester, where he witnessed his father collapse and die of a heart attack when still a boy, and then moving once more to Vienna, where he himself was involved in a crowd uprising against an unfair court decision in July 1927 during which police had shot and killed 90 people around him. At the time he had felt "elevated… there was something in the air, an evil music" and he admitted he had seemed part of a "tremendous wave". The day had a huge influence on him. Later, in 1938, having established his name as a writer, he relocated to Britain to avoid Nazi persecution of the Jews.

He was a remarkable man, who had also turned his hand to travel writing – which was how I had got to know about him in the first place. His short book *The Voices of Marrakesh: A Record of a Visit* is a brilliant description of life in the Moroccan capital, capturing the sounds, smells and quirks of culture from street level.

Canetti had become a hero of mine and I had not previously realized he was born in Ruse. *Enjoy Every Ruse Minute!* had alerted me to the connection, mentioning Canetti House.

Did the tourist information woman know where this house was?

"I am not familiar with this," she replied. "I have not been."

"Really?"

"Yes, really," she said.

She looked at us both in a manner that suggested: *anything else?*

So I asked her where the old train station was for the line to Varna; where the first *Orient Express* passengers would have gathered.

"It is on map," she replied. Her eyes fell on the map in my hands.

She looked at us again as if to suggest: *anything else?*

There wasn't anything that we could think of.

So Danny and I thanked her for all the booklets and the map and walked down to the riverside, passing the unusually named "Studio Hairfuckers Gentleman Cut and Shave" barbershop, to a tall 1960s tower block hotel that rose by the waterfront: the Grand Hotel Riga.

Our digs for the night looked truly soul-destroying but the rooms had been modernized, even if the décor was in shades of grey that seemed chosen to match the exterior. From the windows, sweeping views across the Danube were to be had. The mighty river looked sedate and slow and murky-green, at peace with itself not far from its journey's end in the Black Sea, 1,770 miles after forming in the Black Forest in Germany (not so far from Strasbourg).

This, along with the unusual station, was the best thing about Ruse so far.

We strolled along the river to the Terassa Restaurant and ate "pork shank with garlic potatoes and carrots" accompanied by red wine while looking across the Danube at Romanian woodlands on the far bank and listening to Bulgarian pop music. This was our superior, expensive meal. It was excellent. Danny seemed extremely content. I was extremely content. Ruse was getting better.

As we drank coffees, I asked Danny if he would like to go to the old train station, also home to Bulgaria's National Transport Museum.

"No thanks," he said.

"Are you sure?"

"I am absolutely sure," he said.

"Really?"

"I have never been so sure in my life," he replied.

So I went to the old station/transport museum alone, only to find the staff were sitting outside on a bench about to go home. It was ten minutes before closing time. They looked at me with horror when I, a tourist who wanted to look at their old trains, arrived. Tourists, I was beginning to notice, appeared to be something of an inconvenience in Ruse. A woman in a red jumper and jeans, who looked as though she was not to be crossed, said to me: "Yes?"

I took this to be an enquiry into what I wanted to do at the museum, so I replied: "I'd like to see the transport museum, please."

"It is five lev, we are about to close," she said.

I felt in my pockets, realizing I did not have any lev yet. I had a five-euro note, though: five euros was the equivalent of ten lev. When the formidable woman in the red jumper and jeans realized this, as I offered the five euros to her, a smile slowly crossed her face and she said: "Lev! Lev! Bulgaria!"

She would not let me in.

I asked the staff sitting on the bench if any of them could change a five-euro note for five lev. The staff quickly and shiftily said they had no lev. Not a single lev between them. I looked at them. They looked back at me, all innocence. It was a stand-off. I again offered the main woman five euros to go in, explaining it was worth ten lev. She shook her head and said: "Lev! Bulgaria!"

So I took a couple of pictures of some of the nineteenth-century locomotives that were out in the yard, much to the displeasure of the museum chief. Then I had a quick look at the damp grey-stone station house, dating from 1866, trying to imagine the stampede of *Orient Express* passengers arriving at this remote riverside spot in 1883, worrying about the journey ahead. Not only were there concerns about potential bandits, a trepidation among these pioneer passengers, perhaps led by Henri Opper de Blowitz, was what they might be served for lunch in such remote parts.

In the event, this turned out to be overcooked partridges provided during a stop at the remote town of Scheytandjik, accompanied by a rudimentary local wine. Edmond About had not been impressed: "We were served partridges that the great devil himself would not know how to cut, washed down with a local wine that is not worth the devil." He nicknamed the town of Scheytandjik "The Little Devil".

Monsieur About was fond of the word "devil".

I returned to Hotel Grand Riga.

Danny asked: "How was the transport museum?"

"Great, just great," I lied.

Then we went out for a meal by the main square, having taken a look at the flamboyant neo-Gothic exterior of Canetti House – which turned out to be where Canetti's father and grandfather had run a grocery business, not where he had lived (and now a cultural centre only open on certain days) – finally finding a restaurant after being turned away from a handful as no tables were free.

It was Saturday night. The square was deserted. Yet the restaurants were full. No room for two Interrail tourists off the 10:50 from Bucharest, except at one restaurant where a solitary man was drinking a beer, looking somewhat glum. He was the only customer. What this said about the restaurant given that every other place to eat in Ruse was packed to the rafters, we could only surmise. We joined him and ordered chicken *kavarma* (pork, onion, red and green bell peppers, mushrooms and parsley in a stew) from the "Traditional Bulgarian Cuisine" menu, the order taken by a waitress who seemed to have majored in carefully-studied-complete-and-utter-indifference at hospitality college.

The chicken *kavarma* took ages to come, despite no other customers initially being about.

The solitary man ordered another beer.

We ordered another beer.

The beer came quickly.

We waited for our chicken *kavarma*.

As we did so, a soap opera on a television in a corner ended and, quite bizarrely, a cookery show by the British chefs Jamie Oliver and Mary Berry flickered on. The duo were discussing how to cook a pasta dish. No one watched it. The solitary man was glued to his phone.

Youths wearing hoodies walked by in the square. Were these the "RUSE OUTLAWS, 100 PERCENT HOOLIGANS"?

As we were considering this, the dead-eyed waitress dropped several plates of food about to be delivered to another table after colliding with a waiter. Somehow these dishes had been prepared ahead of our chicken *kavarma*, despite our having arrived before the other diners. A few customers more had also come. They had been served already, too.

On hearing the plates smash on the floor, an elderly female "controller" of the restaurant, sitting in a booth chain-smoking and waiting to deal with bills when it came to payment, put her head in her hands as though silently weeping.

We continued waiting for our chicken *kavarma*.

The Jamie Oliver and Mary Berry show ended.

Another soap opera began. "You can get this, but you can't get Premier League," said Danny – a Premier League match was on that night. He had wanted to watch it.

More youths in hoodies walked by.

About an hour after our order our chicken *kavarma* arrived, served by the waitress without a hint of expression. They were tasty but we were so ravenous we polished them off in rapid time, surprising the otherwise inscrutable waitress, who seemed to regard our wolfing of the chicken *kavarma* as most uncouth tourist behaviour.

It was almost 10 p.m. The solitary man ordered another beer. We ordered another beer, number three of the evening – followed not long after by bottle number one of wine. There was not much else to do.

The solitary man, our new friend (or as close to one as we were going to get in this remote corner of Bulgaria), looked over at us approvingly.

We nodded at him approvingly in reply.

Then we paid the chain-smoking controller in her booth, signalled goodbye to the solitary man, who seemed in a more cheerful mood though not exactly ebullient, and returned to our communist-era hotel.

To be absolutely honest, we had not – you may have gathered – been totally won over by Ruse.

On the sauna train
Ruse to Sofia

Into the gloom of the ticket hall of Ruse's Socialist realist station muffled announcements were being made in Bulgarian.

"They could be saying *everyone go home* for all we know," commented Danny, quite accurately.

Rain pelted down outside.

The departures board clicked into place for the train to Sofia: platform one.

We went to platform one with its view of a space-age-style radio tower to the south and black-and-white patterns painted on the edge of the platforms next to the tracks.

These patterns were also to be found across Romania and it was hard to explain why they had been added, but they did give stations an orderly look: perhaps that was the point of them, as well as to warn passengers of the tracks.

A grimy cranberry-red BDZ (Bulgarian State Railways) train with a saffron stripe appeared out of the gloom. This was our train. No other tourists were on the platform, just us.

"I'm glad we came here," said Danny, out of the blue. Maybe it was his subconscious expressing euphoria at leaving. He was wearing his "poor man's" beanie once more. He paused and added: "Not many people can have said that."

We boarded the 07:53 to Sofia, due in at 2.43 p.m., via a change of trains at Gorna Oryahovitsa station.

Between Ruse to Sofia were 20 stops. A cheerful ticket inspector checked our passes. They were, as ever, in order. We had a compartment fitting eight passengers with royal-blue seats and pistachio-coloured walls to ourselves.

It was hot, really hot. We disposed of jumpers and adjusted to the Saharan conditions as the grey skies of Eastern Europe rolled by through mud-streaked windows.

Beyond the smeared glass, a pallet depot emerged on the outskirts of Ruse, then a garden ornament shop selling striking ten-foot-wide concrete eagles and life-sized concrete bears; perhaps all the rage in the suburbs of north-eastern Bulgaria. We rattled out of town into ploughed farmland and soon pulled into Dolapite station, where a large black dog woofed at the train. Hills arose, something of a surprise; for such a long time through Romania to Bulgaria the landscape had been flat. I went to the toilet and then tried to exit the toilet and for about a minute thought I was stuck in the toilet of a Bulgarian regional train dating from the mid-twentieth century rolling towards the Bulgarian capital. Then, after what seemed like a very long time but was hardly any (during which it appeared I could well be in need of being rescued by early-twenty-first-century

Bulgarian train staff in the toilet of this mid-twentieth-century Bulgarian train rolling towards the Bulgarian capital), I realized you did not twist the handle. Instead, it slid to one side.

At Morunitsa station there was no dog, but a ginger cat was peacefully asleep on the stationmaster's windowsill. In these parts, disembarking passengers hopped over neighbouring lines. It was noticeable that black leather jackets, black trousers and black jumpers were all the rage among local men of a certain age, who tended to carry possessions in plastic bags, while women of a certain age preferred black almost knee-length puffer jackets with fake fur hoods, black jeans and, often, dyed red hair. Stationmasters wore red peaked hats with a gold band and held aloft wooden batons with a circular red symbol attached to the end. These were bandied about until all passenger business was complete – embarkations, disembarkations – before dropping to the stationmasters' sides and the train would continue. The stationmasters, aside from the red and gold of their hats, wore black uniforms, sometimes with navy-blue jackets to keep warm.

Close to Polski Trambesh station, a workman was attending to the maintenance of a municipal park in the company of a horse pulling a cart carrying his tools. Near Radanovo station mud roads connected a neighbourhood of modest wooden houses. We reached Yantra station and clattered on past buildings with tiled roofs that seemed about to collapse and through long rolling landscapes of dark brown ploughed fields that appeared to go on forever.

We may have been in the European Union, but it did not feel much like it.

The compartment was still piping hot and we had worked out that scorching air was emanating from a chute directly below my seat. I moved as far away from this chute as possible. We had left the door of the compartment open in the hope of dissipating some of the Saharan heatwave, after trying a battered triangular heating control panel on a wall that had initially offered hope of reducing the sauna-like conditions. *Chaud* (hot), *froid* (cold) and *moyen* (average) were written in faded French. But the old device seemed to have seized up.

Sweating, I read the latest news in the British press.

Strikes were raging in the UK now as well, with National Health Service junior doctors announcing a four-day strike meaning patients waiting for life-changing operations were facing cancellations. "NEW NIGHTMARE FOR PATIENTS", ran *The Sunday Times* headline. Meanwhile, somewhat bizarrely given our recent visit to Bucharest, Andrew Tate, the "misogynist influencer", had chosen to speak out the day earlier about his "plight for justice". He was reported, again in *The Sunday Times*, as having said: "I think these statements against me are given by those jealous women who know nothing and just ask me for money to go shopping."

The *news* – all sorts of news – would not go away.

Even on an old Bulgarian train on a rainy day in central Bulgaria, in a compartment that seemed to be touching 40°C, the "world" was in our pockets – which brought a new dimension to travel, if you thought about it. No point in pretending the "world" did not exist. It had become a part of the journey, always there. The "world", if you let it at least, had moved in.

We arrived at Gorna Oryahovitsa station, where the passengers for Bucharest disembarked.

Gorna Oryahovitsa station was dull and utilitarian, a concrete box of a place with a small café. Outside was a "SLOTS, POKER, JACKPOTS" joint and a square where men in black seemed to be discussing business transactions on a corner. Depressing-looking apartment blocks arose near the track, with well-wrapped elderly women sitting on benches beneath the apartments exchanging gossip. The temperature was about 10°C.

The station café offered Hell Energy drinks, sold in a corner with a cut-out picture of the actor Bruce Willis, who was looking both raffish and quizzical simultaneously while clutching a can of Hell Energy drink. Also on sale were shelves of cakes covered in chocolate and pink icing. The café was empty. We bought two coffees and boarded the 11:00 to Sofia, where we joined a table that seated four occupied by a woman wearing a pink Adidas top who was watching a film on her phone.

Facing backwards, we rattled by dark brown ploughed fields beneath a sky that had turned an almost perfect blue. The day seemed to be warming up, although the train carriage was – this time – a reasonable temperature. The landscape became hillier. We stopped at Levski and Pleven stations. Beyond, solar energy farms emerged from time to time giving the muddy landscape an orderly look. Mainly though, the scenery had a tumbledown aspect, particularly near towns where destroyed remains of factories, half-collapsed smokestacks, battered old grain silos, derelict buildings and rotting rail sheds were commonplace. Bulgaria was not short of concrete communist-era apartments either, washing flapping in the breeze on balconies as though offered up by residents as flags of surrender.

The fourth seat of our "four" by the table was taken by a woman wearing a t-shirt that said: "THE LESS YOU TALK, THE MORE PEOPLE THINK ABOUT YOUR WORDS". True to her message, she said absolutely nothing. A conductor with a drooping moustache came to check tickets. He did not bother scanning our passes.

"Maybe he doesn't have a scanner," said Danny.

The landscape became more rugged, mountains arising with beautiful folds of pink and red rock and steep granite cliffs. Villages of dwellings with terracotta roofs clung to the foothills. If you stared at the cliffs long enough, gargoyle faces began to peer out making the landscape feel haunted. We traversed the meandering river Iskar, at first a rush of foaming white water before becoming becalmed in a gentle green flow. The train had settled into a rhythmic clatter, like the sound of a drummer practising a marching beat.

A woman with her daughter sat across the aisle. She wore heart-shaped sunglasses that she never took off, a red t-shirt that said "RECKLESS" and a miniskirt that was more like a napkin wrapped around her waist. She clicked on her phone a great deal and seemed in the middle of an important text exchange.

We snaked slowly through a ravine and began to move downhill, the drummer steadily increasing the marching beat. More derelict buildings came and went. More concrete apartments shot up in the suburbs of Bulgaria's capital. It may have been a long time since 1989, when Bulgaria's leader Todor Zhivkov was ousted and a multi-party democratic system was installed – Bulgaria later joined NATO (in 2004) and the EU (2007) – yet the legacy of the regime of Zhivkov, not as ruthless or flamboyant as Ceaușescu but far from a "nice guy", was clear to see and the country continued to suffer badly, just as Romania did, with chronic, widespread corruption.

The train slowed down and stopped at Sofia Central Station.

"One of those moments when all is good"
Sofia

Neither of us had visited Sofia before. Would it be another Bucharest? More depressing multi-lane boulevards, concrete jungles, fast cars with tinted windows and risqué nightlife with stag and hen parties?

First impressions were not great. After the tower blocks of the suburbs, Sofia Central Station itself was a concrete monstrosity featuring a large atrium and an ugly, jagged rocket-like concrete monument outside. On this monument a bronze of a seemingly "ideal" communist-era mother and a child had been placed three quarters of the way up. The symmetrical faces of the mother and child were perfectly balanced, with high cheekbones, widely spaced eyes and absolutely no expression at all, other than maybe a hint of smugness and steely inner strength: *we will struggle on under communism and not complain*, seemed to be the message.

The area around the station was run-down. Shops were boarded up and ugly graffiti depicted women with guns and messages such as

"XL CREW!" We crossed a busy multi-lane boulevard and followed it to the Princess Casino, outside which we paused for a rest. The casino had a gimmicky Greek temple entrance with a red carpet. Nearby, a tall woman in a miniskirt and fur jacket was hanging around and a bouncer dressed in black who might have been a former weightlifter gave me a look suggesting that the new interlopers in his life (us) had better move along. I took a picture of the "Greek temple", causing the bouncer to twitch as though flexing his muscles in preparation for imminent use – which we took as a sign that it was probably best to do what his body language was telling us: i.e., go away, *now*! No point in upsetting Bulgarian casino bouncers so early on in a visit to the country's capital.

It was not far onwards across a bridge guarded by bronze lions, adverts for Bushmills whiskey (the Northern Irish liquor seemed popular locally), a mosque, and the grand, neoclassical Palace of Justice to our little business-traveller hotel: the Sofia Palace Hotel.

Hostels were a thing of the past (we were never going to compete with David, the budget guru). So were one-off apartments that might or might not have heating or hot water. Fancier hotels were beyond our budget. We had discovered our natural slumbering milieu: inexpensive, inoffensive business hotels of the type favoured by down-at-heel travelling salesmen and small-time company reps. Should someone choose to produce a directory of these, or perhaps create an app, it would prove extremely useful. Our rooms came in calming caramel-brown colour schemes with tiny horseshoe armchairs, coffee tables and desks with plug-ins for phones and laptops. We could not have been happier with our choice.

We did not, however, hang about in our caramel-brown rooms. As we had turned into Sofia's old town, crossing the bridge with bronze lions across the river Vladaya, a wonderful sight had arisen: Mount Vitosha. This mountain, part of a massif, was snow-capped and soared to an altitude of 7,520 feet; skiing was possible at the top. It formed a fine backdrop to the city and, along with the tight grid of narrow lanes and old-fashioned houses, immediately made you like Sofia's old town.

This mountain had a magnetic allure. We walked towards it in warm sunshine soon coming to a long, thin rectangular park dominated at the end closest to the mountain by the grim, bulbous National Palace of Culture – the park was named the National Palace of Culture Park. The presence of this communist-era conference and exhibition centre, the brainchild of Todor Zhivkov's daughter, was grating yet its looming bulk did not detract from the enjoyment of the rest of the park, which was full of skateboarders, dog walkers, strolling lovers, mothers pushing prams, children kicking footballs, and parents watching on from benches. Students and youngsters sat cross-legged drinking beers on the lawns or at endless benches along a spider's web of paths. Middle-aged and older people were doing the same too, we noticed.

We also noticed a trail of Bulgarians leading down a path to a street on the side of the park, and a corresponding trail returning clutching bags of beers.

We followed this trail to an off-licence called 1001 Beers, where we bought four of the 1,001 and returned to a park bench where we sat and watched the world go by in the sunshine, as dazzling light captured the snowy peaks of Mount Vitosha. We did not say much. We did not need to. People were taking off coats in the afternoon heat. For the first time on the trip, a hint of spring proper was in the air. Leaves were breaking out in a soft green fuzz. A distinguished-looking woman wearing shades strode past on the cobbled path with a perfectly coiffed poodle in tow. A pair of students joined our bench and began whispering endearments to one another.

"This is one of those moments when all is good," said Danny.

I could not have agreed more.

The long, winding tracks from Ruse had taken us 200 miles south-west and seemed to have delivered us to this sun-baked bench in the National Palace of Culture Park as though the outcome was a fait accompli. There was also a neat, rounded feel to our location: after all, the whole idea of going to Istanbul by train had begun on another park bench.

We stayed until the sun began to drop low, stopping afterwards to regard the simple stone Temple of Bulgarian Martyrs with a black granite memorial listing 7,526 people who died at the hands of the totalitarian communist regime that ran the country from 1944 to 1989. An Orthodox Christian cross graced the roof of the temple; many of those who had been persecuted had stood up for the faith.

Then we grabbed a burger in the old town, went to the RocknRolla Bar, listened to a frizzy-haired singer with a tight backing band play a few songs in a dark basement, and made the acquaintance of an incredibly inebriated Bulgarian wearing camouflage trousers and a camouflage cap who told us at some length how he had once visited Liverpool, before returning to our caramel-brown business hotel.

We had not seen much of Sofia, but the city was proving to be a definite step up from Ruse (most of the time).

In the morning, though, we would see much more.

* * *

You may have gathered by now that, although a tale of a train journey, trains were not the be-all and end-all. What was the point of going from A to B, then to C to D if you did not take look around B, C and D? Even if these were brief stop-offs: make the most of them. This was not always proving straightforward, given timetables. However, in Sofia the sleeper to Istanbul departed at 18:40, so we had the best part of a day to explore.

With this in mind we joined a "free tour" of Sofia.

A "free tour" is one in which you tip your guide according to how much you have enjoyed the experience at the end (nothing, if you think the guide was useless). I had only ever been on one "free tour" before, a guided walk around Lviv in western Ukraine during *Slow Trains to Venice*. That had been both illuminating, enjoyable and sociable ("free tourists" tend to be chatterboxes). I managed to persuade Danny, who seemed somewhat reluctant despite the price tag, to give one a try.

This was how a Bulgarian "free tour" went.

You met outside the Palace of Justice at 11 a.m., beside the rumble and screech of passing trams. A woman wearing shades and brandishing a sign saying "FREE SOFIA TOUR" then corralled your group into a tighter pack (there were about twenty of us).

"I retain the option as a free agent to peel off and meet you later," said Danny, as we gathered at the back. "We'll have forgotten all this stuff by next week anyway."

This was quite out of character given that we had so far paid absolutely nothing. He was not showing an enormous amount of early "free tour" spirit.

The guide was a small, no-nonsense thirty-something woman named Dessi who wore a large white polo-neck jumper that covered the lower part of her chin, blue-framed sunglasses and a puffa jacket. She smiled broadly and assessed her flock. She had seen it all before. "Feel free to leave if you are bored or hungry. I will try not to cry," she said, seeming to glance our way.

Then she began her spiel. Dessi was born and raised in Sofia. She owned a dog. She was licensed by the Bulgarian Ministry of Tourism to give tours, which she had been conducting for 13 years. She had had a tough time during the pandemic when there were no tourists but had somehow survived. These personal preliminaries conveyed, off we went.

We tramped in the direction of some Roman walls dating from a period when Sofia was known as Serdica. These walls had a sideways train connection: they had been discovered when a metro line was being dug ten years earlier. Dessi talked about nomadic people living many centuries ago in the Sofia region until the Romans came, and how the Ottomans arrived in the fourteenth century "and didn't leave until about five hundred years later" in 1878 after the Russo-Turkish War that had also wiped out the Ottomans in Romania.

Thus began the Third Bulgarian Tsardom, which lasted until 1946 "when communism happened". During World War Two, Bulgaria sided with the Axis powers but did not send Jews from within its boundaries to concentration camps, we are told, although it is recorded that more than eleven thousand Jews were transported from territories Bulgaria had taken in Greece and Macedonia at the beginning of the war. After the fall of the Nazis, the Russians seized control of the country.

"Then in 1989 the Berlin Wall happened," Dessi said. "Then democracy happened. In 2004 we joined NATO and in 2007, the European Union, we joined that, too. That's seven thousand years in five minutes, if you can survive that you can survive the whole thing."

She meant the free tour.

We arrived at a large stone church with archways and a dome with lead windows.

This was St Nedelya Church, where "in 1925 there was a terrorist attack at a general's funeral and five hundred people were injured and two hundred died... the person who was the target of the attack wasn't even there, he was late. This is the stereotype of the Bulgarian people, by the way." She meant that Bulgarians often had issues with keeping time, not that they were known for bombing churches.

Dessi strode on, talking about the transfer of power from communism to democracy in 1989: "Unlike in Romania, things were much more peaceful. It was announced that Zhivkov would resign. He may not have known that he was going to resign. But he did. In July 1990 we had our first democratic elections."

Dessi took us to the solitary minaret and copper-topped dome of Banya Bashi Mosque, which we had walked past the day before, near the Princess Casino: "It's the only functioning mosque in Sofia now. For five centuries we were part of the Ottoman Empire, but only

At the beginning: the Eurostar to Paris awaits at St Pancras International station, London

Anti-pension reform flyer featuring President Emmanuel Macron on Place de la République, Paris

Author at Gare de l'Est, Paris, about to board train number two to Strasbourg near the German border

All calm at Gare de l'Est, Paris, a day after major riots in the French capital

Strasbourg cathedral

Pedalos on Dutzendteich lake with the Congress Hall at the Nazi Party Rally Grounds, Nuremberg, in the background

*Rail strikers'
march,
Nuremberg;
the sign reads:
"Do it like they
do in Italy.
Weapons down,
wages up."*

Sign outside café in Nuremberg

Bratislava-Petržalka station

*Train at Budapest
Nyugati station*

*Budapest Keleti station, Hungary, with a statue
of pioneering British rail engineer George
Stephenson to the left above the entrance*

*Hungarian parliament, Budapest, on Kossuth Square, where Soviet tanks
bloodily put down an uprising on 25 October 1956*

Mural inside Timișoara station, Romania

Housing estate on outskirts of Bucharest, Romania

Old locomotive at Bulgaria's National Transport Museum, Ruse

Propaganda images of the Ceaușescu at the Communist Consumers Museum, Timișoara, Romania

Beatles album on sale at stall by St Alexander Nevsky Cathedral, Sofia, Bulgaria

Café at Gorna Oryahovitsa station, Bulgaria

Arrivals hall designed by Prussian architect August Jasmund in "oriental style" at Sirkeci station, Istanbul

Pera Palace Hotel, Istanbul, where Agatha Christie allegedly wrote parts of Murder on the Orient Express

Author at Orient Express *restaurant at Sirkeci station, Istanbul*

Bar at Pera Palace Hotel, Istanbul

The 20.00 sleeper train from Istanbul at Kapıkule station, Turkey

Sign in lounge for Ukrainian refugees at Sofia Central Station, Bulgaria

Finix Hotel at the remote border town of Kulata, Bulgaria

Early locomotive preserved outside Thessaloniki station, Greece

Catching the overnight ferry from Patras, Greece, to Bari in southern Italy

Busy traffic outside stately façade of Bari station, Italy

A short, exhilarating ride from Naples offering fine carriage-window views of Mount Vesuvius takes you to the ruins of Pompeii

Railway crossing in Tirano, Italy

Author at Tirano station, Italy, at 1,407 feet, about to join rail enthusiasts on the Bernina Express

The 14.24 Bernina Express *from Tirano, Italy, to Chur, Switzerland*

The Glacier Express, *Switzerland*

Interior of a second-class carriage of the Glacier Express

Lake Geneva, Switzerland, seen from the train on the way to Lausanne

The 12.23 TGV Lyria from Lausanne, Switzerland, to Dole, France

The Wellington Museum in Waterloo, Belgium, where the Duke of Wellington masterminded the Battle of Waterloo in June 1815

War memorial at Luxembourg station

Mural inside the ticket hall at Ghent station in Belgium

Connection at Antwerp Central Station, Belgium, on the way to Rotterdam from Ghent

Frites and planning where to go next in Ghent, Belgium

Rotterdam station, the Netherlands

Glorious expanse of the beach at the Hook of Holland, the Netherlands

Ferry from Hook of Holland to Harwich, England

one mosque. You might have expected more." There were 500 in the country, she said.

The tour moved on to a beautiful old bathing house with a dome, distinctive burgundy stripes on its walls and mustard-yellow adornments surrounding arched windows. It looked a bit like a marzipan cake. The baths, which were created above a spring with 37°C water – one of the reasons the Romans had been fond of Sofia – had closed in 1986 as they had not been maintained by the communists, perhaps as they may have been seen as places where dissidents could meet to socialize and plot.

Many locals had been distraught about this and protests among regulars had ensued. This unsuccessful "robe revolution" had witnessed demonstrators wearing their bathing gowns and waving placards. In recent times, other former baths in the city centre that had also closed were due to reopen, but this one – the Sofia Central Mineral Baths – had been turned into a history museum. This was still a burning issue: many locals resented the museum and wanted the central baths back.

In Dessi's family, she said, there had been a split about communist rule: "Some loved it, some hated it. This is the same across the country. In my family they adored communism. My grandfather was one of the best aviation engineers in the country. Communism gave him many opportunities. At one time he used to bathe in the river. Then he owned an apartment with a bath. The communist regime did this. Yet intellectuals were sent to concentration camps to die. So if you ask the relatives of those people, they have a different opinion about communism. So we don't say it [communism] is in the past: we are still polarized. There are still many different opinions."

Danny and I joined Dessi at the front of the group as she walked towards St Sofia Church and St Alexander Nevsky Cathedral, the final part of the tour.

She spoke frankly about the current setup in Bulgaria: "This is the poorest and most corrupt country in the EU." The latest GDP per capital was £10,799 or £30 a day (Romania's was £34). "Young people question the way things are now. They say that some countries have a mafia. In Bulgaria, the mafia has a country."

Outside the red-brick façade of St Sofia Church, with the golden domes of St Alexander Nevsky Cathedral gleaming in the background, Dessi told the group how the Cyrillic alphabet was invented in Bulgaria in the ninth century: "So I want you to leave this tour with two important facts: fifty thousand Jews were saved in Bulgaria during the war, and we started an alphabet that three hundred million people now use worldwide." She paused and then added: "Oh, and one other important fact: Sofia is pronounced Soaf-ia, not Suf-ia." She looked around at us to see if any of this was sinking in, then she said: "I thank you for being with me and now I will officially shut up."

She had been a great guide, and quite a motormouth. The group dispersed, everyone tipping Dessi.

Danny, a "free tour" convert, and I thanked her, and idled around for a while looking at the church and the glittery cathedral. Outside the cathedral, a canny elderly man wearing a red baseball cap was running a street stall with a few knick-knacks spread on a low table. Danny and I quite liked his style of salesmanship.

"What is this?" Danny asked, holding up an interesting-shaped stone that looked as though it consisted of minerals.

"A stone," he replied.

"What is this?" Danny asked, pointing at a medal.

"A Bulgarian medal," he replied, before relenting and looking at it closely. There was an image of a man with a receding hairline and a moustache on the back. "Georgi Dimitrov," he said, the Bulgarian communist leader from 1948–1949. The medal must have been awarded for some form of communist achievement.

"And this?" I asked. I was looking at a small decorative box.

"Arghh," he said, shrugging. He was not sure. After examining it, however, the man in the red cap said tentatively: "For jewellery."

He gave me a take-it-or-leave-it look. I bought the small decorative box for Danny's daughter (my god-daughter).

Danny paid for some other knick-knacks dating from the communist period. The elderly man in the red cap had become animated and was showing us quite a few of the items on his stall including an array of old communist-era watches that looked quite nice in a retro sort of way but did not work. He also began to flick through some old communist-era vinyl records including Elvis, Rod Stewart, Michael Jackson and Beatles LPs with the songs on some listed in Cyrillic.

Holding up one of the latter, the stallholder said: "Under communism, Beatles not allowed." Yet the LP existed.

We retraced our steps to the hotel, passing huddles of elderly men playing chess on park benches. They were engrossed in the contest and a few of the many onlookers were drinking vodka and Cokes, making a party of it with the bottles tucked beneath the benches, though players stuck to coffees. Digital timers were being used. It was serious stuff. Everyone was wrapped in leather and puffa jackets. Everyone was of a certain age: retirement age.

It was a touching scene. It was cold, but sunny, and they were having a great time.

You could dream up trips around Europe on park benches in London's West End. You could play chess on them in little parks in capitals of former communist states while wrapped up to keep warm with onlookers crowding round drinking vodka and Cokes if you wanted, too. Both courses of action, highly recommended.

CHAPTER FIVE

SOFIA TO ISTANBUL IN TURKEY

BANDITS, SPIES AND SHISH KEBABS

Istanbul, the grand climax of the old *Orient Express*, was within touching distance, looking at our trusty, tattered copies of *Rail Map Europe*. We were about to arrive, as almost all the articles and guidebooks and so on ever written tell you, where *East meets West*.

It was a fantastic feeling – an almost puzzling sensation of unexpected middle-age accomplishment – to have conquered the initially bamboozling Eurail app, reserved seats as appropriate, avoided stagnation at the hands of French and German rail strikers and zigzagged more or less as we pleased across Central and Eastern Europe with no particular responsibilities. At the back of our minds, the tale of *Three Men in a Boat* penned by Jerome K. Jerome had been looming large – the story published in 1889 (just six years after the first *Orient Express*) of a trio of friends who escape London to potter about on a boat along the River Thames seeking: "Rest and a complete change... The overstrain upon our brains has produced a general depression throughout the system. Change of scene, and absence of the necessity for thought, will restore the mental equilibrium."

Our equilibria were happily in restoration mode. Our overstrains were dissipating, quite pleasantly. Our general depressions (or just plain worries) were lifting. The tracks had been at our disposal, waiting to be explored. And this we had duly done, in a somewhat haphazard manner – Henri Opper de Blowitz, as mentioned back in Ruse, occasionally popping along to "join" us metaphorically, making up our own unusual "three".

Istanbul, the former HQ of an empire that had ruled great swathes of Europe from the mid-fifteenth century to the 1920s, was sitting by the shimmering waters of the Bosphorus down the long winding line. We were travelling to *the east* of the Earth, having walked out from our homes in *the west* of the Earth one late March morning and caught the underground to St Pancras International in the London Borough of Camden amid commuters heading to the office.

Interrailing was not just for young backpackers, and we were proving it.

We were not young.

We were Interrailing.

The idea after Sofia was to weave onwards to Istanbul, where Danny and I would spend a day looking about before he would fly home and I would continue solo by trains back to Britain forming a big circle of Europe along its railways: a snapshot tour from the tracks.

After Turkey, I wanted to visit Greece. Athens seemed like a sensible stop on the way to the Greek port of Patras, where you could catch a ferry across the Ionian and Adriatic seas to the south-eastern tip of Italy (these ferries were very helpfully included with the Interrail pass). From southern Italy, I would head north to Switzerland, then onwards through the Low Countries aiming for the Hook of Holland in the Netherlands, where the idea was to board another ferry to Harwich in Essex followed by trains home to my corner of south-west London.

Initially, a ferry from Turkey to Athens had appeared possible, but no such services were available in early April. So, after Istanbul, I would backtrack into Bulgaria before turning south towards Thessaloniki in Greece.

Carriage 485
Sofia to Istanbul, Turkey

"So this is where all the EU money is going," said Danny as we took the Sofia metro from near the National Palace of Culture Park to Sofia Central Station.

The metro was sparkling clean with wide platforms, plenty of places to sit and lights that snaked artily in a swirly pattern along the ceiling. Dessi had told us to expect good things on the tour and also tipped us off about its background and funding. "The metro was meant to be completed in the 1970s, but it was postponed and finally opened in 1998," she had said. "The problem was that Bulgaria was bankrupted several times during communism, that's what caused the delays. Through EU money – obviously, that was the only way anything was going to happen – we have opened the latest line and improved the others. This new line started three years ago. It has a/c. It's amazing."

The cost of a ride anywhere on the network was 70 pence. Of which both Danny and I approved.

Sofia Central Station, we discovered, had a mezzanine level that had been set aside at the time of our visit for Ukrainian refugees fleeing the conflict with Russia. A "Sleeping Room" and a "Relax Room" had been arranged, while a "Computer for free use from [sic] Ukrainian Citizens" was available as well as free Wi-Fi with the password of "RefugeE#". A noticeboard said that Ukrainians were allowed to use public transport for free in Sofia for three months.

The area was completely empty, not a soul in sight, not even a station employee, although the United Nations had estimated that 1.1 million Ukrainians had entered Bulgaria since Russia had, on 24 February 2022, invaded territory beyond the land it had seized in the east of the country in 2014. Most refugees had already dispersed from Sofia, many moving on to other nations.

Looking round properly, Sofia Central Station was much better from the inside than its Soviet-brutalist exterior suggested. The station, built in 1974, had enjoyed a makeover in 2016. It looked slick with a peculiar "palm tree" of lights in the centre of the atrium, curving tables with seating, and modern art that seemed to blend in with the old Soviet-era mosaics. The ceiling had an odd, fish-scale-like look that had been introduced during the recent renovations, perhaps to improve acoustics.

A couple of old steam locomotives were to be found, one to the left of the main entrance and another, a shiny little red-and-green loco, in the lobby. Hardcore rail enthusiasts may be interested to learn that this locomotive dated from 1918 and was built by Henschel & Son in Kassel in Germany and was number: 16012. Come to Sofia and tick it off!

We ate slices of pizza in a little café occupied by members of the Bulgarian transport police and boarded the 18:40 sleeper to Istanbul, Danny clutching his "overflow" plastic bag as ever – which he had picked up in Paris having realized his backpack was way too small.

The train was white with red-and-blue stripes, operated by the State Railways of the Republic of Turkey (TCDD). Crescent moons with stars from the railway's logo were marked on the windows. We found our lilac-coloured couchette in Carriage 485 and discovered we were sharing it with Hugo and Roxanne, a bright, mid- to late-twenty-something couple from Grenoble in France.

We launched straight into conversation.

The couple were remarkably open and keen to talk. Danny and I were keen too, having set the world to rights several times during the preceding rides and having maybe run out of new ideas for the re-establishment of the global order (for the time being).

They asked what we did for a living, and we asked them.

"I quit my job as a lawyer the day I started my job as a lawyer," said Roxanne, who was considering her next move, hence the Interrail trip.

So far they had travelled from Grenoble to Zurich, then on Switzerland's *Bernina Express* through the Alps to Tirano in Italy, onwards to Venice, Trieste, Ljubljana, Vienna, Zagreb, Split, Dubrovnik, Belgrade and Sofia – the journeys in Croatia and into Serbia had involved a few buses as trains did not run along those routes. "And now we are here," said Roxanne, looking out of the window.

Our current train had already moved away and was passing various derelict factories and grain silos splattered with graffiti.

Roxanne was trying to figure out what to do in her career; she had studied criminal and family law for three years and wondered what use this might ever be to her. "Anything really is possible," she said.

Hugo said: "I'm a farmer, but I don't own a farm. I'm trained as an engineer." Part of his job involved figuring out how to maximize crop yields, which could require genetically modified (GM) crops as well as pesticides in appropriate dosages. Previously he had worked as a product engineer for Decathlon, the sports and outdoor pursuits shop, but he had thrown that in to try farming. "You see, we are from the same page," he said, looking over at Roxanne. They beamed at one another: both seemed to enjoy radical changes so far as employment was concerned: *chuck it all in, move on.*

They were also doing Interrailing on the cheap, perhaps even cheaper so far as overnight stays were concerned than David, the German thrift guru. They had signed up to the website Couchsurfing. com, which put them in touch with people who were happy to accept guests for free on sofas or in spare rooms.

"Some people just want company. Others just want to help you out," said Hugo. "In Belgrade we lucked out, we had a big room with a king-size bed and a lovely parquet floor. In Zagreb, we got chatting to the guy who met us – hosts tend to be guys in their thirties – and he gave us a beer, then we all went to the university restaurant and it was only one euro for a meal."

For the journey to Istanbul they had booked a better quality sleeper than on the Timişoara–Bucharest train, as had we without quite realizing. So the couchette we were in had two bunks on each side, though both were slotted away and the compartment comprised four seats until the bunks were unfurled.

Hugo talked for a while about his job. "Coding or microtechnology, these are the way forward," he said. "I'm an intellectual guy who likes to do practical things. In farming it's always about trying to do things better. As an engineer I see it is a good thing to use GM to make rice with more vitamin A and the same with eggplant. This can be done in a good way and I think research needs to continue. It's the same with pesticides. The president of Sri Lanka said there should be no pesticides and what happens when they implement this? They lose a quarter of their production. They wanted to be the first organic country. But they got very poor yields. Tea producers demanded that this stopped and it has been. If the government says to 'go organic' in the future the tea producers will ignore them."

We discussed the ethics of GM crops for a while. Then we talked about the French strikes over President Macron's changes to the pension age. Hugo was quick off the mark once more: "Politics in France is completely crazy."

Roxanne nodded and waited – she could tell Hugo was on to a favourite subject.

"I'm a heavy leftist," he said. "For me, I am quite happy [with the disruptions in France]. I did not expect the French to rise up. Macron is like a centre-right politician, not a leftist. People are calling for reforms to his programme. The French have decided: *this is too much*. Now the unionists are coming in. In France the unions used to be super strong, then they went downhill and now they are back. Macron, he recently gave an interview to a kids' magazine. I mean: *what the f****? In the middle of all of this. Then his female minister [involved in the pensions negotiations], she gives an interview to *Playboy* magazine. I mean *what the f****, too? I thought it was April Fool's Day."

He was losing me somewhat about the minister and *Playboy*. Danny and Hugo, however, continued to talk about Macron and strikes and this ministerial soft-porn magazine debacle, while Roxanne showed me a feature of the Eurail app that neither Danny nor I had previously appreciated.

It was possible in a "statistics" section to see how many countries you had visited, how many kilometres you had travelled and how many trains taken. Roxanne and Hugo had gone 2,416 kilometres (1,501 miles) on 27 trains taking one day, 18 hours and 48 minutes precisely, using up to 90 per cent less carbon dioxide than flying, a statistic that was also offered for the green-minded. I peeked at what Danny and I had managed, not so far off, but vowed not to start looking at this "statistics" section all the time as it was the journey not the stats that mattered, as interesting as they might have been (but definitely worth a check at the end). Roxanne also pointed out a "map" part on the app, showing your route. Danny and I had completely missed this, too.

Being French and interesting, Roxanne began to talk about Jean-Paul Sartre.

Roxanne had picked up one of the deep-thinking French philosopher's books, entitled *Nausea* somewhat unappealingly, in Italy. "It was the only book I could find in French in Italy," she said. "It's so well-written. You read one sentence and you are totally in. It's so clear. It looks so easy…"

But as she began to sing the praises of the lucidity of Jean-Paul Sartre's detached-yet-super-observant writing style and approach to life in general, the conductor popped his head in the door, interrupting the political and literary rolling salon. There was an empty first-class couchette next door, would Danny and I like it?

We had been upgraded by the State Railways of the Republic of Turkey.

Cutting short Roxanne and Jean-Paul Sartre, we relocated, saying goodbye to them and setting up next door, where we promptly opened a couple of cans of Bulgarian lager, reverting to less elevated topics of conversation and watching the sodium lights of south-western Bulgaria scud by. Darkness had fallen and all that could be seen apart from the sodium lights were television screens flickering in the occasional apartment near the tracks. Rain began to pour, running in rivulets from the roof when we stopped after some time at the deserted, custard-yellow stucco of Plovdiv station, about halfway to the Turkish border.

The conductors were eating beans, cabbage and ham at a compartment at the end of Carriage 485. There was no dining car on board, or else Danny and I would have gone there. We made the beds and laid down. There was no bedside reading lamp. I mentioned this to Danny.

"Why don't you write to Turkish Railways and complain? See where that gets you," he said. Very amusing.

We continued in silence listening to the pitter-patter of rain on the roof. At 11.45 p.m. there was an announcement: "Passport control! Passport control!"

We had stopped at a place called Svilengrad. It was a desolate spot. Outside were yards fenced with razor wire bathed in sodium light – and not much else. The smell of cigarettes wafted down the corridor.

At 12.25 a.m. a scowling, bulky Bulgarian immigration officer silently took our passports and returned a few minutes later and said: "Daniel? Thomas?"

We nodded at him. He seemed satisfied that we had recognized our names, scowled at us once more and left.

At 12.30 a.m. the train moved on, creaking beyond more razor wire into a no man's land blanketed in litter. We crossed the river Maritsa, less than a mile from a place known on Google Maps as Triangular Point, where the borders of Bulgaria, Greece and Turkey met. We had moved into Turkey, and out of the European Union for the first time since Kent. We began traversing an enormous yard full of lorries.

At 12.45 a.m. we arrived at Kapıkule station and the conductor went down the corridor saying in a sing-song voice: "Passport, luggage, passport, luggage."

We disembarked, hauling their luggage from Carriage 485, and filed across a gloomy platform into a grim pale brown building with a chipped granite floor, flickering lighting and a couple of mangy cats. In a corner was an immigration booth. Danny was ahead of me at the booth and was significantly longer at the window than others before him. Then he passed through to the luggage X-ray area. I went up to the same booth and a young immigration officer, who seemed full of beans despite the hour. He flicked through my passport. I had been worrying about this. Post Brexit, most European countries had begun stamping British passports rather than just glancing at them and passing Brits through. The reason for this was that Britain had become a "third country" so far as the European Union was concerned. This meant that my passport only had half a page clear of stamps. I had been intending to order a new one before the trip, even though the passport had two years' validity left, in case of any problems but had not got round to it.

The energetic young immigration officer looked immensely pleased that my passport was irregular. You must have a full blank passport page for entry to Turkey, he said. It was within his power, he said, to deny entry. The energetic young immigration officer kept me in suspense, flicking through the passport and lingering on stamps for Sudan, Iran and Libya. He looked at those closely. He looked at me closely. Then, in a flash of a moment, he seemed to decide *oh, what's the point, I'll give him a break.*

"Passport full, get new passport," he said, waving me through.

Danny was in the queue for the X-ray machine. I joined him.

"That guy was checking my face against wanted faces on his phone, no doubt about it," Danny said.

So we had dodged two bullets: declined entry due to invalid documentation and detainment due to mistaken identity by Interpol.

Considering ourselves lucky to be through, we waited for the X-ray machine.

In the queue were three British women: Alice, who worked as a station controller at Morden Underground Station in London; her daughter Stephanie, an assistant for adults with learning disabilities, and Alice's friend Christine, a retired registrar

They were travelling from London to Istanbul over five days, from where they were considering flying to Italy and taking trains up through Switzerland back to the UK: a route not dissimilar to my own (except I wouldn't be flying).

Christine said the Eurail app was "user-friendly" and that their favourite stop-off had been Veliko Tarnovo, a former capital of Bulgaria that was "very scenic" and had a "nice ambiance", although she had not been a fan of the scenery between Stuttgart and Budapest, which had "varied in standard": too many industrial zones.

Stephanie said their couchette on the train to Istanbul was "a little bit stuffy, you can't open the window". Alice complained that the carriage had "two different standards of toilet", the worst standard being at their end of the carriage. She had found Bucharest "quite seedy and grey and depressing". Christine said there had been "a lot of beggars continually at the supermarket", where she "couldn't understand how they [Romanians] could afford chocolate spread and pineapple", which were particularly expensive items in Romania's capital. All this said, they had been having a great time.

A thirty-something Polish woman named Aleksandra had been listening to us. I recognized her from the platform way back at Ruse station. She wore a tan mackintosh above a thin red puffa jacket and had an enigmatic manner as though concealing a big secret that amused her, or perhaps, more likely, she just found us (the Brits) in some way comical as we exchanged moans in the rich tradition of British travellers abroad since the days of the Empire (and no doubt even earlier than that). Danny and I had been telling Stephanie, Alice and Christine about a few of our travel woes: train strikes mainly, plus the hostel with the earplugs in Bratislava, the insalubrious goings-on of massage parlour representatives in Bucharest and mysteriously closed train lines in Serbia. It had been a veritable moan-fest.

Aleksandra was on a long Interrailing trip of her own. She had been all round Romania to Braşov, Timişoara, Bucharest ("I not so much like"), Cluj-Napoca, Sibiu and Sinaia.

"It was quite a relaxed journey," she said. "You don't have to care too much about logistics on trains." By this, I took it she meant the timetables were easy to follow. "Places are well connected by trains in this part of Europe."

She had a month-long pass that she had bought in the "big promo" celebrating Interrail's fiftieth anniversary. "I'm interested in ex-Yugoslavian countries, their conflicts, their histories." She was going there next.

"I quit my job last year," she said. She had worked for a bank guarantee fund in Warsaw. "I was fed up with this and I felt I needed to change my way of life. It was typical office paperwork. I needed an adventure."

So first she had walked from Poland to Santiago de Compostela in Spain on a pilgrimage along the Camino Way. "It was something like five thousand kilometres and I met lots of people."

She paused. "I'm insane," she said, as though this was quite normal to add to a conversation, though she did not look it.

"Maybe just a little," she said after considering this.

"My friends, my parents, they are very proud of me, especially as I am travelling on my own. They say to me: *that's not my vibe*. And I can't explain to them why I like it so much."

She was considering hiking along the "Sultans Trail" from Vienna to Istanbul one day, another pilgrimage route of sorts that would cover 1,500 miles. She had a job lined up later in the year in Flåm in Norway that had been arranged by a woman she met on the Camino Way. "I will work out what to do next [in terms of travelling by train or foot somewhere] when I am there," she said.

I suggested we meet up in Istanbul and gave her my email. At this, she smiled and said: "OK, sure." Though I never did hear from her.

The queues at Kapıkule station proved surprisingly sociable. Perhaps this was because there seemed to be a general euphoria at having reached Turkey by train. This may not have been the *Orient Express*, but something of the old service seemed to have rubbed off on the *Sofia–Istanbul Express*, as this train was officially known.

Another queue had formed after the security X-ray machine. This was for a duty-free kiosk, which was stacked with packets of Marlboro cigarettes and caramel-hued bottles. Close by was a café with a fridge offering water, beer and quarts of Chivas Regal 12-year-old whisky. Many an all-night party must have been had on the *Sofia–Istanbul Express*.

At 2.30 a.m. we reboarded the train, which departed in the direction of Istanbul.

Supper in Sirkeci
Istanbul

Into a suburb of concrete blocks that would have met with Ceauşescu's full approval, Carriage 485 spun forth beneath a lilac-grey early morning sky.

A rubbish dump... sidings of container wagons... a long, empty platform... Halkalı station... 6.34 a.m.

We, the passengers of Carriage 485, filed out and, bleary-eyed, attempted to establish how to purchase tickets on the Marmaray commuter line from this suburb of Istanbul to Sirkeci station in the heart of Istanbul. Sirkeci was where the old *Orient Express* trains terminated, an appropriate enough stop. Journeys on the Marmaray line were not covered by Interrail passes.

The enigmatic Polish woman, the bright young French couple, the trio of Brits and Danny and me poked at buttons on a machine, tickets eventually emerging, and we joined a wide train with pale-blue seats and a corridor that ran without doors all the way along the many carriages.

We dispersed; it was too early for conversation. The train moved off, soon filling with commuters as it stopped in mini concrete Manhattans of identikit apartment blocks equal to anything the suburbs of communist Bulgaria had had to offer. Around half an hour later, having dipped into a long tunnel, the train stopped at the Marmaray commuter line version of Sirkeci station.

This was not the original Sirkeci station, somewhat disappointingly.

The Marmaray commuter line version of Sirkeci station was deep beneath the Golden Horn estuary that met the Sea of Marmara and linked south-westwards with the Aegean Sea. The estuary was also connected to the Bosphorus, which wound north to the Black Sea. A large amount of water lay above us.

To reach the "real" Sirkeci station required following many shiny granite walkways and taking a series of escalators.

Along the way, we made the acquaintance of a grizzled man, who may have indulged in a few early morning "refreshments" (we seemed to have developed a knack of attracting such underground characters). The man turned to us and declared with almost operatic delivery: "I love Erdoğan! I LOVE ERDOĞAN! I LOOOVE ERRDOOĞAN!"

His voice was rising to demonstrate his seeming fervour for the controversial president of Turkey, Recep Tayyip Erdoğan, who had ruled Turkey with an iron fist since 2014 (while clamping down on press freedom and winning elections with uncanny ease).

"I LOOOVE ERRDOĞAN! I LOOOVE ERRDOĞAN!" the grizzled man repeated after a brief pause, even louder for our benefit, while also glancing about to see that his performance was being appreciated and noticed by others in the passageway. His words echoed beneath the Golden Horn estuary, making you wonder what the multiple fish up above must have been making of it all. Perhaps our new acquaintance was hoping his message might be spotted by passing secret servicemen of some sort or maybe a person of prominence. Might a state honour of some description for such a fulsome display of loyalty be in the offing?

"I LOOOOOVE ERRRDOOOOĞAN!" he trilled in a climax to his performance, whereupon he bowed extravagantly and went on his way.

We watched him go, feeling a little nonplussed.

"I don't know whether that was irony or he genuinely liked him," said Danny.

And with that, we ascended some escalators and arrived at the old, proper Sirkeci station.

There, we stopped on a spot on the platform, close to a little railway museum, the entrance of the *Orient Express* restaurant and a monument to Mustafa Kemal Atatürk, founder of the Republic of Turkey in 1923. On this monument was written: "*Ne mutlu Türk'üm diyene*", which translated as: *How happy I am to be a Turk*. This was a quote from the still much-loved politician who had filled the void left by the collapse of the Ottoman Empire when he had formed a modern democratic state a century earlier.

How happy we were to be in Turkey having arrived across Europe from London by train, was more like it.

Sirkeci station felt like a place of pilgrimage for the railway lover. We took pictures of the smooth limestone station platform where the great and the good of *Orient Express* passengers had disembarked all those years ago during the train's golden era: Agatha Christie among their number, of course.

Large wagon-wheel-shaped stained-glass windows cast tangerine and cranberry light across the peaceful, deserted concourse. Iron columns tapered in neat rows down the unused tracks. Since 2013 when the faster, better-connected Marmaray commuter service had begun, the lines had been closed, while the inviting-looking Orient Express Restaurant beside the platform was shut too, yet to open for the day. We would go back there later.

The sense of euphoria felt at Kapıkule station had moved on and reached a whole new level of railway ecstasy at Sirkeci station. And why not?

Our park bench dreams had come true.

* * *

Istanbul was intoxicating enough whichever way you arrived but somehow even more so after all those hard-earned miles down the tracks. We had covered 2,058 in total, if the Eurail app and our sums were right.

We left our bags at a perfect little (very good value) business hotel round the corner from Sirkeci station and went to drink coffee at a café playing gentle string-instrument music. For some time, we just sat there slightly bemused at being in Istanbul. Then Danny broke the silence. He was in a thoughtful frame of mind. "I am very grateful to Clare. I really am," he said, looking out at the streets of Istanbul as trams trundled by. Clare had after all been holding the fort while her middle-aged husband disappeared with his middle-aged friend for more than a fortnight during a challenging period on the home front. We both raised our cups of strong black Turkish coffee to Clare.

Then, for a while, we became tourists proper.

By foot from the environs of Sirkeci station, passing the gold-tipped minarets of New Mosque and crossing Galata Bridge, we were soon on a pleasant promenade by the Golden Horn. This was, we felt, the perfect spot to eat a late breakfast – chicken kebabs (why not? We were in a *why not?* mood) – as boats bobbed by and calls to prayer echoed across the minarets of the famous city.

"Well here we are: Asia," said Danny.

Which was almost correct. Asia began on the other side of the Bosphorus, close to where we were gazing.

Again, we fell into a kind of reverie: daydreaming quite contentedly by the Golden Horn. It was restful down by the waterfront.

After a while, though, we began to talk Turkey, both literally and in the meaning of the phrase too, some might say.

Turkey had been much in the news of late and it had nothing to do with the country's trains, though it had plenty to do with the stability of the continent we had just taken quite a few trains crossing.

It was hard not to visit Istanbul, or anywhere in Turkey, without considering the recent actions of Recep Tayyip Erdoğan. For a start, you might after a short time in Istanbul find fellow travellers on its transport system yelling "I LOVE ERDOĞAN!" at you in an increasingly flamboyant manner, but even if they did not, the Turkish leader's name was never far from politicians' lips or the headlines: not just in his home country, but across Europe.

Erdoğan, after all, held a pivotal role in the European balance of power having taken a neutral position on Russia's war in Ukraine for quite some time. This had been considered his form of "payback" after Russia had offered support when the Turkish president had been faced with a coup attempt in 2016.

Back then, Erdoğan had dealt with matters himself, however, and he had done so in no uncertain manner: closing newspapers supporting the opposition, sacking 4,000 judges and prosecutors whom he believed were sympathetic to the rebels, declaring a state of emergency, and issuing terror legislation against the minority population of Kurds. So he had not really owed Russia anything. Yet in an abrupt turnaround in his relations with Moscow while we had been clattering along on our train rides, Turkey's president had announced he would start supplying Ukraine with weapons to protect Ukraine's ships in the Black Sea.

On top of this, Turkey had just snubbed Russia by also talking about joining the European Union – much to the annoyance of Moscow once again, even though such discussions were merely symbolic as it was extremely unlikely to happen due to the EU needing to prevent migrants from the Middle East passing through Turkey. Did all his recent words really mean anything, though?

Danny had opinions about all of this, which he discussed at some length while we sat there mulling over matters idly and gazing towards Asia (a very pleasant pursuit). "I suppose, though, most people see through his ********," he said in conclusion.

By "his" he meant "Erdoğan's" and by "most people" he meant "Turkish people". And by ********, he was referring to the end product of an aggressive bovine creature's digestive system.

This summary seemed, probably, about right.

A little bit more politics… why not?

We caught a smooth red tram – Istanbul trams are excellent as long as you are not a pedestrian dodging them – to visit the Hagia Sophia Grand Mosque.

From 1935 until 2020 this vast structure, completed in the sixth century with its giant dome and rocket-like minarets, had been a museum. Under Erdoğan, however, who sought to gain electoral support among Islamic factions in Turkey, it had been reclassified as a mosque.

A little bit more politics, again.

We took off our shoes and joined the tourist throng on soft carpets admiring the golden interior with its arches, columns and chandeliers. Light drifted drowsily down from clusters of high windows. In the middle of the main chamber, a friendly woman at a stall handed me a series of pamphlets about Islam including one entitled *The True Message of Jesus Christ in the Qur'an and the Bible*, in which Jesus is referred to as a "pious messenger" who "endeavoured to guide people to the truth" although "many people followed their desires and thus went far from the prophetic teachings".

A further pamphlet on *Prophet Muhammad (Peace be upon him) You should know this man!* informed us of Prophet Muhammad's qualities of mercy, forgiveness, equality, tolerance and gentleness. Meanwhile, *What does Islam say about Atheism?* quoted a line from the Qur'an on the cover: "We (God) will show them Our signs in the horizons and within themselves until it becomes clear to them that it is the truth."

Take a few trains, convert to Prophet Muhammad.

The woman running the stall, who was wearing a headscarf, as all females were required in the mosque, said: "Please read. Please read."

So I did. Danny had wandered off somewhere.

Yet another (particularly curious) pamphlet was entitled *Muslim Contributions That Changed the World*; listed among these contributions: coffee, soap, fountain pens, mathematics, flying, vaccinations, architecture, windmills, and the printing press. Entertaining stories were offered to back up these claims.

For the flying contribution to world advancement, a reference was made to Abbas ibn Firnas, a poet, astronomer and engineer who in 852 AD is said to have used a cloak connected to a wooden frame to leap from a minaret in Córdoba in Spain. The cloak was reported to have acted more like a parachute – "creating what is thought to be the first parachute" (so he had also bagged this world contribution, too). Abbas ibn Firnas had "walked away with minor injuries". Later on, aged 70, the daredevil poet, astronomer and engineer had gone on to create a machine comprising eagle feathers and silk that was said to have stayed airborne for ten minutes although, on that occasion, "the landing did not go well". The seriousness of the injuries was not provided in the pamphlet.

Regarding soap, although ancient Egyptians and Romans had a form of soap that was "more of a pomade", Arabs were much advanced using "a vegetable oil and sodium hydroxide base". They were so used to great cleanliness that when the Crusaders came in the Middle Ages "they earned the reputation of being 'pungent smelling invaders' as they did not bathe regularly". Meanwhile, so far as the printing press was concerned, "in 1454, Gutenberg developed the most sophisticated printing press of the Middle Ages, but movable brass type was in use in Islamic Spain one hundred years prior". Take that, Strasbourg.

We went to the Grand Bazaar.

This was up a short hill and was mesmerizing in a different way to the golden glitz of Hagia Sophia Grand Mosque.

Instead, you passed down a narrow passage into a simple nondescript entrance that did not appear to be "grand" at all. But very "grand" it was indeed inside in a dazzling labyrinthine network of alleys – all neon lights and glittery decorations designed to entice you – in an endlessly, almost confusingly, "grand" way that was somehow tied in with an overwhelming and quite suddenly inescapable, unavoidable urge to *buy, buy, buy*! Of course, if you were about to return to the UK in the direction of Greece with a bulging backpack largely full of books via a long series of trains in a couple of days, you could not *buy, buy, buy*.

You had to refrain from *buying, buying, buying* despite the many temptations: the shimmery carpets, the Givenchy and Christian

Dior t-shirts, the Calvin Klein underwear, the Gucci pyjamas, Prada jackets, Tom Ford handbags, Lionel Messi shirts, ceremonial knives, chess sets, bars of donkey-milk soap, cushion covers, Louis Vuitton suitcases, Rolex watches, Air Jordan trainers, necklaces, beads, Burberry bags, leather jackets and "unique fine jewellery".

CCTV cameras followed you. Echoey voices emanated. Salesmen and customers gesticulated.

"Come in. No charge for looking!" the stalls-men said (no stalls-women in sight).

"May I take this moment to allow myself the opportunity to present for you a carpet, sir?" As well as, more directly: "Carpet? Sir! Carpet!" And: "Excuse me, sir: sunglasses? Sir! Sunglasses!" All repeated many times over.

You could venture a pretty good guess to how much of what was sold was genuine. Yet it all looked real enough. Danny bought quite a lot of "stuff": *why not?* He was flying home the next day.

We returned to our little business hotel and proceeded to the Orient Express Restaurant.

* * *

Mention *"Orient Express"* and something deep within train lovers' hearts melts a little. Why else would some (admittedly with very deep pockets) to this day shell out £17,500 for the lavish once-a-year Venice Simplon service?

The glamour, romance and mystique of the golden era of trains has somehow remained across the years – and this word "mystique", with its aura of danger, seems crucial to its ongoing appeal, almost a century and a half on.

The reputation is rooted in a long-ago reality. Way back in the 1880s and 1890s the trains did indeed represent something dangerous and edgy. As previously mentioned, some early passengers were so wary of bandits in parts of Romania, Bulgaria and Turkey they packed weapons. Quite rightly so, perhaps. In 1891, when the train was still in its infancy, it was famously held up by a group of bandits/ freedom fighters 60 miles outside Istanbul. This motley assortment of characters had sabotaged the line preventing further passage and causing the driver and fireman to leap for safety from the locomotive, which fortunately broke free of the luxury carriages, leaving them upright and passengers unhurt.

All valuables belonging to passengers, however, were soon purloined by the bandits/freedom fighters, while five German businessmen were taken hostage for ransom. They had planned everything in great detail and the heist worked perfectly: the gang was never caught in what must be counted as one of the most audacious train robberies ever, pocketing the equivalent of £8,000 in gold (more than a million pounds in today's money) for the released Germans along with plentiful loot from the train.

The fear during this period was that law and order was shaky in remote landscapes where the Ottoman Empire no longer exerted influence, beyond the area of protection offered by the Austro-Hungarian Empire. And that sense of alarm, as proven by the hold-up, was clearly justified.

Then you had the stories of early almost-disasters. The most famous of these was when a bridge collapsed in Turkey in 1899, during which all passengers miraculously survived, although the incident was widely reported in dramatic accounts accompanied by pictures of the tangled mess of the locomotive lying in the river and the *Orient Express* customers posing almost nonchalantly by its banks in their finery.

Then you had another side of the mystique: rumours (and perhaps truth) of wealthy businessmen keeping mistresses at stations en route, adding a frisson of intrigue as to what exactly went on aboard the early *Orient Express* trains. So much gossip swirled about that by 1898 the trains had become the subject of a risqué show at a theatre in Montmartre in Paris. Posters from the time show a woman wearing a negligee and looking as though she may have had one too many being embraced in a compartment by an officer with his cap tilted back, who may have had one too many as well, while an elegantly dressed gentleman gazes into the eyes of a woman wearing a short dress and high heels as though declaring his undying devotion in another compartment, and yet more women in negligees mess about making beds in a neighbouring berth, one slipping from a top bunk while doing so (limbs akimbo). All very *Carry On Orient Express*.

Then you had tales of journeys through mysterious new tunnels cut through the Alps, transforming the public's mental geographical map of Europe (as well as travel times) and capturing the collective imagination; the important Simplon Tunnel linking Switzerland and Italy opened in 1906. Then, later still, tantalizing dispatches were wired back as the train moved on beyond Istanbul as far afield as Baghdad and Cairo, where reporters waxed lyrical about the recently discovered pharaohs' tombs.

Then you had the stories of spies. In its early years the *Orient Express* became the transport of choice for those keeping an eye on what was really going on around Europe during incredibly uncertain times in the run-ups to the world wars. Governments sent an array of characters to file back reports throughout the turbulent period. Among these was a certain Robert Baden-Powell, later founder of the Scout movement, who travelled as a "military assistant" but was surprisingly regularly on leave on "butterfly-spotting" trips (the drawings of wings of these butterflies in sketch pads cleverly containing hidden colour-coded messages).

But the most famous *Orient Express* spy of all was the Dutch dancer and *femme fatale* Mata Hari. Her many trips on the train were made in the company of, or on the way to, her coterie of wealthy lovers including businessmen and ministers of state, one of whom was Baron von Krohn, high up in the German secret service. For her perceived espionage (not everyone is certain she really did pass on any information), she was eventually arrested and sentenced to death by firing squad in France in 1917.

Throw in a few other "names" to have taken the famous express train: the Maharajah of Cooch Behar (who ordered divans draped with golden blankets in his compartment), the actress Marlene Dietrich, Leo Tolstoy, Lawrence of Arabia, Graham Greene, Ernest Hemingway and Ian Fleming, who set scenes from his James Bond film *From Russia with Love* on the *Orient Express* – plus many, many more.

Add mahogany and teak-panelled compartments with exquisite marquetry, Art Nouveau and Art Deco touches, chandeliers, marble and onyx bathrooms, Italian glass fittings, velvet curtains, silk sheets (changed daily, of course), conductors in smart uniforms with brass buttons and peaked hats, fine dining with finest wines served on crisp white tablecloths with silver cutlery and smart dress codes... and the *Orient Express* was certainly not short of "glamour". Nagelmackers had made sure of that, with his first guests so lavished with gourmet dishes and bottles from his deep cellar, grand dinners held at stations with music and dancing, and even visits to royalty back in Bucharest.

When you put it all together it was a heady mix. Little wonder Agatha Christie was to be so inspired with her murderous tales; she wrote three books on the *Orient Express* in all. A widely reported real-life snow-in during a blizzard near the Turkish border was to become a central part of the plot of *Murder on the Orient Express*.

Finally, consider that it was in a Compagnie Internationale des Wagons-Lits carriage (number 2419) that Germany surrendered to Marshal Foch and the Allies – the signing of the Armistice – at Compiègne in France on 11 November 1918. This was to be followed by Adolf Hitler using the very same carriage at the exact same spot to accept France's surrender to Germany in 1940. History was made on the train, big history and probably much more history that is not even known about during the secret assignations of all those spies who once travelled down the lines. At times of heightened European unrest, when the continent was crawling with undercover agents, some even referred to the service as the "Spook Express".

And the target of all this intrigue, glamour, romance, sex, skullduggery and scurrying intent? Turkey's biggest city, where Europe and Asia met on either side of the Bosphorus. More specifically: Sirkeci station, rebuilt to "*Orient Express* standards" in 1890 after originally opening in 1872.

Danny and I entered its restaurant.

This was a wonderful place. You may not have travelled in *Orient Express* style – impossible anymore except for the truly loaded – but you could savour the ambiance of those days at Sirkeci's Orient Express Restaurant.

Late afternoon light shone through the wagon-wheel-stained-glass windows illuminating framed cuttings from newspapers and magazines on the pristine, whitewashed walls alongside pictures of steam locomotives, photographs of Agatha Christie and actors from *Murder on the Orient Express* and Alfred Hitchcock's thriller *The Lady Vanishes*.

Evocative old Compagnie Internationale des Wagons-Lits posters adorned the walls, too. Some advertised the "*Golden Arrow*" service from London to Dover, Calais and Paris, to pick up the *Orient Express*. Others covered the main route to Istanbul. The most eye-catching of these featured a sophisticated woman in red wearing a pearl necklace while clutching a guidebook. The route advertised on this poster was London–Dover–Calais–Paris–Lausanne–Milan–Belgrade–Istanbul. Near this poster, and a picture of Atatürk, was an amusing drinks trolley in the shape of an *Orient Express* train. Tropical plants in pots were dotted about amid tables with crisp white tablecloths (just like the old days on the trains).

In this agreeable setting, we indulged in full Henri Opper de Blowitz of *The Times* circa-1883 style.

Dish after dish was soon delivered: great heaps of "Turkish shepherd" salads, little bowls of pickled tuna and olives, hearty stuffed meatballs, delicate buttered shrimp, plates of steaming spring rolls, sizzling chicken kebabs and pasta with bolognese (the latter an order too far, perhaps, but who cared). All washed down with copious glasses of red wine. Buttons on belts were eased. We praised the dishes as each was delivered. The dishes kept on coming. We ordered more. The waiter kept a note, unclipping a pen from a waistcoat pocket. He nodded sagely at each request. He scuttled away to attend to the orders. He was a veritable whirlwind of activity, just like the other staff.

From across the busy restaurant came a pleasing clink of cutlery on crockery. We were not the only ones in Blowitz mode.

Danny said: "I have always liked the Turks, ever since I was a kid."

We raised our glasses to toast our 2,058-mile journey to Istanbul, clinked them, ordered more wine, clinked glasses once again, put the world to rights a few final times, clinked again, put the world to rights a few more times just for good measure, ordered more wine and, eventually, quite full and determinedly sated, returned to our good value little business hotel.

It had been an excellent meal. Best of the trip.

Long may the Orient Express Restaurant at Sirkeci station thrive and survive.

Almost duffilled
Istanbul and Sirkeci to Halkalı

In the morning Danny had gone, having caught a cab for his flight. He had been excellent company despite, and perhaps because of, his quirks, and most importantly (to us): we had achieved what we set out to achieve on our park bench. This could not be taken away from us. The shimmying man in the purple velvet suit, we liked to imagine, would have congratulated us with another deep, gravelly "Yeah, man". There is no small enjoyment in setting yourself a travel target, buying all the maps and tickets and so on and actually doing it. We had talked the middle-aged talk and walked the middle-aged walk (or rather, taken quite a few trains).

My journey, though, was about to enter a new phase.

I returned to Sirkeci station and located the International Tickets desk.

The concourse of the old part of the station was as deserted as ever, a real backwater in the busy city of 15 million people. The reason for this was simple: there were of course no trains from its platforms anymore.

The effect was ghostly, the absence of people seeming to conjure up figures from the past with their leather suitcases and portmanteaus, porters pushing through crowds, locomotives pulsing, the smell of sulphur and smoke in the air as spies and sophisticated women in red wearing pearl necklaces ventured forth into the cacophony of the edge of Asia.

There was no queue for the International Tickets desk and the attendant did not speak much English, while I spoke next to no Turkish. From consulting websites, it was absolutely certain no suitable ferries to Greece were running that day. It appeared that travelling to Sofia via Plovdiv and taking a train to Kulata on the Bulgarian–Greek border was the only sensible way.

Kulata was a nowhere-looking spot but handily placed for travelling to Thessaloniki, Greece's second city. The catch was that, although trains stopped at Kulata, a bus appeared necessary for that 70-mile southwards journey. I decided I would find out about that once I got there. I reserved a sleeper to Sofia that evening, the 20:00 from Halkalı station, arriving at Plovdiv in Bulgaria at 5.40 a.m.

Then a connection would leave Plovdiv at 06:26 reaching Sofia at 9.30 a.m. Following this, the 12:30 train to a place called Blagoevgrad would arrive at 2.40 p.m., a train from Blagoevgrad would go at 14:50 to General Todorov, arriving 4.19 p.m., and a final connection from General Todorov would pull into Kulata at 4.49 p.m. What could be simpler? This required something like 22 out of the next 24 hours on the move. That said, quite a few of these hours would be spent asleep and good headway would have been made towards Greece and the ferry to Italy in a few days' time.

The attendant allowed a reservation for the sleeper to Plovdiv but not onwards to Sofia. She tapped on her smartphone and showed the screen from a translation site: *Our system does not allow reserve ticket Plovdiv-Sofia.*

I thanked her for this information, pocketed my sleeper reservation to Plovdiv and considered my options.

With a day to play with in Istanbul I set myself three missions: 1) To investigate the Istanbul Railway Museum; not difficult, it was a few paces away, 2) To visit the much-heralded Pera Palace Hotel, opened by the Compagnie Internationale des Grand Hotels in 1895, a sister company created so well-heeled *Orient Express* passengers could reside in the manner to which they had become accustomed, and 3) To return for an early dinner at the Orient Express Restaurant at Sirkeci station before heading onwards.

The Istanbul Railway Museum was a little Aladdin's cave of trains. You entered through an arched doorway and were confronted by the façade of an old red tram. A panel explained that a renowned Prussian architect named August Jasmund had been commissioned by Sultan Abdulhamid II to design Sirkeci station, into which he incorporated an "oriental style" to capture the atmosphere of East meeting West that must have been even more potent back then during the Ottoman Empire.

Thus stone portals, Byzantine red-brick stripes and distinctive star shapes in the stained-glass windows had been incorporated – all intended to resonate with architecture adopted during the Seljuk Turco-Persian empire of 1037–1194. This was classic *Orientalism*, a Western take on what was considered Eastern: what passengers on the *Orient Express* might have had in mind when they considered the "East". Three large restaurants and a "big beer garden", not from that period of the Seljuks, but deemed necessary for those rail adventurers, were also slotted in. After dining, or drinking beer, early *Orient Express* passengers could walk off excesses along well-tended terraces to the sedately lapping water of the Golden Horn.

Suffice to say there was plenty of *train stuff* at the Istanbul Railway Museum: old station clocks, chief conductors' horns, ticket pliers, waiting-room stoves, stationmaster caps, silver service crockery and champagne buckets. Evocative photographs in one corner showed the first economic migrants sitting by suitcases at Sirkeci about to head to Germany in the wake of the Recruitment Agreement between the Federal Republic of Germany and Turkey in 1961. Germany had faced a post-World War Two labour shortage and "guest workers" from Turkey helped solve the problem. Sixty years on, more than 3 million people with Turkish roots lived in Germany out of its population of 83 million.

Sirkeci was where it all began.

* * *

Via a tram through Karaköy and over Galata Bridge, beyond the Galata Tower, a medieval landmark built originally as a watchtower, I ascended a narrow lane up a hill that led to the Pera Palace Hotel.

This felt like another train pilgrimage, being where so many of the great and the good (and probably not so good) of the *Orient Express* passengers had stayed. It was a prominent structure in an Art Nouveau style that would not have looked out of place by the Champs-Élysées in Paris, from where a great number of guests would have begun their journeys. Through a polished teak revolving door, you entered a grand tiled reception glittering with crystal chandeliers and brass fittings. Marble steps led to a ballroom adapted into a lounge decked out in full *Orientalism* style with skylight cupolas high above as though you had stepped into a Turkish bathing house. Striped-pink stonework, archways, exquisite carpets, and screens with geometric patterns completed the "look".

Soft violin and cello music played. In a library-like side-lounge with gilded mirrors, wine-red walls, shelves stacked with *Sherlock Holmes: The Complete Works* and books with titles such as *Luxury Trains: From the Orient Express to the TGV*, American businessmen were discussing deals on burgundy velvet sofas.

"They sure did some crazy stuff that day," said one, referring to a business transaction of some sort as I passed.

"Sounds like us," drawled the other.

They both laughed and sipped pink cocktails from tumblers. They might have been characters from an Agatha Christie or Graham Greene book.

Old-fashioned wooden globes topped mahogany tables. A varnished grand piano stood in a corner waiting for the cocktail hour (the Americans had started early). Tall candles flickered. You were immediately struck by a frozen-in-time atmosphere that could not have changed much since Pera Palace opened in 1892 and the golden era of the old steam trains.

From the side of this side-lounge you came to yet another lounge, this one with pink velvet armchairs, flowing tessellated curtains, high windows and a long, mirrored bar stocked with a wild array of bottles of liquor. What a place to check into after a long train journey across Europe (Danny and I had examined the rates and quickly reverted to our usual little business hotel horizons).

After asking at the concierge desk, Mr Eris, an employee with slicked-back hair and a long black coat, kindly took me to inspect the first electric lift in Istanbul (a metal cage, still operating on special occasions), and Room 101, where Atatürk stayed many times between 1915 and 1917. This had become a little museum to the founder of the Turkish Republic. A waxwork of the modernizing, forward-thinking leader wearing military fatigues and a tall black hat stood in the middle of a carpeted suite beside a polished teak bed and a writing desk in their original spots. A cover of *Time* magazine from 21 February 1927 had been framed on one wall depicting Atatürk with a furrowed brow, as though he had much to contemplate.

Then Mr Eris led me down marble stairs to the Agatha Restaurant. Christie had often stayed at Pera Palace, usually in room 411, her favourite, in which it is said she wrote some of *Murder on the Orient Express*. This is, however, a matter of debate as some historians doubt the claim after examining the timings of her travels.

Christie had first stayed at Pera Palace after taking an impromptu solitary train ride on the *Orient Express* in 1928 following the failure of her marriage to Archie Christie. From Istanbul she had travelled on a connecting train, the *Taurus Express*, through Syria to Baghdad in Iraq, meeting her second husband, the archaeologist Max Mallowan, 14 years her junior, at an archaeological dig along the way.

Room 411 was occupied, so we could not enter where the great mystery writer once slept, but the Art Deco restaurant in the famous author's name seemed to resonate with the period she captured so brilliantly in her stories.

For those interested in "names" who had passed by (as I was), the far wall of the restaurant was covered with them. Framed pictures of illustrious former guests included Christie herself, Alfred Hitchcock, Sir Edward Elgar, Greta Garbo, Ian Fleming, Jacqueline Kennedy, Ernest Hemingway (who stayed as a young war reporter in 1922), Sarah Bernhardt and Giorgio Armani. Other guests had included the ill-fated Mata Hari, King Edward VIII, Queen Elizabeth II, Josip Tito, Zsa Zsa Gabor and Austro-Hungarian Emperor Franz Joseph.

Before jet planes arrived post World War Two and travellers, Christie included, chose to fly on newfangled de Havilland Comets and Boeing 707s, the *Orient Express* had been *the* way to go if you wanted to see faraway places quickly in style. Securing private compartments was key to the latter, often requiring bookings weeks in advance. Film stars, aristocrats, diplomats and royalty were all at it, revelling in the requirement to wear evening dress for the seven-course dinners and the feeling of wheeling across a continent, desperately poor in many places, while enjoying the height of luxury. The train back then represented the age of the engine and industrialization set in motion, steaming down the tracks: the pinnacle of elegant living and a proud symbol of "progress". They really were the golden days of rail travel, even if way beyond the earnings of most.

When the flying machines came, though, everything rapidly changed.

The rail historian George Behrend has shown that by the early 1960s a return fare on the *Orient Express* from Paris to Bucharest cost £112 in a single-berth compartment or £83 in a double compartment, while a return flight from London to Romania was £70. And this was well after the peak of the train's popularity. Before World War Two, it has been estimated by the Dutch rail enthusiast Arjan den Boer in his *Orient Express History*, a return ticket from Paris to Istanbul was equivalent to a quarter of the annual income of the average Frenchman. Which gives an indication of its exclusivity back then, although in separate calculations the rail historian, Christian Wolmar, has worked out that a return fare of six hundred francs would have been equivalent to about a month's wages for a manual worker at the time. Not quite as much as a quarter of the annual income, but still a pretty large outlay.

Over the final faltering years up to 1977, however, this sense of exclusivity (and superiority) had long gone.

During those dying days train writer Paul Theroux, heading for Istanbul on the service, wryly commented that "the *Orient Express* really is murder" on his epic journey from London's Victoria station to as far as Japan, recounted in his book *The Great Railway Bazaar* (1975). On that journey Theroux had been initially surprised to find he was sharing a cramped compartment with an unknown passenger. His new companion was a curious, shambolic elderly man named Duffill, who shuffled into the compartment apologetically and was vague about his background, failing to say whether he was travelling for work or pleasure – a mystery man who was down-at-heel and a far cry from the sophistication of the woman in red with her pearl necklace in the advert from the good old days.

In Italy, after a single night on board, Duffill found himself stranded at a station after popping into a shop to buy lunch during a stop to pick up new passengers. Theroux's *Orient Express* in the 1970s had no dining carriage, the service being a shadow of its glory days, with passengers reduced to picnics in compartments. Theroux was never to see Duffill again and adopted a word based on the character: to be "duffilled" (left behind at a station).

These days, however, the whole *Orient Express* felt somewhat *duffilled*.

Mr Eris pointed out the various pictures on the Agatha Restaurant walls, then told me that Netflix had run an eight-part behind-the-scenes series about the Pera Palace Hotel recently, although he had not appeared in it.

"Tourists they always knew about us," he said. "Now the Turkish, after they watch Netflix, they come, too."

I thanked Mr Eris, returned by foot to Sirkeci station past the fishermen on Galata Bridge, and ate shish kebabs at a table with a view of the Golden Horn at the Orient Express Restaurant. Then I looked at my watch. I was running late. I did not want to be *duffilled* before even making it on board in the first place. So I hurried to the Marmaray commuter line to Halkalı station – only just catching the 20:00 to Plovdiv – and entered a compartment where a small elderly Turkish man with a moustache, a squint, and olive-green waterproof walking trousers with a matching hunter-style vest appeared crestfallen he would be sharing.

He had clearly considered it highly unlikely anyone could possibly board so late. The whistle blew as I put down my backpack. It really had been touch-and-go. A conductor checked our tickets. I asked him if there was a dining car. There was no dining car. I asked him if you could buy beer and he replied: "It is Ramadan, no alcohol. Tea, Turkish coffee." I ordered a Turkish coffee and, as he jotted this down, noticed on his list of passengers that our carriage contained Germans, Bulgarians, Turks and Russians. Maybe there were still spies on the line from Istanbul all these years on.

We moved slowly away towards Bulgaria, curling on a north-west diversion into the Turkish night.

CHAPTER SIX

ISTANBUL TO THESSALONIKI IN GREECE, VIA KULATA IN BULGARIA

SLEEPERS, GAMBLERS, TRUCKERS AND SAINTS

Travelling solo, Theroux once said, had its benefits. "Being alone, self-sufficient, and anonymous", he believed, was the "surest way of… gaining experience". Real travel required "total immersion" and if I was to discover the truth, according to Theroux, I needed to surrender myself to movement and simply report what I saw.

Theroux's view was that this was best done alone, though Danny and I had discovered a few truths of our own along the way, such as don't trust French and German trains too much when unions are playing up, check you disembark at the right station in Vienna, steer clear of all hostels when you are middle-aged and do not want to wear earplugs, do not drink too much liquid before bedding down on sleeper trains (requiring traipsing to the toilet in the dead of night), always be nice to border guards, do not encourage representatives of massage parlours in Bucharest, use railway lockers whenever possible to avoid lugging backpacks around even if they are quite often tricky to work out, stay overnight at cheap little business hotels if available, and always trust the Eurail app, even if you did not when you began your trip.

Admittedly, none of this was particularly profound.

So I was more than ready for Theroux's *vanishing act down a pinched line of geography to oblivion* – whatever that meant. I was prepared and very much looking forward to embracing the unknown *sans* sidekick seeking licensed venues, preferably with dartboards and showing live Premier League football matches, obscure karaoke establishments and late-night Bukowski bars.

Though I had been just as guilty of all that.

I put my hands up to all such charges.

Twenty-seven miles an hour
Istanbul/Plovdiv to Kulata, Bulgaria

The elderly man with the moustache and the olive-green waterproof walking trousers left the compartment for a bit. When he returned, he squinted and said something in Turkish. He was leaving the compartment for good, I gathered, to take an empty berth next door. For the first time I would have a sleeper entirely to myself. He collected his possessions, squinted a farewell glance, and departed. I looked around.

The compartment was nothing special: small fridge, slide-out desk, mirror, wider-than-average forest-green seats with armrests, sink with a soap dispenser, clothes hooks, blackout blind and beige curtains. Yet I was deliriously pleased. The conductor passed by and distributed a packet of pretzel sticks, a carton of water, a multi-fruit drink and a Hobby chocolate bar. I was deliriously pleased with these, too. This was more like it. I appeared again to have unwittingly purchased a higher-class sleeper than a Timișoara–Bucharest level sleeper, even higher in standard than the one from Sofia to Istanbul, which had been quite good. I looked at the ticket. It was second class and I was in Carriage 484. The reservation was £9. This was extremely good value (Danny would surely have approved).

The conductor returned with a cup of coffee and put packets of lemon-scented refreshment towels to cool in the fridge. Was there no end to the luxuries of Carriage 484? I thanked him profusely and he regarded me oddly. I slid shut the door. Darkness had descended, though I left the blind up. We stopped at a place called Çerkezköy, close to where the *Orient Express* had been snowed in for five days inspiring *Murder on the Orient Express*. There were voices in the hall. We began to go seemingly very fast, juddering a great deal, and then went seemingly extremely slowly. This pattern was repeated. Someone walked past loudly jangling keys as though it was lockdown time in a prison. I made my bed, pulled down the blind and fell fast asleep to the sound of creaks and twangs as though the suspension was under great strain. The carriages bounced in a swaying motion that was conducive to weird dreams. I had found some of Theroux's *oblivion*.

Temporarily. At 1.15 a.m. the conductor knocked on the door.

"Twenty minutes, passport control," he said.

The passengers soon exited the train and descended a tunnel leading to another platform with a station manager's office, a line coordinator's office, a yardmaster's office and a couple more offices for bigwigs. Peering into the yardmaster's office, I could see that the yardmaster was snoring gently with a blanket pulled up to his neck as he lounged on a swivel chair. The passport office was beyond, and again I was nervous about all the stamps, but the immigration officer did not seem to mind.

We reboarded the train, rolling out of Kapıkule station into Bulgaria, where a pair of Bulgarian passport officials in blue uniforms tapped on the door and shone a torch under my bed as though hoping to find a body. It was 2.50 a.m. We were at Svilengrad station. The officers took my passport, returned it and the train moved on, I fell asleep and before quite knowing what was going on we arrived at Plovdiv station. It was 5.40 a.m.

The station was deserted. The idea seemed to be that you wandered about for a while beneath sodium lights trying to find somewhere to eat (impossible without Bulgarian lev, cards not being accepted anywhere that was open so early), before attempting to locate your train and realizing only one train existed at Plovdiv station. You then boarded that train and discovered you had to make do in a threadbare second-class compartment for the rest of the ride.

Men with hammers clinked the wheels of the carriage checking for cracks. A woman with a yellow jacket, yellow shoes and large yellow headphones joined my compartment, which seated eight and had stencils of butterflies and bamboo shoots on the windows to jolly things up. The 06:26 to Sofia due in at 9.30 a.m. departed and the day began to dawn in Bulgaria, with soft lead-grey and lemony light rising on the horizon as the train passed old, derelict factories. To the right, a jagged ridge rose like a long crocodile's back. I stared at this in an early-morning daze as the sky began to mutate sending shafts of tangerine light into the second-class carriage.

Then I clicked online to check the morning news (a habit I just could not shake).

Things, as ever, were happening.

On *The Times*' front page: "PUNISH THE FBI TO AVENGE MY ARREST, DONALD TRUMP TELLS PARTY", all about allegations that former US president Donald Trump had paid hush money to a porn star. "COULD TRUMP GO TO PRISON?" asked another headline, while a third reported that President Zelensky of Ukraine had been granted Poland's "Order of the White Eagle", the country's highest honour. Tales of two (very different) leaders. As the trains rolled down the dusty tracks, events elsewhere were moving on, too.

To be travelling by train across Europe during a war in Europe was, frankly, extremely odd.

Smoke rose from chimneys in valleys. We traversed silver birch woodland. The landscape widened to farmland. Hills rose with blossom like snowdrift on lower slopes. I offered the woman in yellow a piece of gum.

She replied: "No thank you," and said nothing else during the journey.

Ruined houses that might or might not be occupied appeared by the line, piles of tyres, too, and graffiti saying: "FEED THE PIGEONS". I rather liked that (although disapproved of actually doing so as pigeons could be quite annoying).

Shortly afterwards we arrived at Sofia station.

As before, no Ukrainian refugees were to be found. I shuffled around looking for a bureau de change for Turkish lira. This took me to a bus depot where services to Thessaloniki were available for 15 euros. Instead of taking the train to Kulata, where I had booked the ancient Egyptian-looking Hotel Finix Casino beside the no man's land between Bulgaria and Greece, you could reach Thessaloniki in a few hours by road. It would cost less. I would have made more "progress". But that was not the point. This was not a race around Europe. I wanted to stay a night at a little border town best known by truckers plying Bulgarian–Greek trade along the highway south.

I wanted to slip off the map.

* * *

Two British holidaymakers were standing by the arrivals board on the concourse in Sofia station, looking confused.

They needed to catch a train to the airport for their Wizz Air flight home. I pointed out they were inspecting the arrivals board.

"Ah yes, thank you," said Keith. "Quite right, quite right."

He was with Marina. The couple had stayed at a hotel above the snow line on Mount Vitosha where they had enjoyed "really nice meals" at "half UK prices".

Keith and Marina both had opinions about higher education in the United Kingdom and, before I quite knew it, they were talking about them.

"There are going to be big changes," said Marina, sounding as though those big changes would not be good big changes.

"Unless there are big changes, students face a financial black hole," said Keith.

But, before I quite knew it again, and before they could expand on their opinions about higher education and its big changes, their train was called and they rushed off. I would never learn what the changes would be.

I boarded the 12:30 to Blagoevgrad from platform two.

From the outside this was another graffiti-splattered Bulgarian State Railways train, although inside the carriages were graffiti-free with purple seats sewn with the wings-shaped pattern of BDZ's logo. As the train pulled away from Sofia station, a long trail of concrete housing estates followed the tracks to the left with the inky foothills of Mount Vitosha rising beyond.

So began a series of trundles south.

Lots of little apricot- and ochre-coloured stations with names like Zaharna Fabrika, Batanovtsi and Dupnitsa came and went. Handfuls of passengers embarked and disembarked; mainly wearing black, mainly clutching plastic bags. At Dragichevo station, an unscheduled stop, the train slowed sufficiently that a man in his twenties, evidently a friend of the driver, was able to leap off. More ugly housing estates sprawled forth, followed by litter-strewn rivers and warehouses with smashed windows. The scenery was grim and depressing, but then pleasant rolling countryside opened out marred only by the odd stone quarry.

A group of teenage guys joined the train by Pernik and sat in the opposite set of four seats, occasionally lazily staring at me as though assessing whether I might in some way be useful to them but mainly glued to their phones. From these, music sometimes emanated and they would hunch over watching a friend's screen. I could hazard a guess at the content that had them so rapt. At least they were not bothering me.

At Blagoevgrad those continuing to General Todorov were told to stay on the train. The "connection" meant doing nothing at all.

The youths disembarked. I was joined by an elderly woman with pink hair and a small dog and a woman in her thirties wearing jeans that were so fashionably shredded it looked as though she had just survived a tornado. Each nodded at me and then steadfastly minded their own business. After ten minutes, the carriages creaked forward into a sunlit ravine winding through a peaceful range of jagged mountains dusted with the emerald buds of spring and sprinklings of little yellow wildflowers. Towers of granite poked up like church steeples. Birds of prey swooped by looking for lunch. The landscape felt remote and wild.

This alluring, dramatic scenery soon ended, however, arriving at a wide plain with vines and fields of caramel cattle that was attractive in a more sedate, gentle way. The road the bus from Sofia would have taken came into view as well as a service station with a restaurant named "HAPPY", which you could not help but feel round those parts, so far removed from anywhere and with nothing in particular to do.

Then the terrain transformed into a shrub-land of low rolling hills, as though the train had passed into a different microclimate altogether, and we entered a tunnel and arrived at General Todorov station. This was a desolate spot with multiple platforms, where a team of painters was touching up the black-and-white patterns on the edges of the tracks and no one else was about.

The locomotive pulling the train from Blagoevgrad switched to take the carriages back to Blagoevgrad and the handful of passengers for Kulata joined another train. This one had windows decorated with butterflies and bamboo shoots just like the Plovdiv train earlier. From General Todorov it was a 14-minute ride onwards to Kulata, the topography changing yet again from rolling hills towards more rugged landscape leading to a jagged ridge of mountains.

As the crow flew, the distance from Kulata to Istanbul was 293 miles, except no railway went that way. By train the journey had covered 599 miles.

This was at an average speed of 27 mph over 22 hours.

Slow trains indeed.

Low roller
Kulata

Chickens clucked in a yard by the platform, where pieces of paper had been pinned to the walls in memory of locals who had recently passed away. A policeman in a patrol car watched the only tourist exit Kulata station (me). I walked along a dusty lane in the direction of Hotel Finix Casino, the patrol car passing and two moustachioed officers turning to observe more closely the only tourist off the 16:35 from General Todorov. *Has this person really decided to go on holiday in Kulata*, their looks suggested. *Yes, I have*, I could have told them if they had rolled down their window to ask.

Storks had established nests on many of the electricity poles of Kulata, which consisted otherwise of a square and a grocery shop, ramshackle wooden abodes and dogs attached to chains that barked at you and looked as though they dearly wished to tear you from limb to limb even though they were wagging their tails. No one else was on the streets of the "town", although at the section of Kulata that was on the highway by the border, where a line of traffic comprising about a hundred vehicles was waiting to cross into Greece, a few people were inspecting a run of makeshift duty-free shops offering "NON-STOP: TOBACCO, ALCOHOL, FOOD, 24/7" as well as brown-and-yellow ceramic pots, olives and olive oil, washing detergent and tacky porcelain garden ornaments. These seemed to be the go-to purchases for Greek border hoppers, although trade was slow.

Hotel Finix Casino was a squat warehouse-like structure with a filthy stone exterior designed to resemble (extremely sketchily) the temple of Karnak in Luxor, Egypt. The entrance broke the warehouse-look with a small pyramid shape, sliced off at the top with neon lights popping up saying "FINIX CASINO", and flanked by a pair of cross-armed pharaohs. A huge bouncer pointed me to the reception across a smoky, dimly lit carpeted lounge of pinging slot machines and green-baize blackjack and roulette tables.

At the reception desk, before I could say anything, a smartly dressed bottle-blonde receptionist asked: "Thomas?"

I must have been the only guest yet to check in. It was six o'clock.

Aware that the train line went no further (Kulata station was a terminus) and having resigned myself to the fate of catching a bus for the 70-mile journey south to Thessaloniki, I asked the receptionist about this. She looked alarmed and called over a man dressed in black with slicked-back hair who listened to my request and said: "Take taxi."

"What about the bus?" I asked.

"No bus. Take taxi," he replied and walked away.

The long and the short of it was that the bus to Thessaloniki did not stop at Kulata. The last pickup point for the bus in Bulgaria was in Blagoevgrad, requiring going backwards on the train tomorrow. I did not want to do this. I did not want to catch an expensive taxi either. I was stuck in a casino themed on ancient Egypt in a remote Bulgarian border town. I went to my little industrial-chic room, where the pharaoh theme had been dropped entirely for some reason, and contemplated matters while doing the washing.

It is an inconvenient though unavoidable truth (and preoccupation) of a long backpack journey across Europe that from time to time, every three days in my case, you must do your laundry. You will not, after all, have brought enough fresh clothing for a month's worth of travel. You would need a very large, very heavy suitcase for that. So you have to do the laundry, which is a pain. I only mention this here as the Hotel Finix Casino had excellent hot towel racks in its rooms, which allowed all the various garments to dry especially quickly. Some may visit casinos to launder money, I reflected: I was laundering the contents of my backpack.

I went for a night out in Kulata.

This required negotiating the cavernous interior of Hotel Finix Casino, which was almost empty of customers.

Walking through the casino in a loop, I was aware I was being observed at almost all times by various smartly dressed casino staff, who were unobtrusive yet always somewhere close by. "Mighty Ramses" slot machines blinked and clinked. A few hunched figures were playing these, hands slapping buttons as though a special slap, a perfectly weighted slap at just the right angle and force, might somehow make the computer inside the "Mighty Ramses" slot machine wake up in some microchip deep within and, finally, come to the decision: *now is the time to let the four King Tuts align, now is the time for the big jackpot payout, what on earth have I been waiting for, here we have a player worthy of the big jackpot payout who knows the special slap technique.*

An image depicting the Sphinx at Giza hung over the empty seats of the cocktail bar. I went to look at the "stud poker" table. No one was playing and, while pausing for perhaps five seconds to assess how the game worked, a smartly dressed croupier asked if I would like to buy some chips and begin to play stud poker. I mumbled *no thanks* and quickly moved on, feeling as though I was letting down Hotel Finix Casino by being such a disappointing "low roller", or more accurately "no roller".

Smoke was stinging my eyes, so I walked briskly to the door, where another huge bouncer nodded at me, and I joined "The Strip" of Kulata.

It was a pleasant evening. To the south lazy mellow sunshine illuminated rolling Greek mountains where wind farms dotted the slopes looking like faraway thistles. "The Strip" at Kulata was slightly different to the more famous Strip in Las Vegas, there being only one casino and the few knock-down *non-stop* shops.

Across the road was a truckers' café named "CKAPA". Fluorescent tube lighting gleamed off beige glass-topped tables. Three truckers wearing hoods and jackets were eating dishes piled with meat and chips. They looked as though they were enjoying the food. A pellet-burning fire blazed in a tangerine glow in a corner. At the counter two women in charge of culinary matters took my order of meat with something stuffed inside, shredded cabbage and carrots, sliced tomatoes, a roll and a Heineken beer. This was a very good, "low roller" price: £4.83. A trucker with a hood under his jacket came to the counter as I was paying and asked in Bulgarian and then English: "You trucker?" As he said this, he made hand movements to indicate steering a truck. I said I wasn't, and he seemed disappointed.

Sitting at a beige table, eating my food while wondering what the meat was, I tried to work out how to reach Thessaloniki in an affordable manner with no trains or buses available. A horrible conclusion seemed to be making itself evident: given that getting a taxi such a long distance was out of the question (and I didn't fancy another BlaBlaCar), I might have to hitchhike for the first time in my life. I ate my trucker's meal watching a purple-and-orange sunset beyond a truck parked outside the CKAPA truckers' café, contemplating the prospect of hitchhiking.

Then I texted a friend who had hitchhiked across Europe many times, explaining that the first town with buses was 15 miles beyond Kulata in Greece, which I could feasibly walk to if I got up early.

His swiftly issued advice went thus: "I have never paid for hitchhiking! Seriously – don't pay – or if you get desperate, then ask people *how much to take me to X.* If possible, make a sign. And, of course, avoid the dogging lay-bys. I can't believe you have not hitchhiked. Stare people in the eye till they pass, make sure there is an easy parking spot for them to pull over, avoid hitching on a bend (drivers can't see if they can pull over). Keep your passport on your person and not in your bag. Smile. If you are at the border and there is a border post, people will be in a queue and will be a captive audience for your request." Then he added: "Of course fifteen miles is not that much. You could always walk." He was quite a hardcore hiker as well as a hardcore hitchhiker.

This was reassuring. Hitchhiking appeared the way forward to Thessaloniki in this dead-end train town. It seemed unlikely that "dogging lay-bys" existed at the border crossing, so it would be OK on that point. I resolved to write a hitchhiking sign when I returned to my room.

First, though, I took another gamble. This was an ill-advised move. After being so pleased by the affordable nature of my CKAPA dinner, I returned to the casino, headed for the blackjack table (where two others were playing, possibly truckers), and changed twenty euros into four red casino chips from the smartly dressed croupier. Blackjack was, aside from roulette, the only casino game I really understood.

To buy the gambling chips required showing my passport, which was handed to a gruff, smartly dressed man who seemed to oversee what the smartly dressed croupier was doing. He nodded approval and came to hand back my passport, while at the same time a waitress in a short skirt and high heels from the Sphinx cocktail bar asked me whether I wanted a free drink, while at the same time too, the croupier seemed to want to know whether I would like to place a bet. As I was holding up the two trucker gamblers, I quickly placed five euros while simultaneously receiving back my passport – the gruff man saying "welcome" as he did so – and requesting a double espresso from the waitress. It was all a bit overwhelming.

In the meantime, I had been dealt a three and a four. The dealer had a king (worth ten). I asked for another card and received a ten. So I had seventeen in total. In blackjack you aimed for a perfect score of twenty-one, however, I did not want to go "bust" by requesting an additional card and scoring more than twenty-one. So I "held" on seventeen. The dealer pulled a ten. She had twenty. I had lost and so had both the truckers, who seemed to blame me for some reason for this (as my card selection affected theirs).

So it went for perhaps five minutes. I lost every hand and the croupier looked sorry for me as I said *that's it, thanks*: twenty euros down. I walked towards the Sphinx cocktail bar and sat on a sofa near a "Zodiac Wheel" slot machine, where the waitress gave me my free double espresso, looking surprised I was not at the blackjack table and somewhat sorry for me, too. Who wants to spend five minutes losing twenty euros while upsetting hard-nosed south-east European trucker gamblers who, even during what was an exceedingly short spell, clearly deemed you to be a complete and utter jinx on their own cards and fortunes? Which was the impression I had been getting. It was perhaps the first time in her casino waitressing career that a customer at Hotel Finix Casino had gone "bust" so quickly. I may have been the lowest and unluckiest of low rollers ever.

I drank the coffee, returned to my room and scribbled a hitchhiking sign using a biro and a piece of A4 paper. It read: "THESSALONIKI – Please!" Beside the words, I also poorly drew a thumbs-up universal hitchhiking symbol.

No Eurail app tomorrow.

This piece of Hotel Finix Casino paper had become my new ticket to ride.

Mini odyssey
Kulata to Thessaloniki, Greece

To enter Greece from the Hotel Finix Casino you walked across a parking lot and along a road for about 100 feet, passing a Bulgarian passport kiosk with no Bulgarian immigration officials, entering a no man's zone between Bulgaria and Greece on a short road bridge over the river Pirinska Bistritsa and observing a stone on the bridge that is painted half in the colours of the Bulgarian flag and half in the blue and white of Greece, marking the precise border.

It was 7 a.m. Sheep were baaing in a transport lorry heading to Greece and a line of vehicles edged forward towards booths. The Greek passport officer waved me through, and I went to a café next to an empty Ukrainian refugee information kiosk, where a woman said a bus for Thessaloniki did in fact come at "ten or eleven". Where, I asked. "Here," she said, pointing outside the café. I drank a cup of tea listening to "How Deep is Your Love" by the Bee Gees, "Liberian Girl" by Michael Jackson and "Englishman in New York" by Sting – I may not have been Sting's "illegal alien" but felt like one with my piece of A4 paper and its almost illegible scrawled request.

Outside the café was space for vehicles to stop, it was not on a bend, my passport was in my pocket, and I was smiling at drivers entering Greece trying to establish eye contact. A man in a large silver Mercedes empty of passengers regarded me somewhat disdainfully and sped away, a couple in an Audi seemed to think about it, then a white Bulgarian-licensed lorry stopped and the driver, a shaven-headed man in his thirties wearing a hooded top, gestured me over. *Is this for real*, I was wondering. I had been hitchhiking a couple of minutes.

It was for real. Rosco was a Bulgarian fruit and flowers exporter from Kresna, about thirty miles north of Kulata. He showed me a picture of his current load, which included twisty-shaped trees and small plants with red-and-yellow flowers. He made deliveries in Greece every week. For eight years he had owned a small supermarket in Kresna – "a little business" – and he would bring extra-virgin olive oil back from Greece "because we don't have any olives". The "we" meant "Bulgaria". The olive oil at the run of non-stop shops in Kulata must have been for Bulgarians.

His lorry had no working seat belts. To close the passenger door, which lacked an indoor handle, you had to slam it and flick a latch after reaching deep inside the door panel. It was quite pleasant having a "high up" view of the empty highway curving between the mountains and the increasingly arid landscape in the direction of Thessaloniki, where Rosco said he could drop me at a slip road on the edge of the city where I could catch a short bus ride the rest of the way.

"1913," said Rosco, who then wrote this down – he had a bit of English, which was how we communicated.

"What about 1913?" I asked.

"Bulgaria–Greece fighting," he said.

This was a reference to the Second Balkan War, when Bulgaria had launched attacks on Greek and Serbian forces to attempt to gain land considered its due after the First Balkan War against the Ottoman Empire. This earlier conflict had resulted in Greece and Serbia, who had been allies against the Turks, gaining an undue share of territory (in Bulgaria's view). The result was an ill-advised offensive followed rapidly by a humiliating reversal of fortune as Greece and Serbia subdued the Bulgarians and approached Sofia as though about to finish off Bulgaria for good. At this very moment, the Ottomans and Romanians seized the opportunity to make advances on Bulgaria, which was finding itself under attack on all sides. Bulgaria hastily arranged truces with the various warring nations it had stirred up. Treaties recognizing new official boundaries were signed that were more to the satisfaction of these countries. It had not been the proudest moment in Bulgaria's history.

Somewhat abruptly, the topic of conversation switched – as it seems it can at just about any moment just about anywhere on the continent of Europe – to Premier League football.

Rosco supported Arsenal in the Premier League as well as Levski Sofia in Bulgaria's own league. He asked my affiliation.

"Ah Chelsea!" he said and started chanting in the style of Chelsea supporters: "*Come on Chelsea! Come on Chelsea!*"

Then he said: "Good luck next week." He was referring to a game against Real Madrid in the Champions League.

We paced onwards down the highway, beyond a sign for Sidirokastro, where I might have walked if hitchhiking had failed.

"I lived for two years in Athens," said Rosco, with his eyes on the road. He had a charming, open manner, a wide grin and stubble that almost matched the length of his hair. The impression he gave was of someone who enjoyed company. Passengers helped break the solitude of the drive.

"Oh yes, I liked Athens," he said. "I was on the sea. It was a beautiful life. Good work. Good sea. Beautiful women. Disco." He took his lands off the wheel of the lorry and made some rave-style dance moves with his arms. The lorry swayed from side to side a little alarmingly. He regained control of the wheel.

He paused. Then he asked about Brexit. "You," he said. "You understand Brexit?"

I said I did not.

Rosco said "Brexit" again and gave a silent whistle and rolled his eyes.

A police patrol car was by the side of the road ahead. "Belt!" he said. "Belt!"

We both pulled our seat belts across us as though they were fastened. The police car did not give chase.

"Phew!" said Rosco.

We discussed Russia's invasion of Ukraine: "The truth! The truth, Tommy! United States! NATO! This is NATO versus Russia, Tommy!" Rosco had started to call me Tommy. He pointed to his eye with one hand, the lorry only slightly swaying: "The United States! NATO! I see!"

Rosco turned to the subject of Turkey's President Erdoğan: "Hagia Sophia is now a mosque, you know? No good. It's history, Tommy. Erdoğan killing history!" Rosco shook his head. "Erdoğan very powerful. No chance he goes."

He turned to his own life. Rosco was 36. "I am very young. I don't have family. I want family," he said. He showed me a picture on his phone of a pretty woman with long brunette hair. "Classic beauty, Tommy. Her name Varnia."

I asked what she did for a living.

"Nails, nails!" He pointed to his nails, the lorry swerving once more. "Fingers. Scrub fingers!" He showed the picture again: "Oh Bulgaria!" He pumped a fist in the air, the lorry swerving quite a lot. "Yes! Forever!"

He turned on the radio. "This Bulgarian music," he said. It had a melancholic-yet-upbeat violin and percussion sound. He showed me a picture on his phone of him playing chess. "Here in Balkans: normal. Normal also: cards. Here life: easy. No traffic. Slow, easy, easy, slow. This is normal. *Rakia* [the strong liquor] for breakfast, beer, wine: no problem!"

I asked him what happened if the police breathalyzed drivers who had been drinking *rakia* for breakfast?

"Ehhhhh," he said, tilting his head back as though this would be extremely unlikely, but he would cross that bridge if he ever came to it.

He went on to recommend Alfa beer in Greece and ouzo: "A good drink, Tommy." His favourite whisky was Bowmore single malt.

I asked him if there was money to be made import/exporting alcohol and cigarettes. "Very dangerous business, Tommy," he said. "Prison very bad place in Greece. Oh yes! My friend in Greece went to prison for three months. He died, Tommy. A Bulgarian. Dead." He paused. He had become quite emotional. Then he continued: "In the Balkans, we are one people, one heart!" He thumped his chest. The lorry swayed. "One heart! Different language: Greek, Bulgarian, Romanian. In history, we sometimes not friends. But the people, Tommy, no problem."

He seemed to be saying this as if to accept that what had happened to his friend in the Greek jail had been nothing personal.

We reached a tollbooth and Rosco said *yassou* (hello) and *kaliméra* (good morning) in Greek to the tollbooth attendant.

Rosco asked me if I had been to Greece before and I mentioned a happy holiday on the island of Ithaca. "*The Odyssey*, Tommy," he said. "You know?"

I said I did.

"Homer?"

I nodded and he looked pleased. Ithaca was the legendary island home of the mythical Odysseus, hero of Homer's epic eighth-century-BC poem about his wild adventures round the Mediterranean. Rosco seemed pleased about Odysseus and what he stood for, which might be described, very simply, as: *overcoming great troubles and returning home.*

He knew ancient Greek poetry. He had an eye on current geopolitical affairs. He had thoughts on the modern history of his country and its relationships with its neighbours. He had opinions about Premier League football. And he was able to convey all these in a foreign language while driving down a highway in a slightly rickety lorry full of fruit and flowers. This was not, dare I say it, typical perhaps of every lorry driver you might happen to encounter on a hitchhiking venture. Though what did I know? It was my first try.

Rosco dropped me at the slip road, refusing any payment for petrol, pumped his fists a few times, saying with each pump: "Bulgaria!" Then he drove off to deliver his twisty-shaped trees and flowers to his Greek customers.

Hitchhiking had been rather enjoyable. It was 8.45 a.m. and I was on the edge of my destination for the day. I went down the slip road and caught a bus to the centre of Thessaloniki.

Trains, tragedy and ancient history
Thessaloniki

Greek trains were in a dreadful state and had suffered a huge recent shock. A mere five weeks earlier (on 28 February 2023) the country had witnessed its worst rail crash ever when two trains on the Thessaloniki–Athens line collided head-on near the town of Tempi, about 130 miles north of Athens, during which 57 people died and dozens were left injured. The northbound train had been carrying many students returning to colleges late in the evening from a festive weekend in the Greek capital. On contact with a southbound freight train its front two carriages, a passenger carriage and a dining car, had disintegrated killing the drivers of both trains instantaneously and forming a huge fireball. Passengers were hurled through windows. Some bodies were found 100 feet from the train. Survivors in back carriages, many badly hurt, had to smash their way out to safety as flames engulfed the interiors.

A three-day period of national mourning was declared by the Greek president as answers were sought to what had caused the tragedy.

Initially, the collision was blamed squarely on "human error" as the stationmaster at Larissa station, near Tempi, had failed to notice two trains were on the same line. The country's prime minister Kyriakos Mitsotakis described the crash as a "terrible train accident without precedent" adding that "everything shows that the drama was, sadly, mainly due to a tragic human error".

Yet this position was somewhat undermined by the resignation of the Greek transport minister, Kostas Karamanlis, who said in an impassioned statement that the nation's train network was outdated and belonged firmly to another era: "It is a fact we [the New Democracy party] took stock of Greek railroads in a state that did not befit the 21st century. In these three and a half years [since taking office] we have made every effort to improve this reality. Unfortunately, those efforts were not enough to prevent such an accident."

Railway trade union leaders were quick to pick up on this very public division of accountability: that the prime minister was focusing on a mistake made by a station employee, while his transport minister believed railways were such a "state" that such an accident was waiting to happen. Unions were clear: the blame for the crash was a failed electronic safety system that had heaped responsibility on stationmasters, who had no choice but to check all train movements along lines, a job the system should have covered.

This electronic backstop had not been functioning for years and Kostas Genidounias, president of the Greek train drivers' union, said that the accident "would have been avoided if the safety systems were working". The requirement for manual checks on the important line from Athens to Thessaloniki, the country's second city, was at fault: "We travel from one part of the line to the next by radio, just like in the old days. The station managers give us the green light." This put huge pressure on those working at stations. Meanwhile, one of the main railway unions, the Association of Rail Workers, said that a recent study had shown there should be 2,100 railway workers across Greece, not 750, as there were at the time of the crash. This chronic understaffing had contributed to creating the conditions in which such a disaster could happen.

In the wake of the crash, unions across Greece went on strike in protest: civil servants, doctors, bus drivers, ferry workers and teachers joining railway workers in solidarity. Rail unions had for many years complained about lack of investment in safety and poor staffing levels – and look at what had happened.

Violent demonstrations were held in Athens, where 40,000 people took to the streets and petrol bombs were thrown outside parliament. Banners were waved stating: "IT'S NOT AN ACCIDENT, IT'S A CRIME… IT COULD HAVE BEEN ANY OF US ON THAT TRAIN". Police fired tear gas at them to disperse, as they did to stone-throwing protestors gathered outside Thessaloniki station, where a van was torched. Anarchists in both cities had joined the demonstrations, many leading the clashes.

This huge public backlash led to backtracking at government level. Changing his tune, Mitsotakis, the prime minster, said that "it should not be possible for two trains moving in opposite directions to be on the same track and not be noticed by anyone". The stationmaster at Larissa station had been working alone during a busy holiday period. Mitsotakis declared: "We cannot, will not, and must not hide behind human error." Greece, he added, would be seeking advice from other countries and seeking European Union funding for investment in tracks that were still nationally owned, although the train operator, Hellenic Train, was operated by the Italian group Ferrovie dello Stato Italiane. Hellenic Train had been sold off to raise national funds during a recent national debt crisis.

"We all know the nation's railroads are deeply problematic," said Mitsotakis. "They are perhaps the extreme expression of a Greece that doesn't befit us and which we want to leave behind."

In short, the crash had sparked a national crisis in confidence regarding how the state sector was serving Greece.

Veteran commentators said the episode highlighted an ingrained "careless mentality" that needed to be urgently addressed in all areas of public life.

* * *

This was the background to taking trains around Greece when I arrived by bus outside Thessaloniki station, 17 days after trains had resumed running in the country following a three-week shutdown to the entire rail system after the disaster. The Athens–Thessaloniki train, covering 189 miles, had only resumed a week earlier and the full restart of the Greek rail network was not due for three more days. I was about to take trains across a country in the middle of a full-blown rail crisis.

At Thessaloniki station, where clashes had been held with police not so long before, protestor slogans had been spray-painted on walls by the entrance. "THEIR WEALTH, OUR BLOOD, OUR LONG-TERM STRIFE, WE HAVE TO FIGHT", said one in red paint beside a red communist star, while another declared: "REVENGE ON THE MURDERERS, JUSTICE FOR THE DEAD, POWER AND SUPPORT TO THE FAMILIES", accompanied by an anarchy sign. The dull concrete façade of the station was ugly enough without these hastily daubed messages, although a small, very old steam locomotive sat on a rusty piece of mounted track in the courtyard at the front; evidence there must be a rail enthusiast or two lurking about in Greece's second city.

Inside the station it was empty and quiet with a subdued atmosphere. Passengers had been slow to return to the rails after the accident. There was no queue at the information office, where I initially asked whether a train was available to the city of Drama, about 100 miles to the north-east: a detour to Drama looked intriguing. However, the friendly assistant said: "No trains to Drama. Take bus." So I reserved a seat (for free) on the following day's train straight to Athens departing at 10.00 a.m.

The station was echoey and almost deserted. To one side of the box-like ticket hall was a tiny Greek Orthodox chapel. Thin candles were lit in sandy boxes in alcoves and a sign etched into a marble panel said in both Greek and English: "The holy metropolis of Neapolis and Stavroupoli wishes you a good trip". For a few moments I stood before the chapel, where a brass gate led to a prayer room, and thought about the lives lost on the tracks I was about to travel.

My little business hotel, also popular with tourists, was named Telioni Hotel and was close to the station: the perfect combination.

You reached it down streets of simple concrete apartments, evidence of urgent rebuilding after destruction by an earthquake in 1978. The hotel receptionist, a young man named Nick with extraordinarily prominent eyebrows and a gentle, helpful manner, provided a rundown of local tourist sights and then said of the national train problem: "Now safety is at the maximum, but many people are not taking the train. Not much. But people are like goldfish, they forget, and they start taking trains again, or maybe they think it is so soon after the accident safety and security is amazing." He paused, considered this, and added: "Every coin has two sides."

I went to have a look around Thessaloniki.

From the Telioni Hotel, beyond a kebab-style restaurant roasting an entire goat on a spit in the front window, you quickly came to the glittering golden splendour of the Church of St Demetrius. This was a striking Byzantine-style structure with high wooden rafters, archways and a crypt, all infused by a lovely sweet smell of honey candles lit in honour of Demetrius (270–306 AD).

This saint had been martyred at the site of the church after being held in the crypt, then part of a Roman baths not a church, and speared to death under the orders of the bloodthirsty Roman Emperor Galerius. Demetrius had upset Galerius by performing a miracle when he had blessed a Christian man named Nestor, who was due to fight at a stadium in front of the Romans. Instead of entertaining the assembled dignitaries by dying gruesomely, however, which was how it normally went, Nestor had against all odds won.

Over the centuries, Demetrius had grown in importance in the Greek Orthodox church and developed a reputation for offering protection to children and the sick. In the church you could light candles (after buying them) and write messages to put in boxes naming people you wished to enjoy good health. I did this (igniting a 50-cent candle for good luck), though some candles were as long as five feet and cost 15 euros. Your devotion, it seemed, could be measured in honey-scented wax.

In a corner was the tomb of Demetrius, which was said to smell of myrrh, a sign that he was especially blessed. I will not pretend I noticed this, perhaps the smell of all the candles obscured it. The church, on my visit, was busy with pilgrims queuing to see this tomb as well as the crypt. Many Orthodox Christians regularly visited from Russia, Latvia and Bulgaria, according to the man in the gift shop.

The Church of St Demetrius was on a long, straight street named after the saint. Continuing along I observed for a while a man speaking to himself and causing traffic to swerve around as though he was a slow-moving, highly talkative traffic cone (nobody honked, he appeared to be a regular feature of St Demetrius Street). Men wearing black sat at tables of endless cafés discussing what seemed to be important matters in deep, gravelly voices, many gently turning over acorn-coloured worry beads in their hands. This looked like such a peaceful pastime that you could not help but wonder why worry beads had not taken off more widely round the globe. Perhaps, with so much to worry about, they might sometime soon.

A bit further on, you arrived at Atatürk Museum, where Mustafa Kemal Atatürk, Turkey's great reformer, was born (in 1881) and raised. This was in an old house dating from the Ottoman Empire with shuttered windows and whitewashed walls, heavily guarded by police as it was where the Turkish consulate was also to be found.

Atatürk's family had fled Thessaloniki in 1912 after it became part of Greece during the First Balkan War. You entered after passing through an X-ray machine into a courtyard with steps to the old house in which displays detailed Atatürk's childhood. There you learned that Turkey's modernizer-to-be was a prematurely grown-up boy who, after his father died when he was aged seven in 1888, decided to become a soldier as he admired the discipline and smart uniforms. At military junior high school, he was distinguished by his excellent grasp of mathematics, so much so he would challenge his teacher with extracurricular maths questions. The teacher was also called Mustafa and he complained that it was confusing that they had the same name. So he referred to the future Turkish leader as Mustafa Kemal (*kemal* means "mature").

This name stuck and by the age of 39 – having risen to general, launched the Turkish War of Independence against the sultans, and negotiated the Treaty of Lausanne in July 1923 in the wake of the collapse of the Ottoman sultanate – Atatürk was named the first president of the Turkish Republic in October 1923. It had been a precocious, rocket-like ascent to the top.

Thessaloniki had been at the heart of all of this. In the run-up to the overthrowing of the sultans, you learn, the city had been a hotbed of activity among the anti-Ottoman "Young Turks", with whom Atatürk had been involved.

The pieces of the complex region do begin (slowly) to fall into place when you take a lot of trains around the Balkans.

I ate tasty grilled sardines doused in lemon beneath a cherry blossom tree overlooking the pink-stone walls of the Rotunda, a grand edifice (built by the awful Emperor Galerius at the beginning of the fourth century). I visited the Rotunda, where inside you find a large, empty space with an impressive domed roof. I examined the Arch of Galerius, notable for its stone friezes depicting clashes between soldiers engaged in mortal combat (Galerius definitely seemed to have had a vicious edge). Then I stopped to visit the Archaeological Museum, housed in a low-level building with busts of gods and philosophers, gravestones, funerary pillars, reliefs and ancient pieces of pottery from as early as the fourth century BC.

By a slab of stone inscribed with symbols dating from the third century BC, discovered within the Thessaloniki prefecture, a tall grey-haired man named Mark from the United States was staring at the stone as though transfixed.

I stood beside him looking at the slab, reading that the inscriptions were musical notes.

"It's incredible how intelligent human beings can be when they're not being stupid," the tall man said, soon after introducing himself as Mark. "This is probably the oldest piece of written music. The Greeks recorded this."

He was softly spoken, carefully considering his words.

"The Antikythera mechanism, do you know it?" he asked. To my shame, I admitted I did not.

"The Antikythera mechanism, two thousand two hundred years ago was the first computer ever made," Mark said quietly, going on to explain that this mechanism had measured movements of the moon and other planets as well as the seasons on Earth. It had been discovered in a shipwreck off the island of Antikythera in the Aegean Sea in 1901. "Just a hundred years ago: if you want to understand how advanced the Greeks were, to appreciate how sophisticated the ancient Greeks really were, you need to know about the Antikythera mechanism."

Mark discussed the Antikythera mechanism for some time, adding: "We didn't catch up with them until the nineteenth century." By "them" he meant the ancient Greeks. He paused, and still speaking very softly, almost mumbling, said: "Aristarchus: well, he estimated the ratio of the distances between the Earth, the moon and the sun. Eratosthenes: well, he measured the circumference of the Earth. All of this, two thousand years ago. Don't ask me how they did it, I wouldn't know where to start."

All the time he was speaking Mark was staring at the slab of stone marked by the old musical notes.

Curious, I asked Mark what he did for a living. He sounded as though he must be a professor of some sort. He became evasive.

"I'm a trainer," he replied.

What kind of trainer?

"I train people," he answered.

In what?

"I am a teacher," he said.

That was as much as he wished to divulge so I asked where in America he was from, as much to be polite and conversational by the old slab of musical stone as anything else.

"Will 'the US' do?" he asked.

I said OK.

"I moved from there a long time ago," he added.

How long ago?

He did not answer.

I asked where he had moved.

"Europe," he replied. "Will Europe do?"

I said it would and we shook hands and I wandered round the rest of the Archaeological Museum, then down to the waterfront where the Aegean Sea was calm and the street-side restaurants packed with people drinking ouzo and eating grilled sardines near the chubby battlements of the city's landmark White Tower. The sun was bright, the temperature was in the 20s. It felt a long way from the snow and frost of Passau. It felt wonderful.

Taking trains round Europe in early spring you are transported to all sorts of places and climates, too.

Drinking ouzo at a bar watching boats bob on the Aegean, where yet more 2,000-year-old computers may still have rested somewhere down there beneath the waves, you could let a little bit of Theroux's *oblivion* sweep in. Stop thinking for a while. Just be in the moment at peace with the water slapping against the shore in a city where music was etched on old stone slabs and saints once performed miracles. As good a reason as any to hit the train tracks.

CHAPTER SEVEN

THESSALONIKI TO NAPLES IN ITALY, VIA ATHENS, PATRAS AND BARI

"WE STRIVE FOR A MODERN RAIL NETWORK"

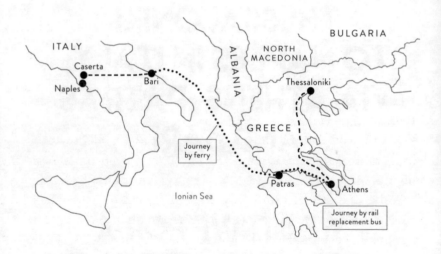

At the information desk at Thessaloniki station, the attendant I had spoken to yesterday was on duty again. She seemed pleased that a tourist was about to take a train in Greece, as though it were a symbol of things to come: the first swallow of spring, a holidaymaking train travelling boom (in the form of: me) about to take off across the country.

I asked her about the departure board. It was terribly confusing, and I could not see the 10:00 to Athens.

"This is because we cannot change the board," she said. It was broken. "These trains," she pointed upwards, "do not exist."

So they are ghost trains?

"Yes," she said, regarding me for a moment, before continuing. "There are only two trains today from this station, not all those trains."

I was to go to platform three where the 10:00 train to Athens was marked on the board as the 10:08 Athens train.

I did so, after lighting a candle to remember the victims of the 28 February crash at the station's little chapel.

The train at platform three was shiny, blue and modern with a haphazard triangular pattern on its side and a "T" logo with the inscription "HELLENIC TRAIN, FERROVIE DELLO STATO ITALIANE GROUP, 120-018" written beside it. Men with wipes attached to poles were cleaning the Siemens-built locomotive and a great number of staff were busy making checks. Passengers, about a hundred of us plus a dog, were told to wait on the platform. Some trains between Thessaloniki and Athens could take as many as six hundred people; confidence had yet to return fully to the service, it seemed.

We were permitted on board and I found my lavender-coloured seat in a spotless modern carriage with lavender curtains. A few moments later a young Greek soldier sat down opposite me. He wore a black parade uniform with polished gold buttons, a polished gold buckle, red epaulettes and a peaked cap with a leafy golden symbol topped by a blue-and-white cross. He was cleanly shaven and named Christos, aged 18, on the first year of a five-year service in a dentistry regiment of the Hellenic Army, ranked second lieutenant. After this period of training, he would be required to stay with the army for a further ten years. He was about to return to his family for Easter. They lived in the village of Tithorea, about three-quarters of the way to Athens, where his parents ran a restaurant and bars.

Christos had dark, placid, steady eyes and a premature maturity – a young Greek version of Atatürk, 120 years on.

We had immediately begun talking. He was a natural born talker, the way some people just are.

He told me that the motto next to an owl motif on his belt was "something about discipline, if you do anything you must have good discipline – here look at this". He pulled out a short dagger-like sword that was attached to a sheaf on this belt. It had a gold-and-white handle and was clearly potentially lethal with a sharp point, even though it was part of his ceremonial uniform.

I asked Christos if he liked being in the army.

"I do like the discipline of it," he said. "I like that we are both scientists and soldiers [in his dentistry division]."

I asked whether he felt comfortable travelling on one of the first intercity trains after the dreadful accident.

"Kind of," he replied. He paused. "One of my classmates was here on the train. She passed away. She was studying medicine. There was an army funeral."

I said I was sorry to hear about his friend.

Christos replied: "Thank you." As he did, he sprang up to help a woman lift her bag to a storage spot.

Then he returned and took off his hat, placing his train ticket inside ready for the inspector. "The railway was closed for a month after the crash," he said. "I think it was a once-in-a-lifetime event. I think it will be better now. We have to move on."

He told me about national service in Greece. Men, not women, had to serve for 12 months, either at the age of 18 or after finishing their studies: "Men are obligated. I think most don't want to join as they don't have a choice."

Christos was in the Military School of Combat Support Officers, which as well as teaching dentistry also covered doctors, pharmacists, vets, lawyers, economists and psychologists. For his year, only six candidates had been accepted for dentistry and 55 to be doctors; he had scored well in exams.

The train was sweeping smoothly through suburbs of identikit apartment blocks with sunshades on balconies overflowing with vegetation and hanging washing. The journey was due to take five and a half hours, much slower than before the February crash, when it was four hours. Strict new safety measures were in place.

I asked about the difference between Athens and Thessaloniki. Christos replied: "Thessaloniki is not as chaotic as Athens. It is by the sea. Everyone from Athens says Athens is better. They have a metro and we don't have one. But I think the view is better in Thessaloniki and it is calmer."

Did he worry about being a soldier and representing the state when a large strand of people – as evidenced by the graffiti on the walls of Thessaloniki station and the violence accompanying the protests in the wake of the train crash – attached themselves to anarchist groups?

"It is a little dangerous, especially if I am dressed like this," he said. "I might be attacked by someone." Though this had never happened.

He had not agreed with the violence during the train protests. "But you are allowed your own opinions," he said. "Being in the army does not mean you have to agree with everything that the state says." He paused, thought about this and added, "But you do have to obey orders."

The train moved into farmland with olive groves, fruit groves and vineyards. Tractors puttered along. Little farmsteads popped up here and there. Christos and I looked out for a while. Pearl-grey clouds hung on low mountains on the horizon and above a canopy of perfect cornflower blue had formed. It was the start of a fine April day.

We talked about his non-dentist duties in Thessaloniki, which included providing security for the military school on night-time patrols.

What were the main concerns of the Greek army?

"Well, sometimes things happen between us and Turkey," he replied. "Especially on the islands, there's always an alert. At Evros, too. It's on alert, close to the border with Turkey." Along the river Evros, known as the river Meriç in Turkey, tension between the nations had heightened recently when Turkey attempted to let refugees from Syria across the border into Greece by breaking a section of fencing. This action had been condemned by the European Union and Turkey had backed down, but animosity remained. "We made a barrier recently between Evros and Turkey. We are always watching out there: the same in Lesbos and Rhodes." These two Greek islands close to the Turkish mainland were another common migrant route.

Christos had some exams coming up so I thanked him for talking, shook his hand, wished him well with his revision and went to the Perfetto Canteen, slogan: "Train Your Taste". This too was lavender in colour, with fixed tables and unfixed chairs at which quite a few students sat, tapping away on laptops. There was also a wizened professor-like character sprouting tufts of spiky locks, a "rock 'n' roll guy" wearing black leather and a chain of some sort hanging from a hip, and a swarthy Greek Orthodox priest slumped in a chair across the aisle fast asleep with his head against a wall and a hand clutching mobile phone charger wires in a fist resting on his laptop.

Shadows of clouds drifted above scrubland on distant inky mountains. We passed the part of the track near Tempi where the tragic accident had occurred and pulled into Larissa station.

Christos joined me for a coffee, but took a call immediately after sitting down, and then another, and another. He hung up on the last call, looking exasperated.

"Everyone's calling because they are afraid of the train," he said. "My father would not let me on it, but the train goes to the heart of the village – the bus ends an hour's drive away – and I'm not scared, it's much safer now it's going slowly."

Over his coffee, he opened up about his friend who had died in the crash and what happened that day.

"Her name was Claountia, she was twenty-one," Christos said. "She was with many other students on the train, many from the Aristotle University of Thessaloniki. Most of those who died were in the dining carriage. This was destroyed. My friends had been in the fourth carriage but Claountia had decided to get a coffee." Christos looked at his own drink as he said this. "Her boyfriend had been in the fourth carriage and she had left him to get the coffee. He was injured in the crash, but not something serious."

He paused. "I actually almost got on that train but my father wouldn't let me." Christos had, fortunately, listened to him that time. "He said I would get in too late. He said to go the next day on the bus. This was at the last minute. I had prepared everything. I said: 'Come on, Dad, let's go.' But my Dad said: 'If you miss it, you miss it.' I still get chills about that. He saved me."

Christos was quiet for a while, pensive, and who could blame him? Then he went on to explain that his father had said that it did not matter if he was a bit late to college the next morning – he would have had a good night's sleep and that was more important. It was as though his father had had a sixth sense.

"I had already told friends in the morning that I was taking the train. Suddenly, when the news broke, I got all these texts: *are you OK?* They thought I was on the train. Luckily, I hadn't gone. It was like dodging a bullet, a really close bullet. On here right now, I do kind of feel nervous," he said. It was Christos' first time back on the rails since the accident. "I am trying not to think about it too much."

Christos and I said goodbye, his station was coming up. He walked with his ramrod-straight gait to the carriage door carrying his bag, peaked cap on, polished gold buttons glistening, dagger bouncing by his side.

Meeting Aristotle
Athens

The 10:00 from Thessaloniki puttered onwards past empty mountains, rolling plains, jagged ridges, great expanses of olive groves, serpentine rivers and mysterious monasteries with cupolas and arches poking up from granite slopes. Apartments extremely similar to ones on the edge of Thessaloniki arose. We entered a tunnel. A whistle blew. A horn hooted. The train slowed.

We had arrived in the capital of Greece.

The swarthy priest had awoken, gathered his black laptop, put his arms into his black backpack, collected his black roll-along bag and was first to disembark, other passengers making way for this Reservoir Dog of the Greek Orthodox church. We disembarked into Larissa station, on the north-west side of the city centre.

Despite being the central station, this was a scruffy, unimpressive place with a platform sign saying: "WE STRIVE FOR A MODERN RAIL NETWORK", as though writing it down in a foreign language would make all the difference. A subheading said: "FOR THE INFRASTRUCTURE AND MODERNISATION, WITH RESPONSIBILITY", and it turned out that this was a promotion still up after the European Year of Rail 2021. The poster, issued by the Hellenic Railways Organization, a public body in charge of Greek tracks, showed a train speeding in a blur through a station. Another nearby was advertising Eleusis, a suburban city just to the west of Athens, as being a European Capital of Culture for the year: a Greek rival to Timişoara back in Romania. There seemed to be a lot of Capitals of Culture on the train lines of Eastern and South-eastern Europe.

I walked towards the neighbourhood of Exarcheia, where I had booked a hotel, enjoying the warmth – warmer than anywhere yet – and the labyrinthine streets between three- or four-storey apartment blocks and small businesses. Even though this was the centre, just as in Thessaloniki, it had a "lived-in" feel: washing hung from balconies, some with well-tended balcony-gardens sprouting flowers. It wasn't pretty – graffiti was scrawled just about anywhere a space to write graffiti existed, but what I could read of the often-English messages seemed to be positive: "NO ONE IS FREE UNTIL EVERYONE IS FREE", "DON'T WORRY, BE HAPPY" (written in a heart symbol), "WAKE UP!" and, perhaps pushing the term "positive" and with a good dose of irony: "EAT THE RICH, FEED THE POOR", accompanied by a picture of a skull and crossbones and a knife and fork.

My route from the station to my lodgings passed one of the most famous museums in the world. Feeling it would be churlish just to walk on by I climbed the steps of the grand façade of the National Archaeological Museum, passed between high Ionic columns, placed my backpack in a locker and soon after began studying statues of long, thin figures with long, thin noses from the Cycladic period of 2800 BC.

This is what can happen to you in Greece, even if you are just a footloose Interrailer obsessed by timetables and the Eurail app: you can find yourself drifting down centuries past, transported and dreaming of ancient civilizations and considering for a while whether things were maybe better back then (probably not if you took into account all the routine massacres, endless wars and generally barbaric state of conducting affairs à la Emperor Galerius).

Cycladic civilization was to be usurped by the Minoans and then Mycenaean civilizations, you discover, as you take in the figurines including a splendid twisty one of a harpist made of Parian marble (from the Cycladic island of Paros). Then you step into the Mycenaean section, which features a great deal of gold discovered by a German archaeologist named Heinrich Schliemann in 1876 including golden octopus- and butterfly-shaped jewellery, golden jugs and golden cups with golden dolphin patterns from the sixteenth century BC. Next up came golden masks, golden staffs, golden bracelets, golden signet rings: enough bling to make certain B-list celebrities of the early twenty-first century want to up their game.

All of this was, of course, just the start. Larger marble statues of Herculaneum women from 320 BC were to follow in bigger rooms, where a bronze sculpture of a horse ridden by a young jockey caught the eye, discovered in a shipwreck off Cape Artemision by the island of Euboea in 1971, yet dating from 140 BC. And so it went, from chamber to chamber within the National Archaeological Museum: growling marble lions from the early fourth century BC; busts of griffins from 350 BC; funerary statues of dogs from 375 BC; muscle-bound bronze warriors from 330 BC; "fighting Gauls" waving their fists from 100 BC.

Busts of the gods and the emperors emerged: Artemis (goddess of hunting, and, seemingly a little contradictorily, chastity and childbirth); Caesar Augustus (founder of the Roman Empire, looking calm and quietly determined); Empress Livia (equally calm and determined, wife of Caesar Augustus); Emperor Caligula (who appeared, and was, a nasty piece of work with a pinched face and thin lips); Emperor Titus (rounder-faced, much more easy-going-looking); Empress Faustina the Younger (wife of Emperor Marcus Aurelius, with tight curls and distant, lazy eyes that seemed to suggest: *why me for this sculpture, could you not please leave me alone?*). Priests, poets, philosophers, "mature women", "mature men", "young men" and, as chance would have it, one "middle-aged man" circa 50 BC, head twisted to one side and looking wrinkled, weather-worn and generally defeated by life. You are tempted, if you happen to be a middle-aged man yourself, to say: *come on, it's not that bad.* But then again, you do not quite know what travails this particular middle-aged man born before Jesus Christ had faced back in 50 BC – it had probably been pretty awful.

Staring at this carnival of characters and wondering about their thoughts and lives was what, for me, made the National Archaeological Museum so special.

Impossible to take all in on a single visit. Like the British Museum, where many Greek treasures that probably ought to return to Athens belonged, the National Archaeological Museum was a place to savour over many visits.

No trains, of course, but quite a few images of chariots carrying warriors to battle on the side of a collection of old urns. Wheels at least existed back then.

* * *

So to the heart of Exarcheia, a district of Athens known for its independence, rebellious nature and population comprising a large number of anarchists, socialists, anti-fascists, artists and intellectuals. Plus one Interrail enthusiast, on that early April day. This was the Greek capital's "alternative" neighbourhood, about a mile north of the tourist district by the Acropolis – and convenient, with pleasingly good value accommodation, for tomorrow's train to Patras, from where a ferry was due to Bari in Italy the following day.

A pit stop in Athens, a pit stop in Patras, a ferry across a sea – and on.

At the risk of becoming obsessed by graffiti, though it is hard not to notice it in Exarcheia (or in Europe in general of late), here are a few examples of messages as the lanes became smaller, increasingly winding and steadily dirtier on the way to the edge of Strefi Hill and the Orion & Dryades Hotel: "PISS ON COPS", "LIBERTÉ, EGALITÉ, FRATERNITÉ" (repeated many times over), "KILL THE NAZIS", "GET IN THE STREETS" (written as a speech bubble coming from the mouth of an octopus), "QUEER-FEMINIST CLASS WAR NOW!", "FUCK THEM ALL!", "FREE PALESTINE", "TRUMP MUST GO: IN THE NAME OF HUMANITY WE REFUSE TO ACCEPT A FASCIST AMERICA!", "THE SYSTEM HAS NO FUTURE FOR THE YOUTH: THE REVOLUTION DOES", "THIS SYSTEM CANNOT BE REFORMED: IT MUST BE

OVERTHROWN!", "DRONES DON'T CRY", and perhaps a little worryingly, if you happen to be a tourist passing through: "TOURIST: STOP FUNDING THE VIOLENCE OF GENTRIFICATION!"

All of this on a short walk, rising up the hill past a litter-strewn street where a market had been held that day and several incongruously smart hipster-ish little cafés/bars were lined with people in dark glasses wearing black who were either in animated conversation or extremely coolly and hipster-ishly sipping drinks while watching the world go by.

The Orion & Dryades Hotel, its name relating to constellations and ancient Greek tree nymphs, was opposite the anti-tourist graffiti, probably not by chance. It was, however, not only excellent value, but the room was first-rate, too; maybe the best yet, with its whitewashed walls, bright modern art and view across a somehow-beautiful concrete jungle of rooftops with satellite dishes and a/c extractor fans to the Acropolis. Beyond, you could just make out a sliver of the milky-white Saronic Gulf by the port of Piraeus. Could not really be better for the price: what a turn up for the books the Orion & Dryades Hotel turned out to be, though I did not spend much time there.

Past the anti-tourist graffiti and down a set of steep steps decorated with a large communist red star – a popular spot for a ragbag bunch of local drunks to gather and volubly discuss matters, quite possibly the overthrow of capitalism – it was a short walk to Exarcheia Square.

There I met the Athens riot police.

They were a friendly bunch, to me at least, standing on a brightly lit corner wearing helmets and body armour, clutching shields and batons. Across from where they were idling, a metal fence blocked off the square's centre in which works were underway to build a new metro station. Having read about this, I already knew of the controversy surrounding the metro station: the gist appeared to be that local anarchists and others did not want Exarcheia linked to other more capitalist parts of the city. However, pretending I did not have any idea, and in the spirit of "train reporting", I asked one of the riot police what was going on.

He was named Aristotle, at least that's the name he gave; apposite perhaps in these parts given many of the fourth-century-BC philosopher's influential thoughts had been dreamed up not far from Exarcheia Square. He warmly shook my hand. He was holding a cup of coffee in the other. The riot police were all drinking coffee. They must have been on a break.

"We are here to protect the square," he said, apparently pleased to talk to someone other than his dozen or so colleagues, who did not seem particularly bothered he was chatting to a tourist. Aristotle had olive eyes and was cleanly shaven, in his early twenties, quite unlike his shaggy-haired bearded namesake of 2,500 years earlier.

I asked him how long they had been on shift.

"Four hours," Aristotle replied. He pointed to the metal fences by the metro development. "If we were not here, they would tear that down."

By "they" he meant anarchists.

"They don't want metro. They don't want to hurt trees," he said. Aristotle was pointing at a few trees behind the metal fence. "But they won't do anything if we are here." The riot police acted as a deterrent.

I asked him about the anti-police graffiti all about the square, including *"TOUT LE MONDE DÉTESTE LA POLICE"* (accompanied incongruously by a heart symbol), and one amusing message that said: "IN MY EYES, THE POLICE AND THE SYSTEM THEY REPRESENT COULD BE IMPROVED". Rather more politely put than by others and probably ironically so.

Nearby, a message fondly remembered anti-capitalist protests at the Hamburg G20 where a 12,000-strong "WELCOME TO HELL" march was held in 2017 to greet delegates of the multi-governmental meeting to discuss the world economy, resulting in clashes with German riot police. Close to this was a banner stating: "EXARCHEIA SQUARE AND STREFI HILL: DEFEND FREE SPACES".

"They don't want us here," said Aristotle carefully choosing his words. He was referring to the local population.

That seemed a bit of an understatement, I suggested, and Aristotle simply shrugged, the gesture conveying: *well, what can I do about it?* Then we shook hands once more, and a little later, when the changing of the riot police guard took place and I happened to be passing on a circuit of the neighbourhood, he waved at me cheerfully as his column marched by with their riot shields at the end of their shift.

Soaking up the "anarchist" atmosphere, I drank a beer at a dimly lit bar, one of many round the square. Dance music with a thudding beat and a chanteuse wailing melodically played softly. The tables were scuffed. The walls were scuffed. Ceiling lamps hung from thick pieces of rope and beer crates were stacked by a narrow bar that was more like a kiosk. Someone had written "ANTIFA" above where I sat, referring to the anti-fascist group Danny and I had seen mentioned back in Bratislava, although on this version the last "A" was in the shape of the international anarchist symbol. The graffiti was next to a charming framed black-and-white photograph that must have been from the early twentieth century showing an elderly man and a woman dancing with their arms outstretched in an old bar (possibly the same bar). Beneath this someone had written in pale ink: "LOVE IS THE DRUG".

Taking a wander about the bar, I peered at fly posters pasted to the walls by groups with names such as RefuseFascism.org and Revcom. us. Then I returned to my seat and my beer, and began to notice that a dishevelled man with a bushy beard was observing me between puffs of a roll-up cigarette from a nearby table. He was about my age and he made no disguise of his stare. This seemed to ask *who are you?* while also affirming *I have spotted you.* He held his gaze, visibly assessing me and not caring whether I knew he was. Was I some sort of undercover officer? Why was I in this bar? He was not aggressive (well, perhaps a bit, *passive-aggressive*), but he was disconcerting. Then again, I did not really care: *let him think what he thinks.*

I had with me *Nausea* by Jean Paul-Sartre, the same book Roxanne had been reading on the train from Sofia to Istanbul. I'd picked up a copy in Thessaloniki out of curiosity even though it added to the weight of the backpack (which seemed about to explode). Ignoring the dishevelled man, I opened the pages, soon losing myself in the story of the protagonist, a young writer named Antoine Roquentin who is in throes of confusion about the direction of his life while on a trip in "Indo-China". He realizes one day that he needs to make big changes. So he decides there and then to leave Indo-China and return to France as he senses an "upheaval" coming in his existence that scares him. Would he wake up "in a few months, a few years, exhausted, disappointed, in the midst of fresh ruins?" Roquentin is not sure although he would "like to understand [himself] properly before it is too late".

Wouldn't we all? Anyway, reading Sartre and ignoring the bushy-bearded man seemed enough for him to accept my presence: I was clearly just another nutcase.

I went to dine at a hipster-ish restaurant further up Strefi Hill.

This hipster-ish restaurant appeared suited to better-heeled anarchists, judging by the prices.

It was not far from the hotel and on entry I was chastised by a hipster-ish head waiter for not having made a reservation – better-heeled anarchists apparently made reservations – although, after a split second's hesitation, he said a table was available "but you must be quick". I sat at this table, close to the clatter of the kitchen in an open space with potted plants, and proceeded to wait an exceedingly long time for a large, overcooked pork chop with couscous to arrive. I ate what I could of the chop and asked for the bill. An exceedingly long time later this bill arrived.

It was delivered by the hipster-ish head waiter who asked: "Is there a problem, sir?"

He could tell I did not think much of the place.

"I would like to pay the bill, please," I replied. I had asked two other waiters before it came.

"Oh, I thought there was a *problem*, sir," he replied.

I was not sure I particularly liked this hipster-ish head waiter.

"Oh no, of course not. What a wonderful restaurant," I replied.

The hipster-ish head waiter looked at me for a moment.

Then he slowly held forward a card machine – all major credit cards accepted by well-heeled anarchists – took my card payment, spun on his heels and wordlessly departed.

I walked up to the hotel.

As I did, it occurred to me that the nicest person I had met all evening had been Aristotle, the riot policeman. It had been a strange evening in Athens.

"There are no trains to Patras"
Athens to Patras

Train travel can take you to places that you might not otherwise visit. Exarcheia was near the station, so I stayed in Exarcheia, which I had been curious about seeing anyway. Good fortune also had it that the National Archaeological Museum was on route. Wonderful: a chance to take a dip into the rich culture of a country and a city known as the "cradle of democracy" (at a time when democracy around the globe was being stretched to the limit). All that said, I was on a long train journey, so it was time to take another train. The many other undoubted pleasures of Athens could be enjoyed on another visit (and I had visited the wonderful Parthenon and Acropolis previously). The only problem with this plan was: *there were no trains to Patras.*

This was announced by the ticket attendant at Larissa station.

"There are no trains to Patras," she said.

"Why?" I asked.

"I wouldn't know," she replied. "Nobody tells me anything. After the crash, for one month the whole network went down. Across the country. It is not totally running now. I do not know why."

There was a replacement bus service, so I was able to take this instead. I reserved a free place (thank you Interrail pass). Then I sat on a plastic seat in the small, grimy concourse and waited for it.

After I did, a woman wearing a railway worker's uniform stepped by. She appeared to be a station supervisor of some description, so I inquired what had happened to the railway between Athens and Patras; it was nothing to do with the ill-fated Athens–Thessaloniki line after all.

This was her reply: "People have been stealing the copper on the electricity lines. They were able to do this when the trains were not running. Now repairs are happening. None of this is official, by the way."

It was not something that had yet been reported.

She continued: "Nobody knows when trains will run again, but they need to fix this. People need to go to work. Now they are spending so much time on buses. Because of the accident there were strikes and protests. Now the trains running to Thessaloniki, they go slower."

I asked her why Greek trains had slumped to such a low.

She said: "Why? Why!" Suddenly she was animated. "Most of the money is being pocketed by the people who run the railways: money for repairs, infrastructure. That's why! That's the reason for the archaic rail system. Payments are made to contractors and they pocket money and don't do the work."

She said lack of work on infrastructure, especially safety systems, made accidents more likely: "There's no communication between train drivers and stations if trains are not close to stations: two or three kilometres away, maybe five. Trains have to be close to stations. Nobody can say what is going on when the train is not close. Drivers often use cell phones to communicate with stations. But then they go through tunnels and have no coverage."

She shrugged. It was not the fault of the Italian train operator, she said, as it was the government that owned the railways on which they ran. She would not give her name and asked me not to describe her visually. She was not a station supervisor, she said, just "another worker here". Then she said: "OK, I'm off now."

And off she went.

I joined the rail replacement bus to Patras.

This was the 12:30 bus arriving at 3.30 p.m. My window seat was broken, permanently reclining, so I found another. The driver had a jolting way of braking. Advertising boards and petrol stations swooshed by and, unlike on a train, it felt as though the horizons had shrunk to the confines of the road.

It was an extremely uneventful ride.

The bus arrived at Patras at 3.10 p.m.

It stopped by a café by a harbour.

Down a noisy road with a string of gentlemen's clubs advertising "live acts" (Patras was, after all, a port), the excellent value El Greco Hotel, my abode for the night, was nestled between commercial premises of a more sedate nature in a tall, thin building. Maybe not quite up to the standards of the Pera Palace back in Istanbul: it was not much of a looker from the outside, or the inside, but I liked its pared-down (if a little worn-down) style that could not have changed much for a decade or two. The receptionist had red hair and a sing-song voice and said she did not know why it was called the El Greco Hotel, only offering: "I think it's because of the name." Which was not particularly enlightening. However, it seemed quite certain that the late-Renaissance painter El Greco, who was born in Crete and moved to Spain, had never stayed: a few centuries too early for that.

"Talk to the boss," she said. "The boss comes at seven."

But as she said this a man who appeared to be the boss arrived. He was early. He looked a bit like the actor James Gandolfini from *The Sopranos*: slick hair, gold chain, blue V-neck jumper, jeans.

To check, I asked him if he was the boss.

"Something like that," he said, and added: "Unfortunately."

I asked him about El Greco. "It's from the sixties," he replied. "Just a name. I bought this business with that name."

This established, I walked along the street with the nightclubs, mopeds buzzing by and goon-like security men guarding the entrances, and then up a pedestrianized road with cafés and clothing shops and quite a few youngsters around: Patras was the third largest city in Greece and had a university. The port had two main attractions, a Roman amphitheatre (closed for restoration) and the Cathedral of St Andrew (open), on the site where it is said St Andrew, one of Christ's 12 apostles, was martyred.

This castle of a cathedral was all cupolas, domes and golden crosses and dated from 1974. An older church, from the fifth century, was to one side where the apostle Andrew was crucified around 60 AD, supposedly on the orders of the then Roman emperor, Nero – another bloodthirsty emperor who also murdered his own mother and two wives. The emperor was, according to a pamphlet you are given at the cathedral, furious that the Roman consul in Patras, Lesvius, had been cured by Andrew of a seemingly incurable disease and converted to Christianity. Nero had instructed the city's vice-consul Aegeates to carry out the order.

Aegeates had a personal grudge with Andrew, who had also cured his wife Maximilla of a terrible disease. Aegeates had offered to pay Andrew for this act, but Andrew had refused saying that any payment would come from God. This holy steadfastness had annoyed Aegeates, especially as both his wife and his brother Stratocles went on to convert to Christianity. This was the final straw. He tortured Andrew with "great fury and brutality", according to the pamphlet, and had him crucified on an X-shaped cross. It is said that Andrew demanded such a cross as he believed that the traditional-shaped crucifixion cross was befitting only of Jesus so his must be different as he was unworthy of comparison (though this might be a legend). Whether true or not, the X-cross shape on the Scottish flag is a reference to the crucifixion of Andrew, the patron saint of Scotland.

Relics at the cathedral in Patras were said to include a part of St Andrew's skull that was once taken to Istanbul and only finally returned to the city in 1964 after being held at the Vatican in Rome for many years after its spell in Turkey.

This is the (very) general gist of the story of Andrew and Patras, as far as I could make out from the material provided in Patras.

Where facts and mythology met was not entirely clear, but to a certain extent it did not particularly matter as that was the story I was told.

There was not a huge amount to do in Patras, frankly, after seeing the glittery cathedral and the church.

"Patras is not really famous for its tourist stuff," admitted the waiter at the Paprika kebab shop, where I went for an early evening meal. "People come here to go somewhere else."

A middle-aged woman drinking an ouzo at a neighbouring table, upon hearing us, agreed. "It is true," she said. "Sure, we have Andrew. But he is not Peter. He is not Paul." Her implication seemed to be that a more famous dead disciple of Jesus might draw a few more tourists. "It is true," she repeated, sounding as though she was defeated by the simple logic of this truth. "People just pass through in Patras."

Yet outside the Paprika kebab shop (excellent kebabs), the city centre had suddenly become busy with locals.

This I soon discovered was because the football teams Panathinaikos and Olympiacos were playing. Groups of fans dressed in green or white-and-red stripes were gesticulating at televisions that had been rolled outside bars with extra seating added. I joined them for a while. Much yelling and groaning was going on in between short spells of silence during passages of play of such tension that onlookers were so utterly transfixed that the urge to yell and groan was temporarily forgotten.

Many of these bars were clustered near the El Greco and at half-time I returned to the hotel for an early night.

The boss was still in the reception.

"Der-bee," he said. "Eet ees local der-bee."

A local derby: Panathinaikos was based in Athens and Olympiacos in the Athens port of Piraeus. The score for any train-loving, football-loving fans: two–nil to Panathinaikos – glory to the greens!

On a ferry, Bari blues
Patras to Bari, Italy

A little bit of fast-forwarding here, as the move from Greece to Italy involved something of a lull in trains.

And also a quick bit of Interrailer background.

One of the benefits of Interrail passes was that over the years non-rail forms of transport including buses, cars (through rental firms) and ferries had either introduced discounts or free passage for pass holders. Around a dozen ferry companies including Hellenic Seaways, which was operating between Patras and Bari, had become involved. Elsewhere, you could also travel on ferries around the Greek islands, from Spain to Morocco, between Finland, Germany and Sweden, from Wales to Ireland, and across the Channel between mainland Europe and Britain. I was intending to catch a discounted Stena Line ferry from the Hook of Holland to Harwich in Essex on the way back. Other Interrail benefits included cheaper rates on hostels and meals at some restaurants (notably the popular Hard Rock Cafe chain). All were listed, handily, under the Eurail app's "Benefits" section.

* * *

The Hellenic Seaways ferry journey to Italy covered about 15 hours.

It left in the afternoon beneath a vapoury sky with mountains rising all around a bay that you do not necessarily appreciate when in the centre of Greece's third biggest city. It was due to arrive at 9.00 a.m. in Bari. The ship was called the *Ariadne*, named after the daughter of the legendary King Minos of Crete, with a capacity of 1,845. On my journey it was almost empty aside from a handful of backpackers and a few truckers.

The *Ariadne* was nothing particularly special: a modern ferry with slot machines, a duty-free shop, bars and restaurants. On board you found a reclining seat and settled there, worrying a bit about leaving your bag, even if it was valuables-free, to look around the ferry.

I made one friend on board, a 21-year-old German backpacker named Jannick, a recent graduate in psychology from the University of Nuremberg. He had been all over Europe, mainly camping or else staying in hostels in bigger cities. He had arrived at Patras from Crete the previous day and his Interrail journey had taken him from Nuremberg to Zurich, Bern, Lausanne, Lake Como, Milan, Venice, Budapest, Ljubljana, Zagreb, Split, Montenegro (where he had had to hitchhike due to lack of public transport), Belgrade, Sofia, Istanbul, back to Sofia, Thessaloniki, Athens, Piraeus and Crete, via other Greek islands.

Jannick had been going for two months and was a vegetarian, living quite often on "tortillas and Nutella". He was lean and athletic (he played in central defence for a football team) and had long blond hair and a sandy beard. When strolling about the ferry he would either wear his baseball cap forwards or backwards, seemingly dependent on his state of contemplation: forwards being generally more withdrawn, as though hiding beneath the rim, and backwards less so.

Jannick had an admirable approach to Interrailing and was almost a walking advert for the younger "finding themselves" crowd.

"I hadn't seen much of Europe. I wanted to make up for that," he said. "Interrail is a good way to get a first impression of countries and big cities so I said: 'Yeah, I got some free time. I will go do Interrail.' If a city is too expensive at its hostels, I just take a train into the suburbs, go camping, then come back to the centre in the morning." This could, he admitted, be "a little tiring".

His approach was to be "spontaneous", following travel leads he picked up from others: "If I meet some people and they say *let's go there*, then I might go there with them." His worst experience of the trip had been a "shitty" bus from Istanbul to Athens. His best experience had been joining a volleyball camp in Crete. He did not like German trains, which were "never on time, everybody makes jokes about them". He was annoyed with the ferry's security people as they had confiscated his gas canister for cooking food. And he said that on return from his Interrailing trip he would train to be a professional psychologist, which would take eight to ten years. Regarding his chosen career, he continued, his preference was for cognitive behavioural therapy: "CBT, not Freud…" He discussed the two for a while in an erudite and carefully considered manner.

Afterwards, I drank a red wine on the aft deck and let thoughts drift along like the good ferry *Ariadne* through the jet-black night. A couple of truckers were (sensibly, given their jobs) drinking tea at a nearby table, not saying much, and I joined their "silence", trying to remember how I had been when I was aged 21. Not as self-assured and "spontaneous" as Jannick perhaps (I never did go Interrailing back then). Not as well organized nor as forward-thinking, either: I had known I wanted to be a journalist and write, but shift rates at my starting jobs at the *Coventry Evening Telegraph* and the *Cambridge Evening News* were not exactly conducive to grand future plans. What would it be like to be 21 again: full of beans and purpose?

Impossible to answer really but nice to consider for a while over a couple of small bottles of Greek red wine (OK, I had three) on a little "solo session" on the sea.

Sleep was fitful in the reclining seats – perhaps due to this impromptu red-wine-fest (which ought to have helped really) – and I woke in the morning wearing my scarf and jacket for warmth with a t-shirt wrapped around my head to keep out the cabin lights, wondering in quick succession where I was and then, after establishing that, where the ferry was. The answer was: Bari.

To be absolutely honest I did not much like Bari.

This is probably because I got off on the wrong foot in the capital of Italy's Puglia region, once an important Byzantine port, and it took a while to get on the right one.

Or maybe it was just because I was tired from the ferry, a touch hung-over and generally a bit out of sorts.

On arrival I discovered my phone would no longer log into my mobile network. I had overused my "data limit", something I had never previously achieved, even though I had no idea how I had managed this feat.

I needed – or, more accurately, felt I needed – the map on the phone to find my way out of the docks to Bari train station. Having cleared immigration I walked along a dusty road, attempted to join what I believed was a shuttle bus to the centre and was told "this bus private", and continued further along the dusty road, took a wrong turn, then a right turn, heading towards what looked like the centre of town and coming to a small square by a large twelfth-century church and hooking into the Wi-Fi at a café next to kids kicking a ball against the church wall. After a while, I established where the train station and my apartment for the night were, looked in the gaunt, cavernous interior of what turned out to be the "cathedral church of San Sabino" (said Tripadvisor), and located a long, squat salmon-pink building beyond a boring pedestrianized street and a park patrolled by officiously alert policemen on the lookout for something, mainly trying to stop kids wheeling by on electric scooters, it seemed.

The salmon-pink building was Bari station and to enter required running the gauntlet of a zebra crossing at a busy junction that the drivers of Bari seemed not to notice in the slightest. Inside was a long queue for tickets, where a group of teenage lads, smirking quite indulgently, pushed by me as I hesitated at the front of the queue as I was unsure if a kiosk was free. Eventually, at a kiosk, I was told by an attendant that the only train to Naples with seats was at 4.05 p.m. the next day. This seemed both very late and extremely unlikely as Eurail suggested a few earlier services: could they all really be full? I took a step back from the kiosk to look at the Eurail app. Some more smirking teenagers, noticing my hesitancy and sensing weakness, pushed by once again, taking my kiosk. I waited for them and muttered at them as they pushed back past me, asking whether they were "VIPs" as they did so. They understood this and one of them replied in Italian and English: "*Sì*. Yes VIPs!" They went on their way smirking and laughing, too. Then I went back to the kiosk and was surprised to find a new attendant had taken the place of the previous one, who seemed to be on a break. The new attendant said there was a place on the 06:10 train to Naples the next day via Caserta, arriving at 9.48 a.m. Why had the previous attendant said the only train was at 4.05 p.m.?

"This I do not know," she said. "Maybe she not notice."

I reserved a ticket and ventured out into the glaring sunshine of Bari. I ate an expensive and not very good pasta dish at a restaurant by the square. I went down a street with a lot of fashion shops, where women and men walked by in tight-fitting clothes and I felt by comparison like a tramp with my bulging backpack and crumpled clothes I had slept in overnight on the ferry. Men wore shoes with shiny gold buckles, Ray-Bans, white trousers and pastel-coloured shirts with buttons undone almost to their navels. Women preferred tight tan leather trousers, sailor's jackets, Ray-Bans and silk blouses – or, at least, quite a few of them. These appeared to be the fashion trends of Bari.

Just about everyone was debonair. They were cool. They were blasé. I heaved around my backpack waiting for the 3 p.m. apartment check-in, not feeling especially debonair, cool and blasé. I visited the church of San Nicola, another twelfth-century affair, built to house the relics of St Nicolas. These were found in a crypt beneath a silver altar to the saint. In front of the altar, people had tossed a few coins, crumpled five-euro notes and folded pieces of paper, presumably with prayers and wish lists of hopes and dreams. A fair bit of barging was going on to get to the front of the effigy, beneath which St Peter's relics were supposedly stored, a bit like back at the station.

Then I continued my tour of the city of Bari by entering an old castle with a museum with a collection of old pots and vases that could not quite compete with the National Archaeological Museum in Athens along with a multi-media exhibition about ancient days set to ponderous, depressing music. I did not spend long in the castle. Outside, a man walking by clutching four bags full of recently purchased grocery shopping asked me for two euros and I looked at his bags pointedly and asked why he needed two euros if he could afford all that shopping – gesticulating to convey this message as he had no English other than *two euros* as far as I could tell.

He looked at me and rattled off something in Italian and shuffled onwards. From his suddenly bulging eyeballs, pulsating veins on his forehead and somewhat forceful nature of the delivery of these words I was guessing his brief tirade was not complimentary.

Further on, past an English language school called Lord Byron College with Union Jacks plastered on the outside, an elderly woman turned to me and cackled and formed a crooked finger symbol that she pointed at me and leered. This was somewhat off-putting (I later established that this gesture probably meant *give me something*). She too did not seem especially pleased with me, as I had not given her anything, muttering what I took to be an unsatisfactory character assessment and hobbling away.

I walked down a street, Strada Arco Basso, where women were said to make pasta twisted into ear-shapes that were apparently famous in Bari. However, most of the stalls in this tiny, cobbled street, little more than an alley, were unoccupied next to houses with flimsy drawn curtains. The owners of the stalls, where the saffron-yellow, purple, green and regular pasta-coloured wares were spread on trays on simple tables, were behind the curtains and could see you but you could not see them. The few stallholders outside were carefully positioning their ear-shaped pastas into more presentable and temptingly buyable positions and ignoring those walking down the lane as though this business of positioning the pasta was a serious matter and they must not be distracted. I considered buying some ear-shaped pasta in case my apartment room had a kitchen, but I checked online and it appeared not to so I did not bother.

Instead, I walked for a very long time attempting to locate a grocery shop for a simple salad and sandwich dinner before the early train for Naples. It was noticeable that Bari's centre had hardly any grocery shops and I ended up returning to Bari station to a small SPAR supermarket I had noticed earlier and where the manager on the till said, on discovering my nationality, that he was going on holiday to Camden in three days' time. I said to him that not many people go on holiday in Camden. He ignored this and asked me what to do in Camden. I suggested visiting the market and he seemed excited by the idea of Camden Market and even said: "Thanks, man!"

So concluded my most in-depth interaction with a fellow human being in Bari.

I located my duplex apartment, having punched in a code for entry (there was no receptionist), ate my salad and sandwich dinner at a circular table in a gloomy room and read some more of Jean-Paul Sartre.

The protagonist, the young writer Roquentin, was in the midst of an existential crisis: "For the first time it disturbs me to be alone. I should like to talk to somebody about what is happening to me before it is too late." He has found himself in such a state that when he discovers a piece of paper on the ground that he would like to inspect, he cannot bring himself to pick it up. He then spends several pages of his diary assessing why he could not do so. In order to exist, Roquentin observes later in his favourite café, sometimes you may need to join others or else you may find yourself unable to act.

After one day in Bari, I seemed to have slumped to a similar condition, reduced to an existential crisis of my own, at least with the master of existentialism to keep me company and maintain spirits – plus the enticing prospect of some lovely trains in the Swiss Alps just a couple of days away.

I cannot pretend otherwise, as I said earlier: I was not overly fond of Bari.

Sunrise spontaneity
Bari to Naples

Loads of seats were available on the 06:10 to Caserta, due to arrive at 8.54 a.m., followed by a connection on the 09:07 to Napoli Centrale station, arriving at 9.48 a.m. Masses of them. Row upon row. What the first ticket assistant had been on about at Bari station, I did not know. Maybe a lot of people had not turned up, but surely not more than half a train's worth.

The carriages of the 06:10 were silver and red with streaks of white and green and "FRECCIARGENTO" written on the side. This translated as "SILVER ARROW". It was not a slow train. It was a high-speed train. It was also simply *a train*. After the hitchhiking, the rail replacement bus and ferry since the Bulgarian border I wanted to keep it that way until the Hook of Holland.

Over the speaker system a message in an extremely upper-class English female voice said: "Those not intending to travel, please get off now."

It sounded as though whoever had been hired for the voice-over was having a bit of fun by being as posh as possible and then abruptly finishing the message. Not: *please leave the train now* or *please disembark from the train now. Please get off now* had a knowing, tongue-in-cheek, posh-yet-coarse feel to it.

The train departed at precisely 6.10 p.m., passing a mural of a figure holding aloft a pride flag. Then, after about a minute, another amusingly extravagant upper-class announcement was made: "If you would like to file a complaint…" This was followed by an email address given in the tones of a lady of the manor. Might as well get that one out of the way, I supposed, although 60 seconds in did feel just a little early. How on earth the voice-over person had been chosen you could not help but wonder. Whomever it was ought to be snapped up as one of Bertie Wooster's aunts for the next audio version of P. G. Wodehouse.

The Frecciargento paced beyond the suburbs, humming into olive groves framed by a ruby-tinted sky. It was a gorgeous morning. But it did not last long. The sun lifted in the east and a tangerine blaze bathed the countryside and the carriage. It had become an even more gorgeous morning. Gazing out of the window as golden-orange olive trees scudded by seemed a very good way to begin a day.

Stops were made at Barletta and Foggia, where quite a few people boarded though many seats remained empty. The train moved into rolling hills and followed a rocky river and series of tunnels. I bought a good-value coffee from the dining car. This seemed to be mainly the preserve of the conductors, of whom there appeared to be quite a few. They were deep in an animated conversation and looked well settled though they were yet to have checked tickets. I returned to my seat. The train tilted onwards through a lush landscape of vineyards. The horn hooted as though saying *hello* to a farmer ploughing a field. Then the train slowed as houses appeared, before stopping at Caserta station in Italy's Campania region. The posh English female voice said: "Thank you for travelling Trenitalia, we will be glad to see you again on board our trains."

It was as though we would all be coming back for another dinner party soon.

As it happened another Trenitalia was a few moments away: the connection to Naples. As I tried to work out the platform for this train, asking one of the station staff, an American woman joined me. She had the same question. We ascertained where to go and walked together to the platform, waiting there a few minutes for the 09:07 to Naples.

This was how I met Keli. She had blonde hair, a deep tan, electric-blue eyes and an infectious, scattergun style of speaking. She was a very enthusiastic person. She was from Washington State and was on a day trip to see Pompeii, having rented an apartment in Puglia outside Bari after letting out her place in Washington State (she also had a home in Idaho) to raise money for a six-month adventure in Italy.

"My rent is my travel budget!" she declared.

She had two children about to graduate from college, was divorced and was in her fifties. I learned all this in about 30 seconds flat.

I said I had been thinking of going to Pompeii.

"Let's go together!" she replied, quick as a shot.

My existential Jean-Paul Sartre phase had come to an abrupt end.

We started looking up how to reach Pompeii from Naples on the internet. It seemed easy, just catch a Circumvesuviana train along the coast to the site of the unlucky Roman town devastated by Mount Vesuvius back in 79 AD. Within the next 30 seconds or so it was all agreed. Just as with Jannick's approach to Interrailing that he had described back on the ferry, spontaneity was taking over. We were off to Pompeii.

CHAPTER EIGHT

NAPLES TO VISP IN SWITZERLAND, VIA MILAN, TIRANO, CHUR AND ZERMATT

INTO THE ALPS

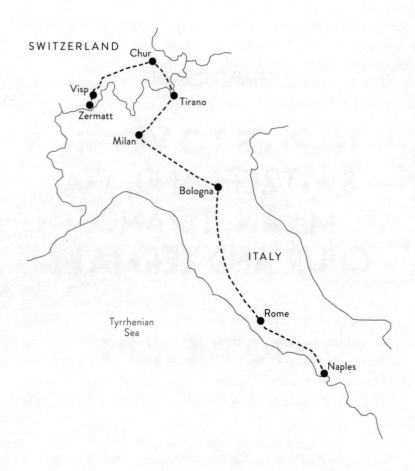

On the 09:07 from Caserta to Napoli Centrale, Keli told me (some of) her life story.

This was relayed in fragments. I did not probe. Her tales seemed to roll out like the scenery by the tracks, which comprised in these parts suburbs followed by farmsteads, then lazy rivers, undulating hills, OTT mansions that looked as though they belonged to old-fashioned landed gentry (or perhaps some other types of extremely well-off southern Italians given to ostentation), vineyards, and long, wide fields with long, thin crops.

Keli, I rapidly discovered, had worked at a "wealth management company for a bank" before being made redundant and receiving a severance payment prior to the Covid pandemic. The worldwide lockdown had ruined her plans for a year's travel on a "mission trip" in Africa. Instead, she had waited until it was over and spent a month "working in a village in Kenya". She intended to go to South Africa later in the year for more of the same. Meanwhile, she was in Italy for six months, having resided in Florence before moving to the east coast and staying in the town of Polignano, south of Bari. Her long day trip to Pompeii would have her back in Polignano by around midnight.

"I do like the trains here," Keli said, catching a breath and looking out of the window.

She had been on lots of similar trips around Italy. "I take trains in the US, too, though one time it took twelve hours to get from Oakland to Los Angeles."

This was a distance of about 400 miles. The train had been badly delayed.

"That was on Amtrak. I took the kids on Amtrak. Once."

She emphasized the last word, even though her children had enjoyed themselves: "They loved it. It was an overnight train. They didn't mind."

"So you like trains?" I asked.

"Oh yes!" Keli said.

I seemed to have uncovered an American rail enthusiast – or as they are called over there, *foamers*, so named as they are said to foam at the mouth when they see a train they especially admire. Keli was not like that at all really, she just enjoyed train travel, not caring particularly what type of train she was travelling on. So she was no foamer, although she was keen to tell me about one of her favourite routes, San Diego to Los Angeles on the Pacific Surfliner service, which she especially liked because of its great ocean views running alongside beaches. She talked about this for a while.

Keli was in her conversational stride, blowing Bari's temporary existential spell well and truly out of the water. She had an American get-up-and-go attitude and was not a mooching Sartre type.

Keli had been a bond trader with her own business for 20 years. "Municipal bonds with a set period interest per year but you can sell out and get the value that year," she said, losing me somewhat. Then she had worked for someone else's company.

"I had to train clients to focus on business hours," she said. "Otherwise, they'd call you the whole time, at the weekend, in the evening. Usually they were respectful."

She had worked at her last job for two years until the one-year severance pay came up. "I didn't even know I had the right to that." She had no idea she was about to be let go either. "Welcome to banking!" she said. "The job I had was *eliminated* soon after it had been created. That was the word they used: *eliminated.*"

The result was that "I was eliminated, too", but this had turned out to be a blessing in disguise as it meant she could go globetrotting on the proceeds of her rented place and nip about on trains here and there if she got the opportunity. She told me at some length about claiming for benefits in the United States and a complicated "same day back" system that meant you had to file tax documents impossibly quickly if you happened to be gallivanting around the globe saving Kenyan villages and taking trains to Pompeii. This clearly rankled.

Then she told me a story about travelling with a friend of hers who worked as an undercover hotel reviewer for a major international magazine. Keli had tagged along for a recent jaunt from Istanbul to Malta, Budapest and Paris, staying free with her journalist companion. The only problem was that in Budapest her friend had mistakenly sent a text to the concierge blowing her cover: "She was devastated. She was like: *Oh my god, this has never happened in thirty years, I'm so embarrassed.*" Service had, naturally, improved after her presence became known: from then on they had been treated like royalty.

On that trip Keli had experienced a fleeting romance in Budapest. She and her friend had been driving when "we had a fender bender [bumping into another vehicle]. There was this guy watching on a corner with his sister – at least that's what I thought she was at the time – and he helped out and was really nice and my friend said: 'Oh my god there are serious vibes between you two. I mean *serious* vibes.' He gave me his number. There *were* serious vibes. My friend was right." Keli and the man went on a series of successful dates. "But he was saying to me: 'I kind of have a girlfriend, we have been together, but we are splitting.'" Keli had not been quite sure what to make of this. "He was younger than me. He installed vape machines in Budapest. That was his job. Anyway, it turned out that he was still with his girlfriend, and I think he might also have been bisexual, too. He had a friend, a young guy in his twenties. The young guy was often around." Keli did not seem particularly bothered that this holiday encounter had led to nothing and was quite happy to tell me all about it.

"Civilization… it is going in reverse"
Naples to Pompeii and back

The train pulled into Napoli Centrale. We exited into a hubbub of manic movement, attempting to locate the platform for Pompeii.

This we managed and squashed into yet another graffiti-daubed train; an epidemic of graffiti/street art appeared to have taken hold in Europe in ways unimaginable in the UK (maybe British street gangs could no longer afford the paint). It was too awkward to talk, and it seemed prudent to keep an eye out for pickpockets. Mount Vesuvius materialized through a heat haze to the left, the top lopped off by cloud giving the mountain the look of a long, sleek submarine. We passed a harbour on the right, where men by a quay were folding fishing nets.

On disembarking at Pompeii station, you needed to catch a short bus to the entrance to the ancient volcano-struck civilization, where we deposited our backpacks at the left-luggage room. "Like everything it's the journey that matters!" said Keli in a fit of even more enthusiasm than usual at having finally made it to Pompeii after departing from Polignano in the early hours of the morning, and seemingly pleased at all the transport hoops through which we had been jumping, the final unexpected bus included. "Oh yes! The journey!"

In this euphoric mood, through a turnstile we joined a sunbaked path comprising rough-cut stones and entered the eerie labyrinth of Pompeii. We were amid a steady stream of tourists who were squinting at the old walls and chambers, snapping madly away as though frightened to miss anything. Some of the ancient houses we were passing were decorated with exquisite mosaics with swirling geometric patterns. Faded murals of wolves, gods, satyrs and nymphs added further decoration, ghostly images that seemed to have seeped out of the stonework rather than been painted on one day a very long time ago by someone employed to jolly up the interior design.

We were clearly in a "fancy" neighbourhood of the ill-fated city. A tourist guide we overheard nearby said: "This bit was like the Beverly Hills of Pompeii… heaven in what became hell."

Hell when the eruption in 79 AD wiped out the walled town of 16,000 people.

"This guy, the guy who lived here," the guide pointed at a particularly large section of ruins, "he was one of the lucky few guys of Pompeii living in an air-conditioned home."

A ventilation system had been devised to make the most of the breezes on its hilltop location.

Birdsong trilled. Lizards basked on old stones. We entered a wide area where another guide was saying: "This entire floor was marble." We were either in the Basilica or perhaps the Sanctuary of Apollo, somewhere close to the Forum. It was all a bit confusing. After seeing a thermal spa where yet another guide was saying "in this room, no water, only hot air" (a very early sauna) we traipsed along a narrow lane to a courtyard where a few figures "frozen" in pumice and ash were in protective glass cabinets: one lying defeated on his side, another sitting hunched over, holding a cloth to his face. It was a grim spectacle.

For a while Keli was silent, then at the amphitheatre, where a sign told us that the pop-rock band Pink Floyd had once played at the setting, she turned philosophical.

"Civilization," she said. "It is going in reverse."

She paused, looking up at the old, crumbling seats. Then she expanded on her decline-of-civilization theme: "There is a story someone told me recently about a fisherman and an industrialist. The industrialist says to the fisherman: 'Why do you stop fishing at the end of the day? If you keep working, you will be rich with more fish to sell and then you will be able to enjoy your lifestyle.' The fisherman looks at the industrialist and then says quietly: 'I'm enjoying it now, thanks.' This is how I feel things should be. For me and for my kids, to be like that fisherman. Now I am like a small business." Keli was referring to renting out her apartment. "I have enough. Enough!" She paused again as though considering that word. "Seventy-five thousand dollars is the perfect amount. The perfect income. You have enough! I worry about my kids. There's so much stress to get a job and then when you save and get a property you have to maintain it." Society, she said, kept pushing people to want more, but was that what people really wanted? The urge for more was "driving us all mad". She looked about the ancient city and repeated: "Enough! Enough!"

Pompeii had cast a spell. Better to live simple lives and be content with less like the people of Pompeii, Keli seemed to be saying – even though, with all the political intrigue, bloody amphitheatre goings-on, slavery, and haves and have-nothings, matters were not always exactly idyllic back then. That did not seem to matter, the setting had affected her in some way that was hard to pinpoint.

We wandered back to the entrance via a small museum with a naked statue of Priapus dating from the early first century AD. Priapus was the Greek god of "male proactive power" and a sign said the statue was a "symbol of prosperity". Keli looked at Priapus' (what might politely be described as) enormous awoken phallus.

"Prosperity?" she said. "I should say so: someone's prosperity."

She was still looking at the enormous awoken phallus.

"They never make it in proportion in these statues," she commented drily.

Then we returned to left-luggage, collected our bags and took the Circumvesuviana train from a closer station across from the entrance to Pompeii, called rather extravagantly Pompei Scavi Villa Dei Misteri station – the previous train had not in fact been on the Circumvesuviana line, it had been a different Trenitalia service – and walked through narrow rubbish-strewn streets with banners hanging from lamp posts in honour of Napoli football club to the pleasingly chaotic heart of Naples. There, we sat at a corner table at a little bar and drank white wine and talked about this and that for a while.

Keli had been a big fan of "grunge" music, in particular Nirvana, when she was younger. She discussed how wonderful Kurt Cobain had been, the lead singer who took his own life aged 27. Then she told me a story about when she had been in Florence a couple of months ago: "I had this beautiful Prada bag – one that was simply impossible to replace."

She pulled a face as though saying: *ah that bag, I will never forget that bag.* "It had my purse and a Chanel lipstick inside. It was taken from me. One minute it was there, the next gone. I was very upset. I was with a friend and we reported it to the police."

Keli received a call a few days later. "They had caught them. We had seen the people we thought took the purse at the café – a man and a woman – we were asked to go to the station and identify them on a computer. It was a Peruvian crime ring. About ten people were involved. The police said they'd try and catch them all and they would be banned from Tuscany and of course serve the sentence for their crime. They had records. This time they would get tougher sentences."

Keli looked at her watch and said: "Oh no!"

She had to go back to the station. After exchanging emails, we parted ways, Keli clutching her current bag, and I sat in the corner bar drinking another glass of white wine. Not much was going on. A smell of marijuana floated in from the street. A pair of female cops with guns in white holsters came in and ordered coffee, leaning against the counter and talking to the barista. Their hair hung loose and they wore shades and lipstick. Napoli football club blue-and-white bunting fluttered in a chaotic mesh above the crossroads of alleys outside the bar. Pictures of Diego Maradona, the late Argentine footballer who once played for Napoli, hung from banners (pictures of this local idol were everywhere, shops sold Maradona posters and scarves and, even, socks and underwear).

Mopeds revved by. Down an adjacent lane, I paid for an odd underground tour of the cisterns of Naples, where I learned that there were a lot of underground cisterns in the city and that they were once very important but were now disused, though for a while a gang of thieves had operated underground, shimmying up through the waterways to rob houses.

The tour came with a voucher for a pizza at the nearby Don Raffaele pizzeria. There, I ate an excellent pepperoni-and-chilli pizza served by a fierce waiter who did not seem particularly pleased by the cistern tour diners with their pizza vouchers from the tour (even though the pizzeria was presumably paid). I tipped him and thanked him profusely, just to see his reaction, and he stopped scowling and grinned a toothy grin and rattled off something in Italian that I took to be: *Thanks, but now get outta here.*

I did so and went back to the corner bar where I ordered a red wine and watched as Napoli lost to AC Milan one–nil. If the people of Patras had taken their football seriously, this was nothing by comparison to the Neapolitans, who crowded round, every seat taken inside and on the street. There were yells. There were screams. There were roars of indignation. Someone let off a blue flare outside and blue smoke filled the bar. The manageress, a young woman with tattoos and multiple gold loop earrings, just laughed. Everyone had tears in their eyes and was spluttering from the blue smoke but the manageress, who ran her team of waiters and waitresses with an iron rod, regularly yelling at them to *hurry up for Christ's sake* in Italian (or words to that effect judging by the impact they had), seemed almost overwhelmed with joy.

This did not last long. Silence reigned when Milan scored. There were angry gesticulations about a refereeing decision connected to this goal. Moped fumes wafted in. A Napoli player was sent off. The bar went bonkers with indignation, even the manageress with multiple gold earrings began yelling at the television, saying something along the lines of: *And now humanity has come to this, I swear to the dear lord who rules us all that this is an abomination that needs to be settled one day from high above, oh referee, oh humanity, what an abomination, what a scandal!*

I returned down a rubbish-scattered lane to my tiny apartment and clicked on the Eurail app for next morning's 11:30, via Milan, to Tirano, on Italy's border with Switzerland.

Italy was due to have a train strike in two days' time. I had had no idea of this before earlier in the day. I had intended to stop somewhere in the middle of the long, thin country on the way to Switzerland, but this was simply not to be. Italy was not quite panning out how I had expected. The Italian trade unionist train gods were scuppering plans, just like their counterparts back in Germany (and almost in France).

The only solution seemed to be: *Uscite velocemente dall'Italia* (get out of Italy fast).

Up Italy
Naples to Tirano, via Milan

At Napoli Centrale you may find yourself fighting through the hubbub of Italian train travellers to reach the Italo train ticket office, whereupon smartly dressed Italo ticket staff will tell you politely but sternly to go to the Trenitalia ticket office across the way, to which you will retrace your steps through the hubbub to find the Trenitalia ticket office, where you will take a ticket for a counter "appointment" and wait for your number to be called and then be informed politely but sternly by smartly dressed Trenitalia staff to go to the "last-minute ticket booth", located in the middle of the hubbub, where another ticket official, looking a bit harassed and exasperated as all the other ticket officials seemed to direct everyone to her, will inform you in no uncertain manner that reserving a first-class seat is absolutely out of the question with a second-class Interrail pass (I had fancied first class even though I knew this rule) and issue you with a second-class seat reservation.

Then, after a slice of pizza for breakfast-brunch from a pleasant food hall in a corner, you may saunter over to a shiny, gently purring red-and-grey bullet-nosed train and find your smart grey leather seat with a wide table and plenty of electricity plugs in second class, feeling a little hung-over once again if you spent the best part of the previous evening in a bar full of Napoli football club fans drinking red wine and vociferously berating referees to fit in with the locals just in case you were taken for a Milanese interloper.

Like the Frecciargento train from Bari to Caserta, the 11:30 to Milan was clearly no slow train. It was an even faster Frecciarossa ("Red Arrow") train capable of 250 mph. Frecciargento trains could only manage a paltry 156 mph. But there seemed little other choice to avoid the train strikes, which I learned were due to Trenitalia staff signed up to the Filt-Cgil, FIT-CISL, Uiltrasporti, UGL Ferrovieri, FAST-Confsal and OR.S.A Ferrovie unions taking industrial action over staff shortages, low pay, unsatisfactory shift patterns and "the critical issue related to the right to a meal", according to the website Napolike.it – motto: "I like loving Naples". The Italian rail workers seemed to have a lot of unions.

The extreme-right-wing-leaning Italian prime minister Giorgia Meloni, the country's first female PM and leader of the Fratelli d'Italia party (Brothers of Italy), was dismissive of their demands, with her transport minister being rolled out to criticize passenger delays. It was not the first such strike. Train employees had already demonstrated and held marches chanting: "*Abbassate le armi, alzate i salari!*" (Down with arms, up with wages!) This had not worked so they were striking again.

Among some trade unionists, this was all part of a defence against recent right-wing internal policies in Italy that had seen tax cuts for profit-making corporations coming at the same time as a failure to support a previous government's Citizen's Income policy to protect those on lowest wages. The World Socialist Web Site, which reported on such matters, backed the train strikes and highlighted reports showing that 5 million Italians lived in absolute poverty, while 10 per cent of people in the south of Italy – where times were toughest – were on the breadline. The population of Italy was 59 million. "The only answer is a common struggle of the European working class against capitalism. To counter the attacks on jobs, wages and democratic rights, the international unity of the working class must be established on a socialist basis," said the WSWS, editorializing somewhat.

All of this was unlikely to go down particularly well with Fratelli d'Italia, which was soaring in the polls on the back of controversial rhetoric to raise fear of migrants, promote national sovereignty and favour "traditional families". Meloni had once pronounced: "Yes to natural families! No to LGBT lobbies!" She had a hard-edged, no-turning-back approach, the electoral support to back her up, and a political symbol for the party she had co-founded in 2012 that incorporated a flame symbol in the red, white and green colours of the Italian flag. This symbol could be traced back to the neo-fascist Italian Social Movement established by pro-Benito Mussolini admirers in the aftermath of World War Two.

In short, it was not a great time to be a socialist train trade unionist hoping for better pay and "critical" rights to meals. Perhaps that was what the group of staff had been huddled round discussing back in the dining car from Bari to Caserta.

As I have said previously, going on trains can open up all sorts of local issues.

Anyway, the train was soon speeding onwards.

Announcements that were not in posh English upper-class accents warned us (the passengers) to watch out for thieves. Suburbs flashed by. According to monitors, the train was scudding along at 185 mph. You could feel the velocity in your seat. Mountains to the right appeared. Mountains to the right disappeared. Olive groves appeared. Olive groves disappeared. As did villages clinging to rolling hills. As did woodlands and fields of rape seed. There were announcements not to leave valuable items unattended. There were more announcements not long after to "keep an eye on your luggage even on board the train". A display flashed up on a screen warning to "be aware of your surroundings while using the self-service ticket machines" at stations. An accompanying diagram showed a figure at a machine pressing buttons while not paying attention to a bag slung over their shoulder. All these messages were enough to make you a bit paranoid.

The Frecciarossa rolled into Roma Termini station, where it was delayed for a while, raising concern about the 16:20 connection from Milan to Tirano, due in at 6.52 p.m. Then the train moved off in the opposite direction, meaning I was facing forwards rather than backwards, as previously, which was an improvement.

Then it paced onwards past rows of cypress trees that looked like strokes on a watercolour painting beneath a mottled grey and blue sky. The elderly Italian couple opposite at my table since Naples closed their crossword puzzle books and had a snooze.

We arrived at Bologna Centrale station at 2.52 p.m., a minute earlier than scheduled – the Frecciarossa had made up good time. Yet good things, I had been reading online using the train's excellent Wi-Fi, had not always happened at Bologna Centrale. In fact, very awful things indeed had happened. Bologna Centrale was where 85 people were killed and more than two hundred injured in Italy's deadliest-ever terrorist attack in 1980. The attack was attributed to neo-fascist militants, many of whom were rounded up and some given life sentences.

Who was to blame remained a contentious political issue still, more than forty years on.

The train pulled away and began to accelerate onwards.

Flat, misty countryside with vineyards on fields lined by more cypress trees appeared. An occasional OTT country mansion popped up. The train hummed gently. Then it slowed into Milano Centrale.

We all got off. I bought a tuna focaccia from a kiosk in a large, airy concourse covered by a wide, curving roof made of steel and glass that dated from the days of Mussolini, who so famously is said to have made Italy's trains run on time (for all his other faults), although many seemingly correctly dispute this, saying trains had already been punctual before the fascist dictator rose to power in 1922. Milano Centrale in its current form was completed in 1931 with elements of Art Deco incorporated into the ostentatiously showy design. The previous station, dating from 1864, had been deemed too small after increased traffic had poured into Milan following the opening of the Simplon Tunnel in 1906; such a key breakthrough for the *Orient Express*, which had sometimes stopped by.

But it was not just wealthy travellers in plush mahogany- and teak-panelled compartments who had passed through.

During World War Two Milano Centrale had been used as a transit point for more than one thousand two hundred Jews sent to concentration camps. These transportations were conducted from a secret underground platform, number 21 (*Binario 21*), where a moving Holocaust memorial with a list of names of those deported was unveiled on the east side of the station in 2013.

Within one of the concourses not far away, however, is an extreme oddity that does not sit especially well with the memorial and the station's dark history: a mural made of tiles that depicts a young Mussolini surrounded by flocks of saluting supporters bearing flags greeting the king of Italy, who is depicted sitting grandly on an elegant white horse. Mussolini's eyes have been chipped away but it is nevertheless almost inexplicable that this former dictator, responsible for the deaths of about a million people, should remain on the station's walls. Would Germany allow such an image of Hitler to stay?

Yet again: where there are trains, there are (usually) stories.

* * *

The train to Tirano was in the green-and-grey livery of Trenord, a regional operator in Lombardy. It had a well-worn look with peeling paint and was packed; the only seat I could find faced backwards again at a table shared with an expressionless late middle-aged man wearing a knitted tie and a blazer who was watching a film on his smartphone that was held extremely close to his face (*please never let me end up like this*, I quietly said to myself).

The train crawled out of Milan and was soon edging along Lake Como. Lead-grey clouds clustered above the slate-grey water and mountains with pointy peaks rose on the far shore. Using the internet, I booked the 14:24 from Tirano to Chur in Switzerland for the next day on the legendary *Bernina Express*, paying a hefty-but-not-extortionate supplement (23 euros).

The wind must have picked up outside. Whitecaps had appeared on the surface of Como looking like strange white fish coming up for air. The Trenord twisted between folds of orange rock and layers of granite into a series of tunnels. Having negotiated these, higher mountains with snowy peaks arose. The first sight of these had a heart-lifting effect: there was something about seeing the mountains up close that roused your spirits.

The Trenord train trundled on, seeming to gain elevation. A baby cried somewhere down the carriage. The man with the knitted tie departed at a branch station, replaced by a twitchy middle-aged man wearing pink fingerless gloves clinging to an umbrella as though this umbrella was somehow key to his survival on planet Earth (*please never let me end up like this*, I said quietly to myself again).

Vineyards led to villages with churches. The mountains grew higher and closer still. At 6.52 p.m the Trenord arrived at Tirano. Most of the other passengers had long since gone. It was chilly. It was remote. The mountains loomed above Tirano station as though watching passengers disembark and keeping an eye on the new arrivals to their valley.

Straight away, it was wonderful being in the Alps.

"Excuse me, geek moment!"
Tirano to Chur, Switzerland

For a committed train lover – such as myself – arriving at Tirano from the south with the railways of Switzerland lying ahead somewhere up there in the crisp Alpine air, feels like Christmas Day and the culmination of a long pilgrimage all rolled into one.

It was an almost religious experience, train-wise: the holy of holies awaited along narrow-gauge lines winding between heady peaks from the little Italian border town (population 9,000).

The 90-mile journey ahead on the *Bernina Express* to Chur was quite simply legendary in rail enthusiast circles.

Train aficionados of the calibre of Mark Smith, founder of the untouchably authoritative website Seat61.com, waxed lyrical: "Fabulous… one of the most scenic train rides in the world, a personal favourite… you can ride it all year round, a completely different experience through Alpine snows in winter and through sunny green meadows in summer. So you should probably ride it more than once!" This was extremely high praise indeed. Smith, with his poker face and neatly trimmed goatee beard reminding you slightly of Hercules Poirot, was not given to gushing.

Another train guru, the travel writer Nicky Gardner, co-author with fellow guru Susanne Kries of a book so definitive about the nuts and bolts of Interrail trains it even includes the word in its title *Europe by Rail: The Definitive Guide*, said it was her pick of the rides on the Continent. She too was careful not to fall into purple prose in her sharp, vignette descriptions of Europe's railways, but her love of the journey shone through: "For the sheer drama of changing mountain landscapes, it's hard to beat. So many Alpine rail routes just don't quite live up to expectations. With the Bernina Railway you have pure theatre: my favourite European rail journey of that length."

Meanwhile, the rail historian Christian Wolmar simply said: "It is the most beautiful train ride ever."

A lot of praise (from lofty heights).

A few stats revealed something of the journey ahead: 55 tunnels, 196 bridges and a high point of 7,392 feet, making it the highest proper passenger railway in Europe. A cog railway existed at Jungfrau in Switzerland reaching 11,332 feet, but this covered a mere five miles. The *Bernina Express* line was in a class of its own, completed in 1910 as a key link between Switzerland and Italy, and operated by the Rhaetian Railway, which was not shy when it came to bragging about the various "helical tunnels" (spiral tunnels) and "stunning" viaducts including the "famous" Brusio Circular Viaduct. The railway's promotional material highlighted that the tracks rose at a gradient of as steep as 7 per cent, straining up a total of 5,905 feet in altitude. Since 2008, the line had been listed as a UNESCO World Heritage Site and was "a masterpiece of engineering… now regarded as one of the world's most outstanding and fascinating railway experiences".

A lot of hype. A lot of height.

Down a cobbled lane, ignoring the temptations of the cosy-looking Buffet Della Stazione, Albergo Meublé Stelvio was a few minutes away. I had booked a single room that a blurb had promised would be "enriched with simplicity and warmth". I entered a lime-green reception with a little 1970s-style bar (not trendily "retro", the real thing) and a bald man who appeared to be in charge, who was exchanging jokes and conversation with a couple of regulars.

The couple was sitting at a table drinking shots with accompanying glasses of beer. They alternated between being animated in a jovial, high-spirited, the-world's-a-good-place manner one minute, and volubly opinionated about various regretful matters concerning local and possibly world affairs the next. Great soliloquies were proffered, and shots and sips of beer taken. Many subjects appeared to be covered, though I could not understand a word. Perhaps they were discussing the next day's train strikes.

A bright-eyed receptionist was behind a counter on one side. She handed me a key and, when asked if many guests came by train, replied: "All of the people," before modifying that to: "Many of the people. Many train people. They come from Milan."

She pointed to timetables for both the railways to Milan and Chur, which were on a wall. A dreamy expression spread across her face. The receptionist herself appeared to be a train enthusiast.

I went to have a look around Tirano.

Walking about for a while you came to a succession of pizzerias and small bars, most empty. The highlights of the small Italian town could be summarized thus: the icy-blue channel of the river Adda, which burbled through the centre, eddying purposefully by boulders and looking extremely cold; the glittery gold sixteenth-century church of Madonna di Tirano with a "famous organ" dating from 1608 ("admire the famous organ" advised a church pamphlet); and of course the narrow-gauge railway track through the centre, past the church, across the main road and up into the mountains in the direction of St Moritz, the swanky Swiss ski resort.

Behind Albergo Meublé Stelvio was a crumbling little hexagonal-shaped chapel with peeling paint, a tiny altar with a single battery-powered candle and an overall neglected look. It was about the size of a town house, and I preferred it for some reason to the flashier church up the hill. I ate a final Italian pizza not far from this chapel at a place called Osteria dell'Angelo, and returned to the hotel where the bald man at the bar served me a shot of the local firewater.

Behind the bar was a strange old-fashioned whip hung on a rack near the spirit bottles. I asked the barman if this was for criminals in former times.

At this he turned to me and somewhat fiercely said: "It eese for clee-ants who do not pay!"

To demonstrate what might happen to such *clee-ants* he took down the whip and performed a slashing motion.

I paid the barman and went to bed in a room that lived up to its billing for being both simple and warm, if rather small. You could not fault the advert.

* * *

The shiny cherry-red 14:24 to Chur was already on the platform. Having arrived early for my second ever ride on the *Bernina Express*

– I had been once before in the opposite direction as described in my book *Ticket to Ride: Around the World on 49 Unusual Train Journeys* – I investigated Buffet Della Stazione. It seemed to have the makings of a good little station café and *good little station cafés* are to be treasured on long rail journeys around Europe, as I had already found in Nuremberg (where Danny and I had discovered one overlooking the central concourse after joining the strikers), Sofia (enjoyed by the Bulgarian transport police, too), and Sirkeci station in Istanbul (although that was fancier by far).

Buffet Della Stazione soon joined the list. Inside it seemed to be home to various local waifs and strays, plus the odd passenger. As with Albergo Meublé Stelvio, the buffet-café had a time-warped 1970s look.

I liked it very much and settled in a corner with a beer.

Not long after, a grizzled man with a florid face and shock of white hair entered and addressed the assembled customers – there were about seven of us – with a flamboyant flourish and a theatrical bow: "*Buongiorno a tutti!*" ("Good morning, everyone!").

It was the afternoon. Nevertheless, his welcome was well-received among the rosé-drinking locals. Rosé appeared to be the tipple of choice. My fellow café-goers included what looked like a mother with a twenty-something daughter furiously exchanging gossip in a *can you believe the sheer audacity of it* manner, a lonely figure with shaking hands smiling to himself while playing the "Mystic Fortune" fruit machine, and a man wearing a cowboy hat who might have passed for a poet and who was eating a sausage and drinking white wine, not rosé. We made a right bunch. I bought two small bottles of red wine for the journey ahead and placed them by my beer – to the approval of the assembled company, who appeared to deem this to be making a statement of some sort – then I watched on for a while as nothing much happened before passing along the empty platforms on the strike-struck tracks to Milan and strolling over to the correct platform for the *Bernina Express*.

What a lovely, shiny cherry-red train. No wonder so many pictures were being taken of it from the platform.

I found my carriage and entered, arriving at a tiny table with four seats.

One of these belonged to me. The other three to Nikki, Aiko and Aiko's father. Nikki was in her mid-forties and English, with swept-back blonde hair, a broad grin, a grey scarf, and glasses hanging round her neck connected to a wire. Aiko was in her early thirties and Japanese, with a short back bob, a broad grin and an orange hoodie. Aiko's father, also Japanese, was middle-aged, had neatly coiffed, spiky greying hair, a broad grin and glasses. They were all grinning broadly at me. They were all drinking red wine. I sat down, rapidly exchanging names and opening one of my little bottles of red wine. We immediately made a right bunch, too, judging by the glances of a middle-aged British couple across the aisle who appeared pleased, however, to be in the liveliest bit of the carriage. There was a generally exuberant, expectant atmosphere on board among the mainly middle-aged passengers. I seemed to have joined a middle-aged party train.

It was a delightfully clear sunny afternoon.

The 14:24 to Chur moved away between looming slopes.

Nikki was very excited. "Oh, oooo! Oh, wooo!" she said, followed by: "Oh, oooo! Oh, wooo! Oh, wooo! Oh, oooo! OOOO! OOOO! WOOO!"

She continued in this vein for some minutes, slipping down the aisle taking shots from various angles through the special "scenic windows" that curved up into the train's roof so you could view the landscape way above. Others in the packed carriage were doing the same. Aiko – but not Aiko's father, who maintained his cool – was doing the same. I was doing the same. We had all, save one or two, lost our heads. We scuttled about *oooo*-ing and *wooo*-ing. After passing the church, the train moved dramatically upwards with snowy mountains slipping into sight, the jagged ridges and granite cliffs looking timeless and perfect. We spiralled around the famous Brusio Circular Viaduct, rapidly gaining altitude. It was as though we were taking a train into the Swiss heavens.

We returned to our seats and drank some red wine.

"Gorgeous," said Nikki. "Just gorgeous."

She sipped some more red wine.

Aiko explained that going on the *Bernina Express* as a trio had come about after her father, on a visit from Japan, declared he wished to see Switzerland. She had arranged the tickets and flights to Milan and out of Zurich.

She was about to explain more about her interest in the *Bernina Express*, but before she could open her mouth Nikki jumped in.

"I'm a train geek," she said. "Oh yes! This has always been my dream [going on the *Bernina Express*]. Like the *Trans-Siberian Express*." She glanced out of the window towards vineyards clinging to the foothills of a snow-tipped mountain: "Here we go! Vineyards! Oh, wooo! Oh, oooo! Oh, wooo! WOOOO! OOOO!"

She paused, staring up and then said: "Excuse me: geek moment!"

She took more photographs.

Nikki and Aiko worked together at a place called the Mount Camphill Community, which had its HQ in East Sussex. Their jobs involved supporting and teaching people with learning difficulties. I never determined Aiko's father's name. There never seemed quite the right moment to ask with so much rail enthusiasm going on.

"It's not that she's always right, she's just never wrong," said Nikki, referring to Aiko's having stuck to her plan to take her father on the *Bernina Express*. She looked proudly at Aiko, who was a prodigy of hers at Mount Camphill Community.

Aiko, who saw this as an opportunity to say something, was about to do just that, even beginning to twitch open her mouth to utter a few words. But Nikki, after momentarily flagging, came bouncing back. "What is it about trains that is so attractive?" she mused rhetorically. "What is it?"

I was about to say something in reply, but Nikki was again too quick off the mark. "I once went on a steam train in Devon. It was… it was…" she said as though answering her own question and pausing extremely briefly to consider the right word: "It was *nice*."

Then she paused for a moment again, most uncharacteristically (even though I had known her so briefly, I sensed this was an untypical occurrence). It was as though she was digging deep into her thoughts on the matter and trying to straighten them out. "Trains are nice," she declared finally.

Trains were *nice*. That was it.

All those years I'd been struggling to work out what it was about them.

I had the answer on the 14:24 to Chur.

They were nice.

She was right, of course: they are nice. And thinking about it, that was about as good, and succinct a description of trains as anyone might need.

Aiko, who had begun reading a book entitled *The Travelling Cat Chronicles* by Hiro Arikawa, noticed a further hesitation in Nikki's dialogue.

"*I'm* not a train geek," she said quickly but firmly.

Nikki leapt straight back in, conversationally, as we passed a station little bigger than a bus stop while the scenery all around began to turn bright white. The train was high up, close to the pass at 7,392 feet (Tirano had been at 1,447 feet).

"Don't spoil my geekiness!" she said, turning to Aiko, who had reiterated that she was not a train geek. Nikki knew she was going off on one, playing up to her audience – all those in the carriage around her. But she simply could not seem to help herself. The *Bernina Express* had tipped her into a zone of train love that she found impossible to contain. "So much excitement! So much! Oh, wooo! Oh, oooo! WOOOO! OOOO!"

She was quiet for a while, pouring more red wine into their small plastic cups. A deadpan-but-authoritative commentary over a speaker began telling us about the formation of the mountains during the Ice Age before quipping that: "*You will see from your window that the train has almost become a plane here above two thousand metres...*"

"Holy crap, we really are going up," said Nikki.

"It is very pretty," said Aiko.

"It's amazing how far we've really gone up," said Nikki.

We were riding right between the peaks. It was pretty "fabulous" (Mark Smith), "dramatic" (Nicky Gardner) and "most beautiful" (Christian Wolmar). All the train gurus were quite right.

The conductor came by. She appeared amused by our end of the carriage.

The British man across the aisle asked the conductor if she ever found the journey boring. He and his partner had also been drinking red wine and *oooo*-ing and *wooo*-ing like the best of them.

The conductor shrugged and said: "Yes," somewhat dampening the growing euphoria.

Nothing was stopping Nikki, though. "Another corner! Look! Look at this corner!" At corners you could see the cherry-red carriages of the train curling ahead. "Look! Look! A tunnel! It's amazing! Just so flippin' gorgeous!"

The deadpan-but-authoritative commentary started saying: "*Before the age of mobile phones, the train driver could order a well-earned drink up ahead by blowing the horn...*" As the Bernina railway through the Swiss Alps was the youngest of the three railways from Switzerland into Italy, finished after the Simplon and Gotthard routes, and because it was narrow-gauge rather than the standard gauge of the likes of the *Orient Express*, it had always tended to be used by locals rather than long-distance travellers, we learnt.

Opening up, Aiko began telling me about *The Travelling Cat Chronicles*. "It's actually by a cat," she said, as in written from the perspective of a cat. "As well as by a human." As in also written from a human perspective. "So far it's a sad story. But it will end nicely. That is what it says in *The Guardian*. It's a good book."

She turned back to the pages. She was not glued to the window like Nikki (and me, for that matter).

The train began to descend below the snow level, beyond St Moritz and Pontresina, where the writers Elizabeth Gaskell and Hans Christian Andersen had once, separately, holed up when it was a literary haunt.

Most of the red wine had been drunk.

Nikki and Aiko began to explain that the Mount Camphill Community involved a close-knit group of "vocational volunteers – some people call us nutters", and that it was "non-hierarchical though we have to have named managers… it's based on mutuality and equity in all you do, you don't get paid, we share everything, we take what we need". One of Aiko's jobs involved teaching weaving. The community had been "started by Jewish refugees fleeing Nazis". It was based on the principles of anthroposophy, which involved trying to uncover and promote the essential goodness within humans based on the works of the influential Austrian anthroposophist Rudolf Steiner.

"Be careful or you might join up after a glass more red," said Nikki.

The train had begun to pass through emerald fields. We crossed the "famous" Landwasser Viaduct, which the commentary informed was 213 feet high and 446 feet long, and particularly "spectacular" (cue lots of *oooo*-ing and *wooo*-ing). Church spires poked up from villages. Chopped wood was stacked beside neat timber chalet-style houses with A-shaped roofs. "All the wood is stacked so flippin' neatly," commented Nikki.

"Oh, wow! Waterfall!" said Aiko's father, breaking his silence. All this time, he had been quite happy to gaze out the window, listening to the various *oooo*s and *wooo*s. There was indeed a pretty waterfall.

He had limited English, but I learned through Aiko that her family lived in Yamaguchi, to the west of Hiroshima, and that her father "worked in the frozen food business including the oyster and the shrimp". He also liked playing golf. As Aiko translated, he gave a little imaginary golf swing.

We polished off the last of the red wine. We crossed the river Rhine. The British man from across the aisle said informatively: "That river flows all the way to Rotterdam." Where I was due in a few days' time.

We pulled into Chur station.

It had been an excellent ride.

I needed a bit of a lie-down.

The world's slowest express
Chur to Visp, via Zermatt

This was not to be. It turned out that Nikki, Aiko and Aiko's father were staying at the same hotel as me.

"Okey koky, karaoke!" said Nikki on hearing this.

We walked as a group from the nondescript modern Chur station to the nondescript not-so-modern Hotel Franziskaner, with its beige walls and basic but comfortable nondescript bedrooms in which (in mine at least), if you turned off the bathroom light, the bedside light would switch on, and vice versa; a system that seemed strangely to work in a useful way and one I had never known in another hotel (having stayed in quite a few).

Outside it was close to zero degrees. Nikki, Aiko, Aiko's father and I all proceeded to traipse shiveringly down narrow lanes to a beer hall – having located Aiko's father who had gone off for a wander ("He did this at Milan station, we almost missed the friggin' train," said Nikki) – where we ate sausages with sauerkraut and boiled potatoes and drank beer and I learned that Aiko's father was a fan of the golfers Tiger Woods and Rory McIlroy and that he had in fact retired six years ago and had played golf every day for the previous three years. He had moved to the countryside to be close to his golf club while his wife remained in the city. His favourite golfers of all time were Seve Ballesteros, Jack Nicklaus and Arnold Palmer.

Ice hockey was being shown on the television in the beer hall.

I asked Aiko's father if he liked ice hockey.

"No," he said as though it was a most disagreeable pastime.

Golf was a far better sport, he said. As though to prove this, he practised another of his imaginary golf swings.

So went the chatter in Chur.

We parted ways and I had a final nightcap at the Hemingway Cafe by the hotel, reading on my phone how Chur was said to be the oldest settlement in Switzerland (from as far back as 3900 BC), German-speaking and on the edge of the Rhine Gorge: "Switzerland's Grand Canyon", said a website. I briefed myself on these basics while sitting on a bar stool drinking a beer among well-groomed, well-dressed romantic couples and groups of singletons sipping elegant cocktails. Having spent a long time on trains traipsing round Europe, I stood out a bit so far as apparel was concerned: jeans that seemed about to fall apart but not in a "trendy" way, old polo shirt, one-euro jumper (bought in Bratislava), and a fleece. But I was getting used to this whenever I went anywhere vaguely "smart", and it did not bother me in the slightest.

* * *

Another cherry-red train awaited on platform 13, the 12:14 *Glacier Express* from Chur to Zermatt, due in at 6.10 p.m.

Having dutifully followed cobbled lanes up to Chur's cathedral and avoided the twin temptations of fridge magnet souvenirs featuring pictures of Albert Einstein offered at a large number of gift shops (Einstein had lived in Zurich, not Chur), as well as *Bernina Express*-branded sunglasses, *Bernina Express*-branded Swiss army pocketknives and 1,000-piece jigsaw puzzles featuring the *Bernina Express* on sale at the station's ticket office, I boarded carriage number 31, where I had booked a "two-course meal (meat)" to be served for lunch as an add-on to my fare.

Why not live it up a bit?

This train was billed as the "slowest express train in the world", which seemed a slightly odd "sell" but also to be almost certainly accurate when worked out: the six-hour westward journey over 102 miles averaged at 17 mph. The *Bernina Express*' four-hour journey from Tirano to Chur was a comparatively speedy 22.5 mph. Surely no other train in the world going slower than 17 mph claimed to be an "express". Hence the *Glacier Express*' claim of global domination of this area of endeavour.

A few more stats and "train facts" here for those so inclined.

The full distance of the *Glacier Express*, which opened in 1930, covered 181 miles crossing 291 bridges and travelling through 91 tunnels. This was the entire route from St Moritz to Zermatt, without the journey north-west to Chur, which shaved off about 80 miles. The longest tunnel, at the Furka Pass, was ten miles long. At its highest point at the Oberalp Pass the railway touched 6,670 feet (Chur's altitude was 1,942 feet). There were first-class, second-class and "excellence class" carriages, the latter only offered on certain journeys with one seat per window so "everyone has a window seat", plus a five-course lunch with free accompanying wines, "personal concierges" and a "private bar area". I was limited to second class due to my Interrail pass but had looked up this "excellence class" online out of curiosity and it showed happy couples clinking glasses in spacious seats while being offered top-ups by waiters in waistcoats and bow ties.

Never mind about all of that. It was the scenery that made the ride and from Chur you were soon travelling along the cocoon-like interior of the Rhine Gorge with pale granite cliffs shooting up all around. Large pine trees and leafless deciduous trees blanketed the terrain that was not exposed rocks. It felt somehow like unchartered territory, a secret gorge that we were discovering for the first time. It did not seem as though you were in Europe. The Grand Canyon comparison of the promo blurbs neatly captured the feeling of otherness, of having stepped – or rather, slid – into a parallel world.

In second class you are allotted a checked mauve–and–aquamarine-coloured seat by a table with fold-down flaps in a carriage with curving scenic windows, just like on the *Bernina Express*. In mine, a group of Germans (or possibly Swiss) was singing happily while drinking beers as the train traversed the gently meandering boulder-strewn water of the river Rhine. A few kids down the way were shrieking. A young couple sat at my table of four. Given the proximity, it felt odd not to at least say "hello". So I did, and I rapidly discovered that one of the pair was from Viana do Castelo in northern Portugal and named Carla, who worked at the headquarters of Burger King in the canton of Zug in Switzerland and had responsibilities promoting the burger chain across Europe as well as its sister brands Firehouse Subs (which sells sub sandwiches) and Popeyes (which sells fried chicken). The other, her partner Jam, from Munich, was in financial services involving "pension funds and property".

Trains do throw people together – Agatha Christie had latched smartly on to that. You never quite knew who you might come across. This was especially so in Switzerland, it seemed, and as the scenery was so eye-catching there was always a common talking point to break the ice; a little more visual inspiration, perhaps, than on the communist-era outskirts of Bratislava and Bucharest.

Like Nikki, Aiko and Aiko's father, Carla and Jam were train lovers. Carla enjoyed her 21-minute commute to the Burger King headquarters from Zurich, where the couple lived, to Zug so much she positively looked forward to commuting. There cannot be many places on the planet where anyone else says that. She described the scenery through the mountains as "just so beautiful", making her life "feel good" whatever the stresses presented by promoting Popeyes chicken that day. Meanwhile, Jam, who seemed enrapt by the swirling water of the Rhine and the jagged rocks and scree tumbling from a cliff above, simply said: "Every train should be like this." It was their first journey on the *Glacier Express*.

Carla and Jam had classic good looks: tanned, healthy, and bright-eyed. They were also relaxed in themselves, and perhaps just a little smug. This was not because they had solid jobs and were happy together with a shiny future. It was because they lived in Switzerland. You could see it in their expressions as they gazed out of the carriage window... the pure joy of living in the mountains. They said as much, and I commented that they were lucky to have found home in between the peaks and the lakes way up in the Alps.

"It is not luck," replied Carla, quick as a shot. "We chose."

Which was accurate – they *had* chosen to come and set up their lives closer to the clouds tucked away in the middle of Europe. Very astutely, I could not help thinking.

Carla and Jam read for a while. So did I (the last of Jean-Paul Sartre).

Then it began to snow. Clouds had settled on the mountaintops and a blizzard had set in. The *Glacier Express*, unperturbed at its steady 17 mph, pottered upwards.

"Now we are really climbing," said Jam, as we entered a tunnel and the Germans/Swiss and the kids began screaming to create a "horror show" feel to the carriage.

My food arrived after a long delay while others had been served. It was not great: an average soup followed by lukewarm pork slices and some potatoes and vegetables. For the soup I was given a knife and fork. For the pork, a soup spoon. This seemed to happen because there were two waiters, who were not quite in sync. One of the waiters, who wore a waistcoat and bow tie, just like the pictures in "excellence class", apologized – it was a very busy train, he said, and "next time we bring you the right cutlery". On another *Glacier Express* journey, one day, I supposed, which seemed quite a likely possibility. Overall, however, I was not sure Henri Opper de Blowitz of *The Times* back in 1883 would have thought much of the culinary provisions on the *Glacier Express*.

The scenery had turned into a white blur. Then we entered the Furka Tunnel and more shrieks began, though they puttered out quite soon as it was so long. Carla started talking about the benefits of Switzerland beyond its spectacular landscapes, complimenting the less than 2 per cent inflation rate, compared to 9 per cent back in Portugal. Jam, turning extremely serious at this juncture, expressed concern that Swiss inflation, if not carefully watched, might increase. The gross domestic product per capita in Switzerland was staggeringly high, however, around double the UK's or six times that of Romania. So the economic situation was generally extremely good.

But not perfect. Jan began to discuss the downsides of Switzerland, of which there did not on the face of it seem to be many. Yet there was one big one.

"Could we buy a place to live in Zurich?" he asked rhetorically. "No! Never! In Portugal maybe. It doesn't make sense here. Switzerland has the lowest percentage of people owning properties in Europe: forty per cent."

"In Romania it's ninety per cent," said Carla.

"In Britain, it's sixty per cent," said Jam.

They knew their country-by-country property percentage ownership figures.

"In Zurich," continued Jam, "a one-bedroom flat in the city centre might cost nine hundred thousand euros. For a decent place, more than a million and you can't be in the centre. No. No. No. This is never happening. We are never buying in Zurich."

We exited Furka Tunnel.

I asked if they would like beers and went to the bar in the dining car to fetch three lagers.

We cracked them open and toasted our good fortune: of being on a train without much to do, passing through one of the most beautiful places in Europe, even though the blizzard had wiped out the view.

Carla said that she had always wanted to be a writer and that when she was younger she had written poetry and loved stories and drawing. Her favourite Portuguese author was José Saramago "for sure, he won the Nobel Prize for Literature, he's very controversial because he takes a situation to an extreme to prove a point". She recommended his book *Death with Interruptions*, imagining what life would be like if everyone lived forever (as quite a few have of late). I was loving these railway book tip-offs, a whole side of rail travel I had not considered previously. I asked Jam what he had enjoyed recently and he mentioned *A Gentleman in Moscow* by the American Amor Towles, which I had already read. So we discussed this for a while. Carriage number 31 had turned into a temporary literary salon, just like Carriage 485 had briefly on the *Sofia–Istanbul Express*.

The blizzard had ceased. The *Glacier Express* had descended. We had turned past Visp into a gully with steep sides and the grubby remains of what appeared to have once been a glacier.

"The last dying bit," said Jan.

"This is not Switzerland," said Carla, almost refusing to look.

But it was – and she was saying it out of sadness rather than denial.

The shrinking lump of ice was just one example of the unavoidable consequences of climate change, of course.

And there were many more all about.

Above Zermatt, where we were drawing near, another melting glacier on the slopes of the Matterhorn had recently unveiled a German climber who had been missing for dozens of years. Unfortunate passers-by had discovered the corpse after spotting a boot sticking up out of the watery ice. Many other bodies were regularly being found in this fashion: dying glaciers revealing the dead with a macabre symbolism. Meanwhile, scientists had found that glaciers in the country had shrunk by half since 1931, meaning less water stored to supply both the Danube and the Rhine rivers, where levels had dropped so low some freight ships could no longer pass and warmer water was killing fish. On top of this, there was less water to irrigate crops as well as shortages for cooling nuclear power stations. Another knock-on effect was quite extraordinary: an international boundary between Switzerland and Italy, based on a water drainage divide point, was changing due to melting glaciers meaning that a part of

Italy that included a renowned mountain lodge, Rifugio Guide del Cervino, had technically become part of Switzerland. Cue delicate diplomatic discussions.

On this sombre note, the *Glacier Express* – which might one day need to be renamed? – rolled on to Zermatt station.

At least the train itself was greener than other ways of getting about.

Carla, Jam and I said our goodbyes, and out of necessity I had a very brief visit to the old mountain town.

* * *

The reason for this was *I could not afford to stay in Zermatt.*

Even the cheapest bunk in a shared dorm was at the high end of my budget. I had already calculated this, so I intended to stay for an hour or so in Zermatt to look around before catching a train out of town back to Visp along the same train line we had just taken. It was cheaper in Visp, another small town, where you could find an en suite room for less than a bunk in Zermatt. Visp also benefitted from good onward train connections. Having examined various of these, I had randomly set my sights on the city of Dole in the *département* of Jura in eastern France. I knew nothing about Dole. I just liked the name. It would, I also realized, be my third consecutive stop at a place with four letters in its name, after Chur and Visp.

Though I was quite possibly overthinking things to have noticed this coincidence. I will put my hands up to that.

There was evidence of skiing in Zermatt.

In the cobbled town centre, opposite the little station entrance, people were walking about in ski costumes between tall, chalet-style buildings lugging skis. I joined the skiers, strolling along an avenue of shops offering gold and diamond-encrusted watches that seemed to promise to transform your life into those of a succession of tanned, healthy, suave models and celebrities. This, frankly, felt slightly unlikely after eating a succession of pork dishes, sausages and boiled potatoes, and endless pizzas in recent days, all washed down with beers and red wines while living out of a backpack in accommodation lurking in the lower echelons of the selection presented by a popular online hotel booking provider. So low, I was finding myself having to take a train out of town to afford somewhere to sleep.

I looked at the watches for a while, though, after all Switzerland was famous for its watches, clocks and general precision; hence the excellent trains, so efficiently run that tardy, unreliable German trains were being barred from rolling late into the main station in Basel and messing up its timetables. As I did so – they were beautiful watches – my primary thought was, however: *I could never leave one of those in the locker at my local pool back home.* I'd be a nervous wreck.

But I suppose with the GDP per capita soaring so high, gold diamond-studded wristwatches of the sort favoured by models and celebrities – no doubt capable of withstanding 200-metre plunges beneath the surface of the ocean – were par for the course in Switzerland. As was dressing extremely smartly, without worrying much about the cost, or so it appeared. More fashionable, tanned, healthy, suave figures gazed out from a succession of fashionable clothing shops: Gucci, Prada, etcetera, etcetera. Then there were the many sleek, eye-wateringly expensive ski outfits. The models for the displays in these shops were not just fashionable, tanned, healthy and suave, however, they were also appreciably sportier and fitter, too.

At the end of the avenue, you could see the pyramid shape of the Matterhorn towering up and looking as though it was saying: *want to try to climb me? Good luck!* Evidence of the difficulty of doing so was to be found a little further on at a small cemetery containing the graves of daring mountaineers who had perished on the mountain's terrifying cliffs or simply died naturally later on. Among the latter were Peter and Peter Taugwalder, a father and son who had guided the Englishman Edward Whymper to the first ascent of the Matterhorn (14,692 feet) in 1865; a feat of derring-do celebrated at the time across the globe. During Whymper's descent, four other climbers in their group were to die in falls, among them Michel Auguste Croz, a mountain guide from Chamonix in France, who is buried beside the Taugwalders. There were more than fifty mountaineer graves in all.

I bought a microwave chicken curry from the local Coop supermarket. I examined some old replica posters advertising Zermatt, one showing an early plane flying above the glacier by the pyramid-shaped peak of the Matterhorn during times more innocent of climate change (less than 100 years ago), sold at a station shop. Then I boarded the train to Visp. It was almost empty save for a few workers from Zermatt commuting home for the evening, some singing and clapping in a far carriage as though a mini party was underway. These Alpine trains seemed to engender joviality. Then I arrived at a large modern station down the mountain in Visp and walked up a hill to Bildungshaus St Jodern, an eerily empty hostel-hotel with long corridors of rooms, chapels for prayers and cards on the reception that said: "GOD LOVES ME ÷ I LIVE APART FROM GOD + JESUS GAVE EVERYTHING FOR ME = WILL I CHOOSE TO FOLLOW JESUS?" At the bottom a website was listed – thefour.com – which reiterated these points. I went to the empty canteen, which had no staff and one other guest, who sat on a burgundy faux-leather sofa.

This was Irma from Rotterdam in the Netherlands. She was short, middle-aged and wore a t-shirt with the logo: "CHANCE, TAKE NO. 5, DROP EVERY FEAR". This was designed in the style of a Chanel perfume advert. She quietly observed me putting my chicken curry in the microwave and after a while asked where I had bought the curry. I explained and she said: "We have Coop in Holland. The curry is very good."

She paused and then began talking about things that popped into her head as though this Coop curry connectivity was enough grounds for a natter. She was quite opinionated. She had worked in human resources for 25 years in "industry and municipality" as well as for some time in "benefit care". She had come to the Valais canton to attempt to buy a place to live so she could move to the area, which she liked as it was "good quality, good food, good mindset, a release of stress, a comfort – this is the problem in Holland, people don't want to pay for better quality as they are used to lower quality, which is not funny as it's only the rich who can afford the good stuff". The mountain air seemed to have loosened her tongue.

After discussing the merits of Coop for a period, Irma turned to the British royal family: "This crowning of Charles, it is good thing. A good thing they are more open, but the family is so damaged by life. So damaged." Irma looked sad about exactly how damaged they were in her estimation. "Where is their dignity? In society, if you think you are above people and can get away with anything it is not good."

Her eyeballs bulged a little as she said this.

"It is the same in society," she said. "Too many people feel they are 'above' other people. They do not care. This is not good situation because you do not have a middle class anymore. In Rotterdam it is a working-class city. People are not afraid…"

She tailed off.

Of what, I asked?

Irma seemed to change tack: "So many nationalities. It's about knowing multicultural differences. I could talk about this for hours…"

She tailed off again.

Then Irma told me how she had visited London but not stayed in the part where the "Russians and the oil sheikhs lived" and continued afterwards for quite some time about the twists and turns of her mortgage negotiations with various Swiss banks for her potential property purchase in the canton of Valais.

This conversation with Irma was just about my only encounter in Visp.

CHAPTER NINE

VISP TO GHENT IN BELGIUM, VIA DOLE IN FRANCE, LUXEMBOURG AND WATERLOO IN BELGIUM

LET THE RANDOM RULE

Travel, like life perhaps, has a delicious quality when you make it up as you go along.

Trains allow you to do that.

Dole in France had been a snap decision. It was about 175 miles north-west of Visp. All I knew about Visp was that it was the economic centre of the Valais region, hilly, and home to both a big chemical company and the Bildungshaus St Jodern hostel-hotel. All I knew about Dole was that it was about three times the size of Visp with a population of 23,000 and that Louis Pasteur was born there in 1822, going on to save millions of lives with his anthrax and rabies vaccines as well as lending his name to the technique of food preservation, pasteurization, that was so important for milk.

What the two places had in common was railways – and I made sure I was on time for the 10:06 to Lausanne in Switzerland, before connecting on the 12:23 from Lausanne to Dole, due in at 1.57 p.m. Swiss trains had something of a reputation for being punctual and I did not want to get stuck in Visp.

Statistics backed up the word-of-mouth stories of the magnificent efficiency of Swiss trains. During the previous year a startling 94 per cent had run on time compared to around 70 per cent in Britain, 85 per cent in France, a shocking 65 per cent in Germany and, as far as Italy was concerned, it was quite difficult to tell. In fact, all the figures seemed based on slightly different definitions of "late" – some "lates" being over five minutes and some over one, with various other provisos – so these are very much ballpark estimations. Yet they did give a rough guide, and it was telling to note that of the troublesome 6 per cent of delays to Swiss trains, most of these were attributed to services beginning in Germany and Italy, so nothing whatsoever to do with Swiss rail operators. In reality, trains run by the Swiss were better than 94 per cent on time.

Expecting a perfect onward journey – just as the narrow-gauge *Bernina Express* and *Glacier Express* had provided – I joined the standard-gauge train to Lausanne. My intention was to rattle and jolt north towards the Low Countries seeing whatever I happened to see.

Very good snails
Visp to Dole, France, via Lausanne

The 10:06 to Lausanne left on time, of course. It was a swish, modern double-decker with little upstairs lounges with sofas and coffee tables that appeared to act as "break-out zones" for those who felt a need for a period of relaxation on a sofa away from their regular seat.

It moved smoothly into and out of tunnels through valleys of terraced vineyards framed by snow-dusted mountains. A silhouette of a castle appeared on a hill: Tourbillon Castle at the town of Sion. The train rolled on beyond Martigny via orchards of blossoming fruit trees – spring was springing – and via Bex station, where the train stopped and a man clutching what could possibly have been his entire earthly possessions in red plastic bags disembarked. Not long after, Lake Geneva came into view, all luminous and creamy in pastel icy blues, the faintest of pinks and soft greys, the surface seeming quietly to breathe while mirroring the milky sky and the hazy mountains on the far shore near Évian-les-Bains in France. Out of the carriage window was a veritable dreamland of gently glowing light.

Another castle appeared on the foreshore, Château de Chillon, with its terracotta turrets lifting through the mist and its famous story of an inmate once held there and immortalized by Lord Byron in his poem, "The Prisoner of Chillon". On a visit, Byron had been inspired by the story of a monk named François Bonivard, who had been incarcerated in chains for his religious beliefs after his father was burned at the stake and his six brothers killed one by one, two before his eyes at the castle. Bonivard had been held at the castle from 1532 to 1536.

"My hair is grey, but not with years, / Nor grew it white / In a single night…" – so begins the long poem, which tells the story of Bonivard with plenty of poetic licence regarding the precise truth of what really happened. Yet as the train rolls by Château de Chillon, the solitary plight of the tragic monk seems to hang in the atmosphere above the lake, especially on a calm, thoughtful, pastel-hued day.

Montreux station with its potted palm trees came next followed by Vevey station. Graham Greene lived his final years in Vevey, where he was friends with another retiree, Charlie Chaplin; Greene was buried in the Corseaux cemetery, just up the hill from the station. Then the bewitching terraces of the Lavaux vineyards with their mesmerizing stone balconies arose, the vines carefully planted on land used for winemaking since medieval days and coming right up to the track surrounding the train as though we, the passengers of the 10:06 from Visp, were all being taken there to begin a shift attending to the terraces.

Next up was the elegant Lausanne station, where we did all get off. This station had an arresting Art-Nouveau-meets-Art-Deco style with a grand hall with a stone clock depicting two stone figures with arms raising above their heads as if in weary acceptance of the ticking of time. A lottery-ticket vending machine rested in a corner (another new vending machine venture after the books at Timişoara station). There was also an Inside Africa shop selling hair extensions and plantain, and a newsagent with plentiful racks of papers. One of these, the *FT Weekend*, was headlined: "MUSK TO LAUNCH AI START-UP TO RIVAL CHATGPT" (which would have been complete gibberish to me six months earlier). A commentator, Nicholas Kristof, was writing about the war in Ukraine and "AVOIDING SUPERPOWER CATASTROPHE" in *The New York Times*. Meanwhile, the local *20 minutes* paper was covering yet more pension demonstrations in France: "*ON VEUT MONTRER QU'ON N'EST PAS DUPES*" ("WE WANT TO SHOW WE ARE NOT FOOLED").

I boarded the 12:23 from Lausanne.

This was a TGV Lyria train with an eel-like locomotive in red, white and black stripes. It moved smoothly away from Lausanne, rapidly entering thick forest between mountains. French immigration officers trailed through the train, and one asked whether I was carrying "cash money above ten thousand euros". I smiled thinly at him and said "*non*" in a deadpan fashion at which the officer smirked. We went into a tunnel. I investigated the "bar buffet" carriage and ordered a red wine at around the time we were pulling into Frasne station. I made a joke to the barman that this station had spelled the country wrong, and he just looked at me as though he found the customers he was required to put up with during his hours of duty quite increasingly unbelievable.

The train tilted quite a lot. After the mountains, it passed many rape seed or possibly mustard fields. At around 1.57 p.m. we arrived in Dole.

* * *

Dole did not exactly ignite the soul. It was something of a "French Bari". The ticket office at the station, where I wanted to ask about the best route to Luxembourg for tomorrow, was *ferme* (shut). Dull roads with launderettes, kebab shops and grey buildings from the nineteenth and early twentieth centuries led to a tourism office that was also *ferme*. Traffic revved by. My phone ran out of battery. I asked a sullen teenager with a crew cut for the way to my place for the night, which was listed as "Dark Room Centre Ville de Dole" on a popular online accommodation provider (I had been wondering what on earth this would be like and could not resist booking). I gave him the street name. He pointed to a labyrinth of roads lined with high-street chain shops, the odd fashion outlet and lingerie boutique. At a confusing junction further on, I asked the proprietor of the Pizz'up pizzeria the way again. He pointed further into the spaghetti lanes of Dole and said: "*Bon chance, mon ami!*" By a stroke of good fortune, however, I found Rue du Prélot and located a darkened hall to a darkened internal stairway above a café. These stairs and a punch-code led to the Dark Room Centre Ville de Dole.

It lived up to its name: the walls were painted black and it was indeed dark. However, there were a few quirks.

The first was that the walls were also hung with neat rows of bags from designer shops such as Gucci, Christian Dior and Louis Vuitton – seemingly for upmarket decoration. The second was a great number of mirrors both on the walls and the ceilings by the bed. The third was a multicoloured lighting system, also above the bed, which slowly flickered between reds, purples, pinks, yellows and greens.

The fourth was a small side room, also painted black, with an unusually shaped inflatable curving sofa that judging by comments I was noticing online was for purposes devoted to nocturnal activities. A massage table was in this side room, too. I read some more of these "verified reviews": *too many mirrors on the ceiling; the coloured lights that changed constantly meant I couldn't read in bed at night; interesting (questionable) equipment in the side room: definitely not a property suited to families!* However, these were niggles and the general consensus was more of the *great location, very clean* variety.

Close by was the birthplace of Pasteur, next to a canal. A pallid-faced assistant at the front desk, however, informed me "the museum is closed". The door to the museum had yet to be locked, she said. She apologized for the confusion.

Out on the streets, it was cold, grey, empty and boring. It was a Sunday afternoon and all the shops were shut. I went to the sixteenth-century Collegiate Church Notre-Dame, another one, like the one in Tirano, said to have an important organ, this one with 3,500 pipes. The interior was impressively Gothic and Renaissance in style with some nice stained-glass windows. I am afraid to say – God strike me down – I could not muster much more enthusiasm after having visited quite a few Gothic/Renaissance places of worship during the trip. I had, if you like, reached peak "Gothic godliness".

Instead, I walked around the streets some more. They were particularly dirty with dog mess (even by French standards of dog cleanliness). I tried to find an unemployment office so I could take a selfie outside and caption it *On the dole in Dole* and post this as a "hilarious" message on social media, but I could not locate one. I had sunk to such a low I was considering such stunts. I was even failing at them.

It began to drizzle. I came to a weir by the canal next to a park where a fairground was shutting down for the day. A few youths were thumping a punchbag machine. There was a smell of popcorn. No one was on the "Shanghai Express" ride. No one was playing games at the "GOOD 777 LUCK" arcade.

I wandered down an alley as the drizzle turned to rain.

Then Dole began to pick up.

This was all because of Restaurant La Demi Lune (The Half-Moon Restaurant).

It was not far from the birthplace of Pasteur, down some steps into a vaulted cellar dotted with potted plants and illuminated by tea candles and side lamps shaped like cats. I ordered an aperitif of gin and tonic from a friendly middle-aged waitress, who seemed most approving of this. Then six garlicky snails were delivered on a sizzling dish by a cheerful chef wearing a ruby bandana. As I ate these, a grey and white cat sidled up to my table and rubbed against my legs as though hoping for a snack. The snails were excellent, if a little tricky to hook out of the shells. Then I polished off a slice of chicken in a mustardy cheese sauce, accompanied by salty little roasted potatoes and ratatouille, a local speciality. On the side I had a vinegary-yet-sweet *salade verte*. All excellent, too, especially the tender chicken with its interesting mustardy taste – and all washed down by some better-than-average Côtes du Rhône red wine (superior to Eurostar's so long ago). I had rediscovered my inner Blowitz.

The friendly waitress, who seemed extremely pleased with her unexpected euro-shedding, early-evening, long-distance train-travelling customer, gave me a glass of a sherry-like drink called *vin jaune*, which she said was another speciality. This was on the house. I said it tasted like sherry and she said: "*Exactement!*" I ate some crêpes for pudding and stayed for a while reading "The Prisoner of Chillon": "There are seven pillars of Gothic mould, / In Chillon's dungeons deep and old..." The waitress occasionally came and topped up my Côtes du Rhône. I paid my *addition* (bill) and returned to my own strange, but perfectly comfortable (and exceedingly reasonable) dungeon-like room and fell promptly into a deep slumber.

Dole had not been so bad after all.

On Rue Joseph Junck
Dole to Luxembourg

The day ahead involved several trains.

From Dole the tracks led to Dijon. From Dijon to Strasbourg. From Strasbourg to Metz. And from Metz to Luxembourg. France felt "done" for the time being, Dole having been the second foray of the trip. The connections would have me in the Grand Duchy of Luxembourg, its official name, for 1.22 p.m. after a 6.59 a.m. start.

A grey and blue SNCF train with "BOURGOGNE-FRANCHE-COMTÉ" written on the side in yellow and black – Dole was in this region – drew up at platform two. I boarded and the train pulled away efficiently on time, soon rattling across fields of vivid yellow crops that must surely have been mustard being so close to Dijon, the French mustard capital.

Long ago on these series of trains I had begun to take great pleasure in these early starts, watching the day begin from the tracks. A pale orange sun was lifting into the thinnest of pale grey skies that was soon to come alive in a curiously delicate harpsichord pattern of rose-tinted light. The motion down the line combined with the shifting of the skies forming a subtle double effect of movement and for a while, as the horizon changed colour casting shades and shapes into the clouds, it was pleasant enough just to gaze out and sense Dijon drawing near.

At 7.30 a.m. the train stopped at Dijon-Ville station.

There was half an hour to kill during the connection so I went out of the station to regard its façade, enough time to observe the rotund beige-concrete exterior of Dijon-Ville station (which reminded me slightly of Hanger Lane tube station in north-west London), drink a coffee and read a discarded *Le Monde* with the headline *"RÉFORME DES RETRAITES: MACRON PROMULGUE LA LOI, LA CONTESTATION CONTINUE"* ("PENSION REFORMS: MACRON PROMULGATES THE LAW, THE CONTEST CONTINUES"). The president of France had finally got his way: the law pushing the age of retirement from 62 to 64 had been confirmed by a constitutional council, although many were still trying whatever they could to challenge this, even though it was too late.

Another grey-and-blue SNCF train arrived, the 08:00 to Strasbourg, due in at 10.27 a.m. In the carriage a mother was attending to five young children who were running wild, clambering beneath seats and popping up unexpectedly here, there and everywhere while conducting various personal vendettas against one another involving the pulling of hair, kicks and slaps that led to intermittent shrieks and returns to their mother, who consoled them briefly before they went out on further missions/vendettas seeking retribution at a higher degree of pain to that originally dished out by the perpetrator.

As amusing as this was to witness at first, the low-level guerrilla warfare, which was becoming noisier and noisier as tactics became dirtier, eventually drove me to the snazzy tangerine-and-purple buffet coach, where I drank another coffee and watched gently rolling hills on the horizon beyond long ploughed fields and the occasional perky chateau poking up with turrets and long rows of high windows: posh little perfect palaces. The French gentry knows how to live, whatever age they are made to retire by upstart presidents (if they actually need to retire from doing anything, that is).

On arrival in Strasbourg station, which felt like déjà vu after Danny and me being there a few weeks earlier, all trains were cancelled going towards Metz. This was frustrating. However, signs with asterisked words in the ticket hall clearly warned not to take out frustration on staff, with examples of former miscreants' language: "*TON TAF C'EST DE LA M****!*" ("YOUR JOB IS SHIT!") and "*ON VA SE REVOIR, F*** D* ****!*" ("WE'RE GONNA SEE EACH OTHER AGAIN…"), and "*F*** D* *****". I had no idea what that meant and perhaps was better off not doing so. There were other examples and these messages at least helped pass the time of day, while you tried to work out what all the mysterious asterisks meant.

After waiting a long time in a long queue in this hall, I reached the front, where a frazzled-looking SNCF employee explained what had caused all the trouble. There had been an accident on a main line; he formed a fist and used it to hit the palm of his other hand to demonstrate what had happened. "One person in front of train," he said as he made this gesture. It was a stark, matter-of-fact message – and it put things in perspective. Who really cared if we were all held up?

There would be a two-hour delay. I sat for a while in the square outside the station reading near a group of guys with laundry bags stuffed full of possessions who were drinking cans of Guinness, discussing matters of seeming great importance (which no doubt they were: *their futures*), and looking as though they were a long way from where they had come. Five tents were pitched by a taxi rank nearby and it was possible these were where they were residing.

Then I joined the 12:47 to Metz, an SNCF Voyageur, which was notable for having the best reading lights I had ever seen on any train, attached to special panels beside the headrests. Aside from this, a woman sitting across the aisle looked remarkably like Tina Turner, the late American soul singer. The train raced past a cluster of home improvement shops and broke free into farmland of crops and creatures: horses, wild-boar-like pigs, geese, sheep and cows. Settlements along the way became steadily more Germanic in appearance: squared off, solider-looking structures. Long rows of tall, bushy trees cut across the landscape like pinned-up collections of foxes' tails. Tina Turner fell fast asleep. A strange sound like a cappuccino machine began to emanate when the train tilted at bends, and soon enough we pulled into Metz and those travelling to Luxembourg crossed a platform for the 14:30 to the small, wealthy country – number one on the world's GDP per capita list, about 50 per cent higher than in Switzerland even, mainly due to its status as a notorious tax haven.

A smartly dressed woman who had sat down near me had a shock after the train doors had closed, but before it had moved away.

"Oh! Looks-em-bug!" she said on hearing an announcement on the speaker system.

She looked at me and I confirmed it was going to *Looks-em-bug*.

"Oh! But I am on the wrong train!" she said.

The train conductor happened to be passing by. He called the driver, halted the train, which had moved a few yards, and the woman disembarked, whereupon the train was held for about a quarter of an hour as this unusual procedure had clearly upset a security setting on the train. Eventually we got moving again, rolled past some apartments with an Eastern European look and began to slide across flat countryside passing the towns of Hagondange, Uckange, Thionville and Bettembourg. At the latter a "Welcome to Luxembourg" text pinged.

I was entering the twelfth country of the trip, on the twenty-fourth day – a Grand Duchy, no less.

We rolled into Luxembourg City at 3.22 p.m., two hours behind schedule.

* * *

Luxembourg station was busy and cramped – just over a mile from the historic centre of Luxembourg City, the country's capital, which was reached along a road and a bridge above a deep gorge.

It had a neoclassical meets twenty-first-century-how-on-earth-do-we-make-this-bigger architectural style. The first element of this "look" was evidenced in columns, archways and decorative stone urns. The second found expression in a curvy conservatory section similar but on a lesser scale to the conservatory at Strasbourg station that had been attached to one side, with the odd piece of modern sculpture dotted here and there in an extended concourse.

An abstract trompe l'oeil mural depicting a sky with a star-shaped sun and swirling clouds had been painted on the curving roof of the main ticket hall, where two memorials were to be found. The first was in memory of railway workers who died in World War Two, with a Socialist realism-like sculpted panel depicting two muscle-bound figures, one clasping a lantern with a flame. The second memorial was a simple plaque to victims of the Holocaust: "You who walk freely, remember that from this station, six hundred and fifty-eight Jewish men, women and children were deported from 1941 to 1943 to the ghettos and camps where they were murdered in cold blood by the Nazis." *Never forget*, on the site of where the transport began.

I crossed a busy street in front of the station and entered Rue Joseph Junck, where I had booked a room for the night.

Sometimes popular online accommodation providers can let you down. This was the case in Luxembourg City, although then again – not really.

The Dark Room in Dole had been odd but OK. The room on Rue Joseph Junck (named after a philanthropist who lived from 1839 to 1922, said the road sign), was odd and perhaps best described as *challengingly OK*.

Walking down the street it was hard not to notice a series of, to use an old-fashioned term, *gentlemen's clubs*, some with pictures of scantily clad women in bunny costumes. These establishments had names like "DREAMS NIGHT CLUB" and shifty figures approached on the pavements asking: "Do you want something, mister?" and "Hey, hey, mister, you lookin' for something, mister?"

To enter my place for the night, in a block in between several of these places of entertainment, meant punching in a code. This was frequently how it went with the lower echelons of the popular online accommodation provider's offerings; it had been impossible to find anywhere else close to Luxembourg City's historic centre for a suitable price, hence Rue Joseph Junck, conveniently close to the station, it must be said.

The code was not working as I was too early and it had not been activated. As I hesitated in the doorway, another shifty figure approached.

"*Ça bonne?*" he asked ("Are you OK?"). He said this with a devious-yet-casual look, loading the words with unspoken meaning in a manner to suggest he could provide a channel of assistance for whatever I might need: *absolutely anything, really, it would be no trouble at all.* He had a shrewd demeanour and was wearing an Adidas tracksuit. From his attitude, he seemed in some intangible way to be *representing* Rue Joseph Junck, chairman of the (underworld) welcoming committee and a neighbourhood fixture.

I said I was fine. He shrugged, not disguising his disappointment in me. Then I gave the code another go – the shifty man lingering, making me cover the display as I pecked in the number. It still didn't work. I cursed punch-codes with timers and left the shifty man to go for a drink of *vin rouge* at Café du Globe on a nearby corner.

Inside it was empty aside from four other customers: a man with dreadlocks who was also ordering a glass of *vin rouge* (and who drank it in two gulps and promptly departed), a bored-looking young woman with lots of make-up, tightly pulled-back hair, multiple rings and a cup of coffee, and an elderly couple in deep discussion on bar stools. The woman on the stool was hunched over and tearfully explaining something to her companion, who was listening sympathetically though you got the impression he had heard it all before.

The barman was no-nonsense. He wore a flat cap and t-shirt with a skull on the front. He had an inscrutable expression and looked as though he might have played rugby at a reasonably high level about thirty years previously. I sat at a simple wooden table and drank my *vin rouge*, the cheapest red wine of this Interrail tour, next to a fake fern and some pink plastic flowers. On a wall near a jukebox was an arty painting of a naked woman reclining on a chaise longue. A television in a corner was showing a pig-farming event being held somewhere in the Deep South of the United States. It may have been unlikely to find its way any time soon into the glossy pages of *Condé Nast Traveller* magazine, but I quite liked Café du Globe: everyone kept themselves to themselves (no *hey mister* enquiries) and it was decent, cheap plonk: *rudimentary*, some wine critics might say, but good enough for me.

A message pinged. The punch-code for my room had become available. I left Café du Globe, walked a few metres down Rue Joseph Junck and put in the code, un-harassed by the shifty man this time. Inside, I ascended a darkened staircase to a tiny, perfectly clean en-suite room that required a second entry punch-code. Through the walls, you could hear the steady, distant thud of dance music from a next-door "establishment", but it was not too noisy even though earplugs were provided by the bedside.

I went out to investigate Luxembourg City. This involved walking across the gorge to its small historic centre. It was past six o'clock and just about everywhere seemed closed. Being perched on a corner of land between two gorges above the river Pétrusse and the river Alzette there was not a lot to the historic centre of Luxembourg City other than government offices (from which workers had already returned home for the day), places of worship, bars/cafés (largely empty) and a few deserted, windswept squares.

The Cathédrale Notre-Dame with its narrow spires and tall, thin windows was closed; at least, the main door I tried was locked. The Bank Museum explaining Luxembourg's importance as a financial tax haven was closed. The Grand Ducal Palace was closed too, official residence of Grand Duke Henri, the constitutional monarch at the head of the House of Nassau who acted as figurehead for the country; elections were held for the Grand Duchy's democratic parliament. The palace was a distinguished building with Flemish flourishes of little towers, intricate stonework and narrow iron balconies. During the summer, guided tours were possible.

Luxembourg had been made a Grand Duchy during the Treaty of Versailles after the fall of Napoleon in 1815 and that status had been reconfirmed after a further treaty in London in 1867. Being in such a strategically important location with great natural defences it had been deemed too much of a regional stronghold ever to fall into either French or German hands, hence the Grand Duchy's survival, although "grand" seemed over-egging it a bit: the territory was about the same size as Derbyshire and its population of 640,000 was about 150,000 less than the Midlands county's.

I walked across a large square with the town hall on one side. Outside this an information panel for tourists said it was in this building that the High Authority of the European Coal and Steel Community held its inaugural session in 1952 paving the way for the creation of the European Union in 1993. So this cream-coloured building with the flags of Luxembourg, Ukraine and the European Union fluttering on its façade was where the EU had effectively begun – and this tradition of being a key place in Europe had solidified over the years as Luxembourg City had become the home of the Court of Justice of the European Union, located in the north-east of the city beyond the river Alzette.

Along fortifications, I came to the gorge. The views across the plunging rocks down into the deep ravine with its winding river were splendid. Arches of a railway viaduct curled in the direction of Trier in Germany, where Karl Marx was born in 1818, about 26 miles away.

Then I made my way back to Rue Joseph Junck and ate chicken noodles at a Vietnamese restaurant with palm-frond wallpaper, run by a woman who came to France from Vietnam as a refugee in 1976.

In 2005, she had moved to Luxembourg, which she said she liked as it was *plus calme* (calmer) than Paris, where she had lived after initially settling in Metz.

"*La vie est trop vite*," she said of Paris: life is too fast.

I learned all this while waiting for my chicken noodles. The Vietnamese restaurant, you could not help but notice, was next door to a club with a black door and a picture of a woman wearing a purple negligee and purple high heels posted on a sign above the door. The sign simply said "ENTRÉE". The establishment appeared to have no official name.

The noodles were excellent. I ate them slowly, watching characters shuffling by outside on Rue Joseph Junck, some possibly on their way to the black door and its discreet-but-not-at-all-discreet sign. Everyone appeared to be on urgent, undefined business, while at the same time doing absolutely nothing at all, rather like those who had been milling about outside Gare du Nord back in Paris. I watched the ebb and flow of people: so much activity, yet not a lot going on. *A metaphor for our times*, I concluded after a while, rather grandiosely and not really knowing what I meant; the red wine accompanying my chicken noodles perhaps prompting such a sweeping observation. Why could not everyone simply slow down? Take it easy. Perhaps go on a few trains around Europe for a while? The red wine was definitely kicking in, rather pleasantly. The truth was you did often feel like an outsider on a long series of slow train rides, wherever you may have happened to roll in (on this occasion Rue Joseph Junck). You went places, you saw what you saw, you formed judgements (good, bad or otherwise). This was just what the slow train traveller did. It was what *all* travellers did. No point in fighting it.

As I paid my bill, I asked the woman running the Vietnamese restaurant about operating next to a club with no apparent name and a black door and a picture of a woman wearing a purple negligee and she simply raised her eyebrows and smiled as if to say *each to their own*. Then she said that her parents had lived in the south of Vietnam and had to escape by boat after the Viet Cong defeated the Americans the previous year as they had been regarded as close to the previous regime. She had only been back twice since then "*en vacances*" and she was about to tell me more about this, but a group arrived, and she rushed to take their orders. What a very nice woman. What a very nice Vietnamese restaurant near Luxembourg station.

Outside, a man was begging using a stick with a plastic cup attached to the end as though fishing for tips. A pair of women in scarlet high heels and miniskirts tottered by. A furtive group of skinny hooded youths had gathered near the corner by Café du Globe for purposes known only to themselves. The *hey mister* men, however, were bothering me less. In a few hours, I seemed to have blended in on Rue Joseph Junck. I had been "clocked" by the street hustlers and deemed quite useless to them.

For the purposes of research regarding life on Rue Joseph Junck – honest guv (etcetera) – I entered DREAMS NIGHT CLUB to see what went on in such a place on the *rue* and found myself in an empty neon-blue-lit chamber with a barmaid behind the bar and two waitresses in short skirts sitting on stools looking extremely bored. All three were startled to see a potential customer. There were no others. It was early evening and perhaps the usual clientele came later. Dance music thumped. The waitresses leapt off their stools, one of them saying something I could not discern and gesturing towards the interior. I looked beyond and could see more neon lights and darkened corners. I had not expected to be the only person who was not a member of staff, so far as I could tell, in DREAMS NIGHT CLUB. I had thought I might swiftly observe proceedings and depart unnoticed. It did not work that way at DREAMS NIGHT CLUB on my visit, though. I was very noticed. At that moment, I was the only customer around possible to be noticed. In the time it took me to calibrate those thoughts, I mumbled "Sorry, I must have the wrong place", spun round and exited DREAMS NIGHT CLUB. In old British tabloid parlance, I *made my excuses and left*, very quickly.

You may wonder what that was all about (so do I, up to a point).

The answer is that, as I was staying on the street (thanks to the popular online accommodation provider), I wanted to try at least to see what I could of Rue Joseph Junck as it was – an odd little lane by the main station in a country with the highest GDP per capita on the planet. Odd little lanes by stations often get overlooked in the glossy travel mags (as I said before) and generally by just about everyone, perhaps for good reasons. Anyway, the popular online accommodation provider had thrown me on to Rue Joseph Junck, no point in closing my eyes, although no point also in paying large amounts for drinks and hoping to find out more about life on the street from employees paid for other reasons who were no doubt supervised, especially when you were the only customer at the bar and had no idea how much the drinks cost.

Then I returned to my box room and read up about a destination that holds a special place in British hearts next up along the line… a few fields in the Belgian countryside just south of Brussels where dreams were both shattered and had come true.

The real Waterloo station
Luxembourg to Waterloo, Belgium

The trains seemed to be sweeping inevitably northward as though drawn by a giant magnet. Before allowing myself to be swept along with them, though, I bought a sandwich at a supermarket close to my abode, where a photograph of a grinning Grand Duke Henri hung behind the counter. For a moment or two I stared at the Grand Duke's knowing-yet-cheery tanned visage. He had a slight gap between his upper front teeth and a hint of a double chin (his only visible imperfections). He was dressed in an impeccable navy-blue suit with a white handkerchief poking out. Things seemed to be going pretty well for him judging by this affable and affluent-appearing official public portrait behind the counter of the supermarket, which reminded me for a moment of one of the Kims in North Korea (which I had once reached by train from Beijing in China and witnessed many such portraits just about every which way I turned). Not to say that Grand Duke Henri with his democratic principality had much, if anything, in common with the secretive East Asian country and Kim Jong Un, but this "sanctioned" picture stirred such thoughts and for a while I simply wondered what life was really like for the grand duke of the world's wealthiest country, GDP per capita-wise. Quite different from most people's, including Kim Jong Un's, I decided as I paid for a ham and cheese croissant.

It was time to move on. As home (London) drew closer, a fatalistic feeling had begun to set in. Whatever would be, would be. The giant magnet had "turned on". I could feel home calling and something inside seemed to be telling me: *from now on, just go with the flow.* Listening to this, I crossed the busy street to Luxembourg station for the 10:11 to Belgium's capital and onwards on the 13:10 to Waterloo station. Not, obviously, the one in central London (just 20 minutes by train from my apartment): the real Waterloo station.

The train to Brussels was a double-decker operated by the National Railway Company of Belgium. The carriage was empty and the train left on time beneath a low, patchy grey sky. There were a lot of flat fields with emerald crops, once the Luxembourg City suburbs were negotiated, and the occasional harrier hawk hovered above hedgerows, golden light filtering between the clouds and catching their lovely stripy chestnut-brown coats and white tail feathers. The train stopped at Arlon station and a "Welcome to Belgium" text pinged.

Around Arlon, I became embroiled in attempting to call my bank to check whether a payment had gone through for my next stay, Hotel Le 1815, which adjoined the site of the Battle of Waterloo where, during the year in the hotel's name, Napoleon Bonaparte was finally defeated by troops led by England's Duke of Wellington. Overnight, the hotel had seemingly reasonably enough (though no other accommodation had during the trip) sought a "verification request" for my payment.

This, however, required using the Wi-Fi of the room on Rue Joseph Junck, which seemed unwise for accessing my bank. Meanwhile, my phone had hit its digital roaming limit again, so I could not use "roaming" to check.

This meant calling the bank, slightly misdialling the first time, thinking nothing of it and then being phoned a moment later by the Belgian police, whom I had somehow called by mistake. I explained what had happened and the Belgian police wished me a good day. Then I dialled the correct number and got through to my bank, which said – after I had gone through various security checks – that the hotel payment had cleared and my card would "probably not be frozen" unless the international "card payment organization" decided to do so.

Finding out about this would require a further phone call that the bank would make on my behalf, but I was put on hold for so long that while this was happening the train entered a tunnel and the line was cut off. I re-called the bank and was put on hold, then through to another assistant, and exactly the same thing happened again. Overnight I had received bank text messages suggesting the card might be frozen due to my failure to confirm the hotel's "verification request". Were it to stop working, I would have had neither money nor means of using the internet except via Wi-Fi. I gave up contacting the international "card payment organization" via my bank (hoping that it would somehow all be OK) and phoned my mobile company to increase my digital "roaming" credit limit.

All of this, I am aware, may seem a touch prosaic, but these are the sorts of reality the modern-day long-distance train traveller faces, especially one coming to the end of a particularly lengthy journey, who is concerned about their overdraft limit having doled out quite a lot of cash, one way or another, on ticket reservations, abodes of varying quality, ham and cheese croissants, *vin rouges* and much else besides.

I will not describe my exact thoughts regarding the consequences of this "verification request", but you may have a very good guess.

I looked out of the carriage window and took a few deep breaths. A fox scurried across a field, frightened by the 10:11 from Luxembourg. A river meandered between villages, looking indecisive. Enormous white cows munched on grass, ignoring the 10:11 from Luxembourg. The green and copper rolling hills were reminiscent of the English countryside, making me think once again of home.

A large middle-aged man wearing gold chains and rings had joined the carriage nearby and begun a long conversation in a deep voice that went like this: "Yeah, yeah, yeah. Ha, ha, ha. Yes, yes, yes, yes, yes. Exactly, exactly, exactly. OK man, OK. This is normal. I haven't tried it, not yet. Sometimes it's like that, you know. I think three or four euros. Oh, la, la. Ha, ha, ha, ha."

For a while I had imagined some kind of big deal was going down, but the "three or four euros" put an end to that speculation.

The train slid through silver birch forests stopping from time to time at Libramont, Rochefort-Jemelle, Marloie and a place called Haversin, where almost every home had solar panels as though the local solar panel salesman had a particularly slick tongue. Small farms with haystacks led to the large city of Namur, reached across the river Meuse, where the run-in to the station featured several yards scattered with accident-damaged cars followed by *Coronation Street*-like rows of terraced houses. A lot of people got on at Namur. A lot more at Ottignies, further down the line. Then everyone got off at Brussels, where I transferred to the railway south to Waterloo. I boarded an empty train with grey seats and very soon afterwards arrived.

* * *

The real Waterloo station was frankly a disappointment: a long concrete platform that looked recently laid and a small ticket hall made of steel and tinted glass. It was in a quiet suburb of grey houses with neat front gardens in the small town of Waterloo (population 30,000) that led to a high street lined with vape shops, waffle cafés, jewellery shops, lingerie boutiques, a cinema named "Cinés Wellington", a "Passage Wellington" alleyway and a pub selling "Waterloo" branded beer, motto: "The Beer of Bravery!" Also on the high street was the Wellington Museum, located in the house where the Duke of Wellington stayed on the nights before and after the Battle of Waterloo on 18 June 1815.

It was at this elegant, whitewashed town house that Wellington penned his letter to King George III informing him of the defeat and capture of Napoleon. Inside, you entered a gift shop selling an almost equal number of gifts shaped like Napoleon and the Duke of Wellington: key rings, stuffed toys, little busts, tin soldier figurines and children's stickers (Napoleon slightly outnumbering Wellington so far as the availability of such gifts was concerned, if you did try to tot up the emperor–duke ratio). There were also shelves of historical books, replica pistols from the battle (presumably not working), bottles of Waterloo beer and tea mugs featuring pictures of Joséphine, Napoleon's wife.

The desk was manned by a young assistant with a friendly-yet-deadpan manner, who showed me on a map where the battle site – and my hotel – was to be found.

Pointing at the village of Braine-l'Alleud, slightly south-west of Waterloo, he said: "I suppose it could be argued that it should have been called the Battle of Braine-l'Alleud."

"The Battle of Waterloo?" I asked, to check I was hearing this right.

"Yes," he said.

"The historians got the name wrong?"

"You might say that," he replied.

The friendly-yet-deadpan assistant seemed to be having a bit of fun.

"Really?" I asked him.

He shrugged and said: "For sure, yes." He paused, pointing at the map again. "It was there."

By "it", he meant the battle.

"Then again," he mused, "had Napoleon won, it would have been called the Battle of Genappe." Napoleon had his headquarters in the village of Genappe.

This was slightly south of the battlefield.

The assistant paused, looked at me steadily and said matter-of-factly: "But he lost."

I liked this museum assistant.

He went on to tell me that the building in which the Wellington Museum was found dated from 1750, that around thirty thousand tourists a year came to see the museum, and that in 2015, the two-hundredth anniversary of the battle, "there was a big show" with re-enactments, celebrations and memorials: nearly fifty thousand troops had been killed or wounded in 1815 and an extraordinary re-enacted version of this had been staged.

The displays in the museum ranged over two creaky floors. Red-and-gold uniforms belonging to officers of the Royal Welch Fusiliers led to displays about how Napoleon had been exiled on the Isle of Elba in April 1814 when Louis XVIII had been restored to the French throne thanks to Napoleon's defeat by a coalition army including Austrian, Russian, Spanish and German soldiers. But his subsequent escape and return to take France in March 1815 had led to the showdown and his surrender at Waterloo in June. From the museum's building, Wellington had masterminded the campaign, after which Napoleon was exiled to the remote island of St Helena in the South Atlantic – no escaping from there – where he died a middle-aged death (aged 51) in 1821.

A small bed in one room was where Wellington's aide-de-camp, Sir Alexander Gordon, died from injuries on the evening of the battle. Wellington said after the victory: "Well, thank God, I don't know what it is to lose a battle; but certainly nothing can be more painful than to gain one with the loss of so many of one's friends." This is written on the wall above the bed, the words of course ringing true forever.

Just a few weeks before arriving in Waterloo, a tearful Volodymyr Zelensky, echoing Wellington, had said: "Almost everyone [in Ukraine] has at least one contact in their phone who will never pick up the phone again. [Someone] who will not respond to the SMS *How are you?* These simple words [gained] a new meaning during the war."

Events had gone full circle in Europe: Russia, whose troops had held off Napoleon's march on Moscow and helped defeat him in Paris in 1814, had become the enemy.

Wellington's white wool cape from the Spanish campaign against Napoleon's forces is in another room. Portraits and busts depict the duke in dignified poses. Pictures of the battlefield show billowing smoke, corpses, rows of thousands of troops, raised swords, charging horses – and general mayhem. All of which took place not too far away.

I said goodbye to the wry museum assistant, who was busy selling a Joséphine mug to a customer, and hiked the couple of miles down the high street and past supermarkets, car showrooms and a drive-through McDonald's – crossing a bridge above a busy road and traversing several farmer's fields – to the memorial hill shaped like a pyramid facing the main battleground.

Hotel Le 1815 was close by, facing the hill.

Inside, I mentioned my problem with the "verification request" earlier.

A receptionist with a stripy jumper said: "We have many problems with [the well-known online accommodation provider]."

I mentioned that I had no trouble during all previous bookings.

"Ah!" he said and pressed a few buttons on his computer, then switching tack said: "You are in the Thielmann room."

"Who was he?" I asked. I had already noticed there were Wellington and Napoleon suites.

"A general," he replied.

"On which side?" I asked.

The receptionist looked at me as though I really ought to know. Perhaps I should have.

"The French," he said, arching an eyebrow.

"Do you have an English general free?" I asked, just to check.

"No, fully booked, sir," he said and handed me the key to a small white room with a window looking across a field towards the pyramid memorial.

This I went to visit, a few hundred feet away. To reach the steps to the top you passed through an underground bunker containing a museum that went into more detail about Napoleon and the French Revolution in 1789 and his subsequent rise. At the top of the pyramid memorial, 135 feet in height and completed in 1826, was a plinth with a cast-iron lion; the "pyramid" is known as the Lion's Mound. Panels explain where the troops gathered on the fateful day.

Back at the hotel, I met some British archaeologists in the bar.

They were digging in the fields to search for clues to how the battle unfolded, part of a project named Waterloo Uncovered supported by the local Wallonian governments and the universities of Utrecht, Glasgow and Ghent, where I was about to go the next day. They wore cargo trousers or jeans, t-shirts, fleeces and hiking boots, looking as though they had not shaved for a while. All were beaming and full of archaeological enthusiasm.

Mark Evans, who headed the team, said the digs had begun in 2015: "No archaeology went on in two hundred years up to that anniversary. Everyone thinks they know everything about the battle, but there are the half-truths of history. It is archaeology's role to find what's actually in the ground and add to research, sometimes finding new things sometimes not." The big mystery of the battle site was what happened to all the bodies. "There are hundreds of accounts and drawings of mass graves but no one's found any."

The team of four was gathered round a table drinking coffee. They had been using electromagnetic machines to search the wide area. To date, they had found a few human remains but not mass graves. Sometimes they would involve veterans of more recent wars to help with digs to "support their recoveries from war".

Did they enjoy such a huge task? The battlefield was massive.

"Oh yeah," said Duncan. "We are doing archaeology on possibly the world's most famous battlefield."

"I'm quite looking forward to putting one in the eye of all the historians," said Steve, who believed that "archaeology will change the story through the little personal stories".

"What happened to *humans*," said Duncan: the everyday soldiers in the rank and file.

"Wellington always won, of course," said Steve.

Their discoveries could not alter that.

* * *

In the morning I retraced my steps to Waterloo station, caught the 10:11 to Brussels, followed by the 10:53 to Ghent.

This short journey across flat, uninspiring countryside seen through grimy windows was memorable for a couple sitting across the aisle. I eavesdropped on them for a while.

The woman, with an American accent, maybe a university student, said: "We are always going to have a hierarchy, even if there are people elected democratically, but one day people will naturally organize and a communal system will develop."

Her male companion, also a student, replied: "No way that's going to happen, that's what people throughout history have said."

The woman replied: "Yeah, yeah." She paused for a bit, then added: "My mate said the perfect leader for the future in a communal world would be a woman. There would be no wars."

The man replied: "What about Margaret Thatcher? She was pretty tough."

They continued in this vein for some time, as they put the world to rights. Danny and I had no monopoly on that – moving along the tracks seems to encourage such thoughts. And why not?

The train rolled onwards across ploughed fields.

It arrived in Ghent at 11.21 a.m.

In three days, I had been "on holiday" in Dole, Luxembourg and Waterloo. Not many can have laid claim to that trio of leisure getaways in quick succession, I could not help reflecting. Let the random rule when Interrailing in Europe and this kind of thing can happen to you.

CHAPTER TEN

GHENT TO LONDON, VIA ROTTERDAM IN THE NETHERLANDS AND THE HOOK OF HOLLAND

SLOW TRAINS HOME

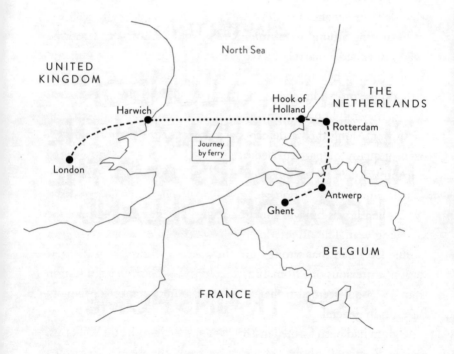

Ghent station was quite a station. I know I have a weak spot for a good station (and perhaps a tendency from time to time to go on about a good station) but this really was an exceptional one.

So exceptional I went back in to have another look about.

Being a little dazed from the long morning hike to the real Waterloo station (not a good station) and the rapid-fire trains to Ghent, having entered the Flemish part of Belgium where people mainly speak French, I had walked out of the station in tunnel vision, wondering what delights lay ahead in this new city.

On turning around to examine Ghent station, however, I realized I had just exited a marvel of a Gothic folly with red-brick turrets and battlements. A bell tower arose on one side looking like a minaret with a spike protruding from the top. Thin windows that seemed as though they might have been designed for arrow-men were dotted on this tower. Along the battlements at the top of the main building a series of quatrefoil patterns had been carved. For a while I just stared at it thinking: *In the old days they really knew how to make a station.*

Gent-Sint-Pieters station, to give its official name, dated from 1912 when it was built in time for a World's Fair held in Ghent the following year. The ostentatious style was regarded as "eclectic" not Gothic (so I had that wrong) and the great expenditure on the new station, a previous one from 1837 ceased to be the city's main station from 1913 on, seemed to hark back to the importance of trains to Belgium in general.

Belgium had been formed in 1830 when the Flemish and Walloons, mainly Roman Catholic, broke away from the Dutch Reformed Church and the United Kingdom of the Netherlands to the north. Leopold I, the first king of the modern Belgium, had been impressed by passenger railways that had begun in England round then. So he invested heavily in early railways, hiring Britain's train engineering guru George Stephenson and building lines that linked the new nation, effectively (and rather cleverly) fostering a form of national unity via the tracks. Blowing a fortune on the station as Ghent was part of a proud Belgian train tradition that sprang from those heady railway days.

I went back inside Gent-Sint-Pieters station. In my earlier daze, I had shuffled beneath grand granite archways and between Doric columns of polished rose-tinted stone, ignoring murals depicting cathedrals and old scenes by docks with smoke rising from ships' funnels by quays and rivers bustling with activity. Swirls of floral stucco, gilded clocks, town-house-sized windows, Art Nouveau tiles, painted coats of armour, mosaic floors, friezes, and long, narrow arched corridors were all about: *eclectic* indeed.

I may never quite become a trainspotter but, I will here admit, may well already have been turning into a closely related species: a veritable, fully signed-up, can't-even-help-myself-anymore *station-spotter*.

* * *

By this stage of this Interrail journey, the end was nigh.

From Ghent to the Hook of Holland and the ferry to Essex was little more than a couple of hours by train.

It was a bright, hopeful day in April. I intended to take it easy from Ghent onwards, or perhaps *even easier* was the better way of putting it. The lure of home, the ferry to Harwich, had put me in a happily whimsical, daydreaming frame of mind.

This desired result – taking it even easier – was quite simply achieved. I began to *drift*.

Beyond station stalls selling sweet-smelling waffles and oniony hotdogs, I drifted down a long street of elegant, thin gabled houses – each one subtly different from the next, seeming to lend the city centre "personality" – to the Museum of Fine Arts, where I ascended some steps into a grand classical entrance, deposited my backpack in a locker room and felt the bones in my shoulder blades shift upwards a couple of inches. My backpack had become out of control with its books, pamphlets, guides and old newspapers.

Light on my feet, I proceeded to spend an indeterminate period drifting about perusing Flemish masterpieces, which proved to be an excellent course of action should you wish to while away some time in Ghent. One after another, the masterpieces came, beginning with a dramatic depiction of *The Crucifixion* by Maarten van Heemskerck (1498–1574), setting the quality bar high with the faces of the many characters surrounding the cross exquisitely and realistically drawn, their personalities captured as though there they were before you, having stepped off the street outside. It was almost uncanny how true to everyday life they seemed: how *normal*, how *modern*, how *timeless*. Ordinary people, not idealized versions of how figures in an "important" picture about a big event ought to be. The paint may have dried on *The Crucifixion* 400 years earlier, but you would never have guessed it.

This was what Flemish art seemed to offer, in the museum's early rooms: *ordinary life*.

It was a delight. Real people getting on with everyday affairs, four centuries ago or so: no pretension, no focus on royalty and aristocracy, no missing out on the simple existences lived by most (who could not have afforded to hire a master painter to portray them) or what might be deemed "lower" matters. Next up after Maarten van Heemskerck came Adriaen van de Venne (1589–1662) and his chaotic and disturbing *Dicing, Drabbing and Drinking Bring Man to Destruction*, its protagonists seeming to do just that. Then Pieter Brueghel the Younger (1564–1638) and his action-packed *Farmer's Wedding in a Barn*, ca. 1616, the bride in a paper hat tucking into a feast based on left-over sheaves of wheat from the harvest. And after this, one from his father Pieter Brueghel the Elder (1525/30–1569), entitled *Wedding Dance in the Open Air*, in which participants are embracing, cavorting, drinking, gambling and generally having a whale of a time. At least I thought it was by his father, until I realized it was a copy of Pieter Brueghel the Elder's famous work by his son, Pieter Brueghel the Younger, according to the small print of a note by the painting. Then, as I was trying to get my head round this, it was back to another piece of the younger Brueghel's original work with *Village Lawyer*, depicting a cluttered office with peasants clasping papers in desperation, pleading to slippery, calculating lawyers who clearly hold the upper hand.

You quickly become a big fan of both Brueghels, one way or another, at the Museum of Fine Arts in Ghent (at least I did).

Drifting further onwards were more modern, abstract works by Victor Servranckx (1897–1965), René Magritte (1898–1967), Gustave de Smet (1877–1943) and Gustave van de Woestijne (1881–1947) that made you stop and wonder *where on earth, from what remote corner of the brain, did that come from*: "harbours" broken into a series of shapes that somehow seem to capture perfectly the essence of an industrial dockside; coffins in place of figures in peculiar, unsettling portraits; the buildings of a town centre captured in a muddle of shadows and intertwining forms as though cast in a heap from above; strange-eyed characters with twisted faces and hard lives that are either going to go badly wrong or move harmlessly, happily forward, depending on the eye of the beholder (you, the visitor, that is).

Further on still came traditional landscapes and depictions of Belgian city centres: Ghent, Brussels and Bruges included. Of the landscapes of the Low Countries, though, the beautiful, stark works of Hippolyte Boulenger (1837–1874) were the ones that really stood out with their grassy plains, skyscapes and silhouettes of horizons that seemed so familiar to the long-distance train traveller who happens to be drifting through the first-rate Museum of Fine Arts in Ghent.

I drifted out of the museum in another daze, this one induced by masterpieces rather than long walks to stations and connections on trains. I drifted to my digs (an unfussy room in "Roxi: the Urban Residence"). I drifted to a corner restaurant and ate Flemish beef stew and *frites*, watching cyclists and trams flow by, of which there are a large number in Ghent. I drifted to the mind-blowingly big Gothic cathedral, where I bought a ticket to drift onwards down a medieval passage to witness yet more (very fine) art.

This came in the form of the 12-panelled Ghent Altarpiece, also known as *The Adoration of the Mystic Lamb*, completed by brothers Hubert and Jan van Eyck in 1432. Again, the details of the faces of the followers of Christ (the dignitaries, the stragglers), of Adam and Eve, of Christ himself, even of the countenance of the lamb at the centre of the composition, as blood oozes into a sacrificial golden cup, are so sharply drawn you cannot but feel they are somehow *there*, hidden in the canvas.

The story of this painting added another dimension to your appreciation. From virtual reality-style information devices you learn of a tale of theft over the centuries, with just about everyone who could lay their hands on the masterpiece seeming to have had a go: Napoleon before he got his comeuppance, Nazis, rioting Calvinists. One panel of the altarpiece is still missing, snatched 90 years ago in a heist that had for a while involved a million-Belgian-franc ransom. The crime was yet to be solved.

Afterwards I drifted to a café in a tight network of old, narrow streets in the Patershol district where I drank a glass of sparkling wine by a little bridge over a water channel. Locals, mainly of retirement age, plus a few workers who had finished for the day, were drinking the same along with beers and glasses of a creamy, bright yellow Dutch drink named Advocaat comprising eggs, sugar and brandy.

In this setting I fell into conversation with an artist named Eline who had a mop of blonde hair, a flowery dress and a good sense of humour. She told me about Ghent: "There are a lot of youngsters coming here, it is quite an artistic scene, you see: more so than Bruges, though you have a scene there, too. In Antwerp, there is design and fashion, more than in Ghent. Here it is all about art, that is the reputation." She paused and sipped her Advocaat. "People will party at the weekend sometimes till eight a.m., when there is a festival," she said, partying till 8 a.m. seeming to be a sure sign of artiness. "Sometimes when there is not a festival, too. Then they sleep till two o'clock on Sunday. I do think we know how to party. Ghent knows how to party, yes we do. We have many colleges, art colleges, regular colleges. Of our population: two hundred and sixty thousand in total, plus seventy thousand students. A lot of students! A lot of parties!"

Eline was distracted, a friend had arrived. I began to talk to Bill.

Bill was sitting at a table on the opposite side to Eline. He was from Odessa in Texas, rather than Ukraine. He was chatty, too. He was, he said, a "digital nomad" who was teaching English online while travelling the world. He could speak Spanish, German and Russian.

"I flew here from Egypt," he said, surprising me. "Six days a week, I work. Then I try and see things."

He had a laptop with him. He was working and also *seeing things* at the bar at the same time. He wore a baseball cap and Reebok trainers and had a windswept, beach-bum look, yet was quite self-contained and sure of himself, as every good digital nomad no doubt must be. He was perhaps in his early forties. His digital nomad-ing had taken him from Odessa in Texas to Britain, France, Spain, Italy and Greece, before Egypt – mostly going by train. In Egypt, he had gone to St Catherine's Monastery on the Sinai Peninsula but "almost got into a fist fight with a cab driver, he said he wanted forty dollars, then sixty, then I made the mistake of going to an ATM, then this other guy came up… I was lucky to get out of there in one piece".

Bill turned to his computer. A message had popped up that needed addressing. He began working, typing away while saying to me: "This is the problem. They want miraculous results. They want to learn a language. They want the glory of having learned a language. They don't actually want to learn it, though."

Bill had to take a call. I left Bill and Eline and drifted back past the old cathedral to Roxi: the Urban Residence. The parties may have been going on all night, but I had a train to catch in the morning.

Of the joy of trains
Ghent to the Hook of Holland, the Netherlands,
via Antwerp and Rotterdam

The 09:27 to Antwerp was late, 19 minutes late. But I did not mind.

I stood on the platform in glorious Gent-Sint-Pieters station, waiting for my forty-eighth ride.

A small grey train soon arrived, and I sat in a crowded carriage opposite a woman with (somehow) permanently arched eyebrows, who smiled briefly before returning her gaze to a newspaper with an article about the Netherlands donating tanks to Ukraine. The train soon passed beyond terraces of narrow houses with steep Flemish roofs before slipping across a hazy flatland dotted with wind farms.

Three women carrying bags containing plastic-wrapped Louis Vuitton handbags boarded at a station, joining the woman with the permanently arched eyebrows and me. The train proceeded to follow a busy motorway before arriving soon after at the extremely ornate station, Antwerp Central Station, where I took a lift to a deep underground platform where the 10:44 to Rotterdam awaited.

This train was buttercup yellow and navy blue, soon rising out of a long tunnel and crossing waterways and passing tower blocks and more wind farms.

My new fellow train travellers comprised a group of men in their twenties who each had handlebar moustaches and wore black leather jackets and were drinking beers. Polite announcements over the speakers kept saying things like: "Good morning, dear passengers, we will be departing fifteen minutes late…" and, "Good morning dear passengers, we have now departed fifteen minutes late due to a technical problem on a train in Brussels…"

The train paced across flatlands making a whistling sound. We stopped at Noorderkempen and shortly afterwards crossed into the Netherlands. The guys with the handlebar moustaches got off at Breda, a little Dutch city with a British connection as it was where Charles II spent much of his time in exile in the 1660s. There, the train swapped direction and reversed northward on a branch line to Rotterdam. A polite announcement said: "Good morning, dear passengers, in a few moments we will be arriving in Rotterdam Centraal…"

And so it proved. We arrived at noon: only ten minutes late.

* * *

Rotterdam Centraal station was a modern angular affair with a giant concourse with a high ceiling interspersed with thin skylights. A striking V-shaped façade by the entrance dominated all, with a futuristic architectural intent that was reminiscent of some of the Socialist realism efforts of the 1960s, but carried off in a deliberately retro manner, as though the chief designer was fond of dry irony. I shall say no more about the station, at the risk of banging on way too much about stations, other than, 1) All these stations were making me architecturally aware in a way I never had been before; there was, increasingly, a frisson on arrival at a new one: *what on earth had the railway bosses dreamed up this time?* and 2) It was extremely tempting at Rotterdam Centraal to catch a Eurostar back to London St Pancras International in business premier class. This was possible. The tickets would cost more than the entire Interrail pass for a month and were the only ones available at short notice. I stood in the giant concourse looking at the departure board, wavering.

Snapping out of this impulsive mood, I stepped forth into Rotterdam.

Across long retro-futuristic plazas, one with a striking sculpture of a perilously balanced pile of empty oil cans, I arrived at the Maritime Museum.

Inside, this chartered the history of the port at Rotterdam, which had shot to prominence in the 1570s when Antwerp and Amsterdam were blockaded. Access to the river Rhine and river Meuse allowed excellent passage of trade and the port continued to be extremely important. On my visit it remained the busiest in Europe and the world's tenth hardest working after Shanghai and several other Chinese ports, plus Hong Kong and Busan in South Korea. Forward-thinking displays at the museum were concerned about climate change, suggesting in one section that "autonomous roadtrains" might be a good idea one day to replace cars. Further displays discussed the possibility of more dikes and dams to curtail rising seas in the Netherlands, and even "floating port islands".

Then I went to have a look at a collection of charming old boats belonging to the museum at a dock at the back overlooking Erasmus Bridge, a suspension bridge that crossed a tributary of the river Rhine beside the museum with a tall, twisted V-shape support that reminded me of the station's façade.

Then I took a boat ride along a canal to the edge of the river with a septuagenarian skipper-guide named Rhinus, a retired captain of a cargo ship, and Caglar, an early thirty-something from Istanbul with a quiff and Ray-Ban shades who worked in the "business finance sector" connected to bottling machine factories back in Turkey. He was the only other passenger. The boat was a small wooden one. Rhinus told Caglar and me about travelling to New Zealand, Australia and Singapore on his cargo ship. Caglar told Rhinus and me that he was about to go on his honeymoon in Zanzibar. Rhinus took us to the dammed river Rotte, formerly a tributary of the main river. This spot had given Rotterdam its name.

Then we returned and I took the Rotterdam metro to the Hook of Holland, stopping after half an hour at a bleak quayside next to a red automated lighthouse on a train that crossed many water channels and was distinguished by strange adverts that seemed to flash up on the windows in tunnels (something I had never witnessed before).

At the station was a sign for Stena Line ferries, pointing passengers in the correct direction for the ferry I would be taking the next day. I walked into the small town – the only tourist as far as I could spot – and checked into Hotel Kuiperduin, where my room at the top faced a church tower where bells clanged every half hour.

On the quiet high street I ate an Indian meal and drank a Dutch beer or two at a bar full of Feyenoord supporters watching a game. It was a key showdown in the European Champions League – just as the game back in Naples had been. "We go crazy when Feyenoord scores," said the woman sitting next to me at the bar, who ran a flower farm. Feyenoord promptly scored and the flower farm woman and the rest of the customers at the bar promptly went crazy for a while. This was my only insight into the Hook of Holland: many of its locals seemed to be extremely passionate Feyenoord supporters. I had run out of ability (if I had any to start with) of even trying to think deep thoughts or any thoughts of much consequence other than: *these Hook of Hollanders like their football and seem a pretty good lot*. After a great many trains, the time eventually comes when you are simply ready to go home.

* * *

That moment had arrived. In the morning I walked to the beach, a wide expanse of sand by the North Sea. It was sunny and cloudy, then cloudy and sunny, and for a while I looked back across the railways of Europe thinking of the glory days of the *Orient Express*, of the nature of companionship and travel, of the comfort of gentle movement, of the great fortune of a place called Europe that exists so close at hand, of clicking time, of park bench dreams, of deciding *let's do this*, of setting off on a train beneath the Channel, of pleasures, of diversions, of freedom, of luck, of seeing things for yourself, of encounters, of surprises, of not always doing things "right", of not caring, of caring too, of finding your feet again, of restoring "mental equilibrium" (and removing "overstrains", too, à la Jerome K. Jerome), of moving on, of returning home, of taking a ferry and crossing a sea and travelling down a few last lines. All these things and most obvious of the lot... of the joy of trains.

AFTERWORD

Back on 4 October 1883, when the very first *Orient Express* passengers were gathering on the platform at Gare de Strasbourg in Paris, anything seemed possible. As crowds milled and steam billowed from the big shiny locomotive – a Buddicom class 500, designed in Crewe (in case you were wondering) – Georges Nagelmackers must have been filled with a mixture of excitement and trepidation.

Would his grand plans for a "MAGIC CARPET TO THE ORIENT", as the headlines of the day were declaring, come off? Would the assembled dignitaries and cream of the European press take to his posh new carriages with their clever state-of-the-art bogies? What might happen if there was a breakdown or some other technical calamity? (In the event, all went swimmingly save for a dangerously overheating dining carriage that had to be replaced in Munich.)

What about concerns regarding bandits in the wilds of Romania and Bulgaria? Might passengers, with pistols packed, be called into action to see off ambushing brigands? Who quite knew? Would transcontinental trains really work in Europe, as Nagelmackers had witnessed they had in the United States on his fact-finding mission in 1869? Or were they just suited to the flamboyant frontier spirit of America's great plains? Was it all a mad pipe dream?

That US trip had been crucial to Nagelmackers' vision, with the swanky carriages and lofty ambitions of George Mortimer Pullman seeming to point the way ahead. It was, after all, in a Pullman carriage, the *Pioneer*, that Abraham Lincoln's body had been transported in 1865 from Washington, D.C. to his hometown of Springfield, Illinois. It was in the very same carriage that Civil War general Ulysses S. Grant had been given a triumphant hero's journey to his own home town, also in Illinois. Pullman had hit the big time. He was a household name. His trains were the talk of the former English colony. But could Nagelmackers with his *Orient Express* do the same?

The answer was, of course, a resounding "yes" – for a while. The golden period glittered brightly until the interruption of World War Two, as described in chapter five. Royalty flocked to its opulent carriages: Bulgarian kings so enamoured they requested to drive the locos through their territory (King Ferdinand himself a few times), Edward VII (who so enjoyed the dining carriage he tried to hire the chef, who could not be enticed away), Indian maharajahs, Haile Selassie, the emperor of Ethiopia. Theodor Herzl, Zionism's founder, went for a spin. As did endless actors including Maurice Chevalier, Sarah Bernhardt, Lauren Bacall, Ingrid Bergman and many, many others.

Telling the story of the *Orient Express* during its heyday it's almost impossible not to name-drop. The opera singers Maria Callas and Dame Nellie Melba were seduced by the on-board glamour. So were Harry Houdini, Charlie Chaplin, and writers aplenty from Graham Greene, Agatha Christie (so many times), and the American novelist F. Scott Fitzgerald. The latter was blown away, approving of how the train seemed to blend in with the scenery better than Pullman trains back home where passengers, he said, were usually "absorbed in an intense destiny of their own and scornful of people in another world less swift and breathless". By contrast, the *Orient Express* was, he thought, far less brash and more considered: a part of the landscape through which it moved, not an alien object packed with cigar-smoking moguls (although there were a fair few of them in Europe, too).

Yet even as the post-war jet plane took over – the advent of low-cost carriers in the 1990s seeming for a while to finish off long-distance rail travel altogether – the memory of those glory days has somehow always tantalizingly lingered.

Perhaps it is all those grandiose stations found in Paris, Antwerp, Ghent, Nuremberg, Milan, and elsewhere (not to mention Sirkeci back in Istanbul) offering a glimpse of those glitzier times that has stuck in our minds, quietly working on the subconscious. All those statues, columns, lofty windows and resplendent halls acting as a reminder that: *trains used to be a whole lot better.*

And the truth is that they were, for those who could afford them. Those old luxurious *Orient Express* trains were marvellous, even if the best carriages were pitched at the upper crust rather than the mass public – while also being utilized by a murky underworld of smugglers, spies, spivs, purveyors of counterfeit currency and, in that old-fashioned phrase, ladies of the night (a regular feature by many accounts).

That period of rail "mystique" – steam, soot and cinders swirling by carriage windows adding to it all – may be gone for good. Train travel has of late, however, been enjoying a resurgence in the form of high-speed networks that have sprung up across Europe from Spain to France, Germany, Italy, Poland, and elsewhere. Even Britain has a good stretch from the Kent coast to the centre of London (probably best not to dwell on the woeful efforts to link the north of the country to the capital).

Alongside the emergence and success of most of these fast trains, has been a growth in sleeper services as passengers swap short-haul flights for overnight berths. Sleek Nightjet trains run by Austrian Railways between Vienna and Munich to Milan, Venice, Rome and Paris (depart Paris 7.30 p.m., arrive Vienna 10.00 a.m.) have led the way. Zurich, Cologne, Hamburg, Innsbruck and Amsterdam have also been connected, and routes planned between Berlin, Brussels and Paris, perhaps linking up to Barcelona soon, too.

"Partner trains" of Austrian Railways travel between Bratislava and Split, Graz and Warsaw and Rijeka and Stuttgart. Meanwhile, the Swedish operator Snälltåget offers links from Stockholm to Berlin via Malmö and Hamburg (depart Stockholm 4.23 p.m., arrive in Berlin 8.47 a.m.). And in France the billionaire Xavier Niel, co-owner of *Le Monde*, is behind plans for a new fleet of "hotels on rails" called Midnight Trains to run from Paris to Porto, Madrid, Barcelona, Florence, Venice, Berlin, Copenhagen and Edinburgh. "The experience being sold by airlines is outdated. It's time to retire the short-haul flight," Niel has said. "The experience of flying around Europe is inefficient and marked by stress and discomfort."

His ultimate aim? To create trains with retro carriages designed to offer "roaring '20s charm" – just like on the *Orient Express*.

All in all, these are heady times for trains in Europe.

Train guru Mark Smith of The Man in Seat 61, one of the resurgent sleeper movement's great cheerleaders and not a train guru given to wasting his words, has described the success of recent overnight services as nothing short of "remarkable". Travelling by Nightjet, he recently declared, is a "real treat".

And he is, as ever, right. As networks improve and people switch to trains for longer journeys, many motivated by green concerns à la Thunberg, it is an exciting time for rail travel and what I have hoped to capture in *Slow Trains to Istanbul* is a sense of that – along with the nitty-gritty of going about and doing it for yourself.

Could a new golden era be round the corner?

Quite possibly.

* * *

There is no right or wrong way to take trains on a long journey in Europe, or anywhere for that matter. Best to let serendipity run its course. Let whatever may happen, happen – as Danny and I agreed on our park bench all that time ago, and I increasingly grew into, eventually drifting my way through the Low Countries, letting sensations and experiences come and go as they might.

No two journeys will ever be quite the same.

Strikes, line closures, availability of tickets may nudge you one way or another. You may choose to speak to other passengers. You may not. You may be interested in the (often chaotic) politics along the way. You may not give a stuff. You may be keen on seeing great art and architecture or archaeological sites. You may be a foodie. You may seek out literary connections. Or you may be a history buff. Or just someone who simply likes trains. Someone who enjoys peering quietly out of the carriage window, dropping in here and there along the way. Nothing wrong with that.

Travelling with a companion or going solo, however, presents two quite different experiences.

Paul Theroux was right to draw the distinction, and to point out the pleasures of solitary rail travel with the greater chances it allows to meet others on board (especially in dining cars) and that feeling of drifting "down a pinched line of geography to oblivion" while enjoying an "experiment with space", as he described in *The Old Patagonian Express*. On your own, anything is possible. With a companion, this remains true, though the "space" is naturally shared making the "experiment" subtly different – and Danny was, as I said in chapter five, great company as far as that went in the "first half" of this book (pick your companion carefully).

Theroux also once said that travel literature tends to neglect the "getting there" side of telling a tale. Travel books, he bemoaned, often begin with an arresting moment of the "from the balcony of my room I had a panoramic view over Accra" variety. Which was all well and good, but how had the writer found themselves on that balcony in Ghana in the first place?

Train travel books by their very nature do not leave this unsaid, allowing for plenty of *getting there*. No shortage of that.

Trains also permit you to see, hear, smell, touch and feel more of the world than other forms of getting about at a time when this seems more important than ever. This was what Danny and I had wanted from the start: our park bench dream. With AI, according to probably pretty accurate doom-mongers, threatening to cast humanity into a virtual existence directed by computer-generated "brain" power far greater than our own, taking a long series of trains could almost be regarded as an act of rebellion, if you like, one step removed from the clutches of this "intelligence" that nobody really quite understands. "HAVE KILLER MACHINES TAKEN OVER THE WORLD?" one of the headlines ran, way back on the Eurostar to Paris.

Not quite, yet.

We saw strikes (we *smelt* strikes in Paris). We were held up, diverted and waylaid by strikes. We witnessed the aftermath of mass migration in Sofia (hearing the echo of our footsteps in the empty station waiting lounges for Ukrainian refugees). We were prevented from passing through a European nation under siege from a neighbour. We squeezed into sleepers. We got slightly lost. We tasted food we would not otherwise have tried (excellent *kavarma* in Ruse, despite the perhaps not so excellent ambiance). We drank rough red wine and put the world to rights. We downed frothy beers and did the same. We witnessed Europe going by and thought about the places we saw as we did so – just as the first *Orient Express* passengers had so long ago. Put the lot together: it was a very pleasant thing to do.

Killer machines taking over the world couldn't give you any of that.

So two fingers to AI and ChatGPT and all the rest of it. And a big thumbs up to watching the world pass by… best done as slowly as you can along the tracks.

November 2023

ACKNOWLEDGEMENTS

I am indebted to the many people who generously shared their time on this journey, many mentioned in the text. Special thanks to Richard Hallmark of the Orwell Society, John Telfer (for his hitchhiking advice), Noel Josephides (for his translations of Greek graffiti), Eleni Skarveli, Mark Palmer, Harriet Sime, Hugo Brown, Laura Sharman, Sarah Hartley, Ted Thornhill, Katie Gatens, Steve Anglesey, Steve Chapman, and Naomi Grimley. Thanks also to Danny and Clare as well as to my parents Robert and Christine Chesshyre, my aunt Meg Chesshyre, my sister Kate and brother Edward. As ever, thanks to the staff at Stanfords maps and travel bookshop in Covent Garden and the Open Book in Richmond. Claire Plimmer, editorial director at Summersdale, has been wonderful as always, encouraging the idea for this book from the outset. Thanks also to Siobhan Coleman for her excellent production edit and to Donna Hillyer for her detailed and insightful structural edit and Ross Dickinson for the fantastic copy edit, Jasmin Burkitt for her tireless publicity and Hamish Braid for the maps.

TRAINS TAKEN

1. London St Pancras International to Paris Gare du Nord – Eurostar, 2 hours and 16 minutes, 212 miles
2. Paris Gare de l'Est to Strasbourg – SNCF, 1 hour and 46 minutes, 247 miles
3. Strasbourg to Stuttgart – Deutsche Bahn, 1 hour and 19 minutes, 94 miles
4. Stuttgart to Nuremberg – Deutsche Bahn, 2 hours and 43 minutes, 97 miles
5. Nuremberg to Passau – Journey by BlaBlaCar, 2 hours and 30 minutes, 142 miles
6. Passau to Vienna Meidling – Deutsche Bahn, 2 hours and 11 minutes, 135 miles
7. Vienna Meidling to Vienna Hauptbahnhof – OBB, 5 minutes, 2 miles
8. Vienna to Bratislava – OBB, 59 minutes, 34 miles
9. Bratislava to Budapest – OBB, 2 hours and 31 minutes, 110 miles
10. Blaha Lujza to Kossuth Lajos – Budapest Metro/BKK, 7 minutes, 1 mile
11. Blaha Lujza to Keleti – Budapest Metro/BKK, 7 minutes, 1 mile
12. Budapest to Timișoara – Hungarian State Railways, 6 hours and 24 minutes, 159 miles
13. Timișoara to Bucharest – Căile Ferate Române, 10 hours and 16 minutes, 333 miles
14. Bucharest to Ruse – Căile Ferate Române, 2 hours and 55 minutes, 83 miles

15. Ruse to Gorna Oryahovitsa – BDZ, 2 hours and 36 minutes, 53 miles

16. Gorna Oryahovitsa to Sofia – BDZ, 3 hours and 43 minutes, 142 miles

17. National Palace of Culture to Central Railway Station – Metro Sofia, 3 minutes, 2 miles

18. Sofia to Kapıkule – Turkish State Railways, 6 hours and 5 minutes, 184 miles

19. Kapıkule to Halkalı – Turkish State Railways, 4 hours and 4 minutes, 152 miles

20. Halkalı to Sirkeci – Marmaray commuter line, 42 minutes, 17 miles

21. Beyazıt-Kapalıçarşı to Galata Bridge – Metro Istanbul, 16 minutes, 1 mile

22. Sirkeci to Karaköy – Metro Istanbul, 5 minutes, 1 mile

23. Sirkeci to Halkalı – Marmaray commuter line, 42 minutes, 17 miles

24. Halkalı to Plovdiv – Turkish State Railways, 9 hours and 41 minutes, 253 miles

25. Plovdiv to Sofia – BDZ, 2 hours and 48 minutes, 108 miles

26. Sofia to Blagoevgrad – BDZ, 2 hours and 10 minutes, 62 miles

27. Blagoevgrad to General Todorov – BDZ, 1 hour and 29 minutes, 49 miles

28. General Todorov to Kulata – BDZ, 14 minutes, 6 miles

29. Kulata to Thessaloniki – Hitchhiked/bus, 3 hours and 30 minutes, 71 miles

30. Thessaloniki to Athens – Hellenic Train, 5 hours and 30 minutes, 313 miles

31. Athens to Patras – Rail replacement bus, 3 hours, 132 miles

32. Bari to Caserta – Trenitalia, 2 hours and 44 minutes, 169 miles

33. Caserta to Naples – Trenitalia, 41 minutes, 25 miles

34. Naples to Pompeii – Trenitalia, 25 minutes, 15 miles

35. Pompeii to Naples – Circumvesuviana, 23 minutes, 14 miles

36. Naples to Milan – Trenitalia, 4 hours and 30 minutes, 412 miles
37. Milan to Tirano – Trenord, 2 hours and 32 minutes, 70 miles
38. Tirano to Chur – Rhätische Bahn, 3 hours and 58 minutes, 90 miles
39. Chur to Zermatt – Rhätische Bahn, 5 hours and 56 minutes, 102 miles
40. Zermatt to Visp – Matterhorn Gotthard Bahn, 1 hour and 9 minutes, 20 miles
41. Visp to Lausanne – Swiss Federal Railways, 1 hour and 33 minutes, 86 miles
42. Lausanne to Dole – SNCF, 1 hour and 44 minutes, 68 miles
43. Dole to Dijon – SNCF, 31 minutes, 27 miles
44. Dijon to Strasbourg – SNCF, 2 hours and 27 minutes, 154 miles
45. Strasbourg to Metz – SNCF, 1 hour and 29 minutes, 80 miles
46. Metz to Luxembourg – SNCF, 52 minutes, 34 miles
47. Luxembourg to Brussels – NMBS/SNCB, 2 hours and 53 minutes, 116 miles
48. Brussels to Waterloo – NMBS/SNCB, 26 minutes, 9 miles
49. Waterloo to Brussels – NMBS/SNCB, 24 minutes, 9 miles
50. Brussels to Ghent – NMBS/SNCB, 28 minutes, 31 miles
51. Ghent to Antwerp – NMBS/SNCB, 56 minutes, 31 miles
52. Antwerp to Rotterdam – NS International, 1 hour and 6 minutes, 48 miles
53. Rotterdam to Hook of Holland Haven – Rotterdamse Elektrische Tram, 35 minutes, 18 miles
54. Hook of Holland Strand to Hook of Holland – Rotterdamse Elektrische Tram, 2 minutes, 1 mile
55. Harwich to Liverpool Street, London – Greater Anglia, 1 hour and 36 minutes, 64 miles
56. Liverpool Street to Euston – London Underground, 9 minutes, 2 miles
57. Euston to Vauxhall – London Underground, 10 minutes, 3 miles

58. Vauxhall to Mortlake – South Western Railway, 18 minutes, 6 miles

Total distance: 4,570 miles on 55 trains

Total distance car-sharing/hitchhiking/replacement buses: 345 miles

Total time spent on trains: 4 days, 7 hours and 46 minutes

Please note: *distances and times are approximate.*

No hospitality was taken for this book.

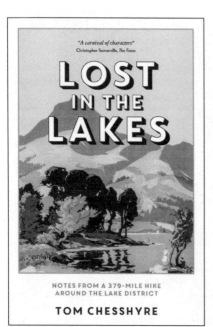

LOST IN THE LAKES

Notes from a 379-Mile Hike
Around the Lake District

Tom Chesshyre

ISBN: 978-1-83799-295-9

Paperback

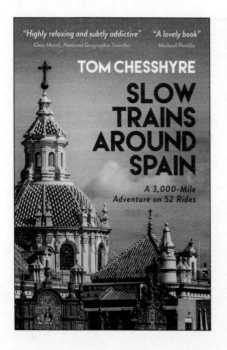

SLOW TRAINS
AROUND SPAIN

A 3,000-Mile Adventure
on 52 Rides

Tom Chesshyre

ISBN: 978-1-80007-263-3

Paperback

SLOW TRAINS TO VENICE

A 4,000-Mile Adventure Across Europe

Tom Chesshyre

ISBN: 978-1-78783-299-2

Paperback

PARK LIFE

Around the World in 50 Parks

Tom Chesshyre

ISBN: 978-1-80007-009-7

Hardback

Have you enjoyed this book?

If so, why not write a review on your favourite website?

If you're interested in finding out more about our books, find us on Facebook at **Summersdale Publishers**, on Twitter/X at **@Summersdale** and on Instagram and TikTok at **@summersdalebooks** and get in touch. We'd love to hear from you!

Thanks very much for buying this Summersdale book.

www.summersdale.com

Tanked